Journey Into
WISDOM

Living Wisely in the
21st Century

Bill Stewart

Journey Into WISDOM

Living Wisely in the 21st Century

JOURNEY INTO WISDOM
Living Wisely in the Twenty-First Century
Copyright © 2013 by Bill Stewart

ISBN: 978-1-4866-0158-5

Word Alive Press
131 Cordite Road, Winnipeg, MB R3W 1S1
www.wordalivepress.ca

WORD ALIVE PRESS
Just Write!

Cataloguing in Publication information may be obtained through Library and Archives Canada.

To my sister, Catherine Soutar—
lifelong encourager, supporter, and friend.

CONTENTS

Prologue

THE JOURNEY REALLY STARTED WITH A SIMPLE BREAKFAST. MY FRIEND PETER AND I were sitting in a restaurant together. My name is Colin Brenner and I've been friends with Peter for many years. This breakfast had become a weekly occurrence. We made it a practice to meet at the same place each week and enjoy one another's company, exchange news, discuss ideas, and share a few laughs together.

On this morning, however, the talk turned serious and didn't follow the normal pattern. We launched into the unfamiliar topic of developing our spiritual lives. From the clumsy and hesitant way we exchanged our thoughts, it was clear neither of us were comfortable or knowledgeable in exploring these matters. Nevertheless, with some determination, we tentatively felt our way along.

Peter was a little more experienced than I. He had been brought up to go to church, although he hadn't attended for some time. With his background, he did have a measure of information. On the other hand, I was completely ignorant. I had never gone to church in my upbringing, and spiritual matters had never been discussed in our home. To me, the concepts of God and spirituality were closed books. In terms of my own spiritual development, I was unskilled and uninformed. It was therefore quite out of character for both of us to be so engrossed in this type of discussion.

The reason for this was quite simple. A few weeks earlier, a friend had invited us to attend some religious services. Although I was entirely unfamiliar with these services, I was, much to my own surprise, deeply impressed. Both Peter and I continued to attend week after week, and I found my interest increasing. While all the talk about God and souls and our relationship with God was new to me, I was strongly affected. It opened up a whole new world I had neglected.

The week before this particular breakfast, We reached a turning point. Our friend, realizing our growing interest, invited us to his home for coffee. While we were enjoying coffee together, he explained to us some of the rudimentary essentials of the spiritual life. He was a Christian man and his understanding of spirituality centered on Jesus Christ and our relationship with Him. I was deeply moved, and decided that night that I should no longer neglect these matters. I committed myself to begin pursuing and developing my spiritual life, especially as it pertained to Jesus Christ. Peter had a very similar response, and so here we were at breakfast discussing how we should go about developing our spirituality.

"If I'm going to do this and set Jesus Christ up as my model and believe in Him, then I want to do it right," I said to Peter. "If I'm going to be a follower of Christ, I want to be a good follower."

"Well, me too," said Peter, "but I don't have any idea how to do it right."

"But you've gone to church. Don't they tell you these things there?"

"Yes, I have gone to church, but I didn't pay close attention and I didn't absorb much of what they were saying."

"Well," I said, "if this is worth doing, it's worth doing well. I want to know how to live for God and experience God in a real way. I'm full of questions. How do you go about it? Is there a right way and a wrong way? How do I know I'm doing it the right way? Who warns me if I'm doing it the wrong way? Lots of people say they're followers of Jesus, but I get the impression they don't handle life any better than I do."

"Don't look at me," Peter said. "I don't have the answers. I'm new to this way of life, too."

So Peter and I continued to discuss the matter. We both felt we had made a life-changing commitment to become followers of Jesus Christ, and that decision had ushered us into a different way of life and a new relationship with God. But where to go from there?

We did, however, come up with some ideas.

"I guess I should start going to church," I said.

"Yes," Peter agreed. Then he added with a smile, "I need to start paying more attention to what I hear there."

"What about reading the Bible? Don't spiritual people do that?" I asked.

"Yes, they seem to make a big thing out of reading the Bible. Praying seems to be important to them, too."

"So if we want to develop our relationship with God, we should start going to church, reading the Bible, and praying?"

"I think that covers it," said Peter.

We were then distracted by a rather strange event happening in the street right outside the restaurant. Our table was next to the window, so we had a good view of the busy intersection. As we watched, a van drove up and parked right at the corner of the busy street. It was an old van and had obviously seen many years of heavy service. What caught our attention was that it was painted in very gaudy colors with bright lettering across the side: "Jesus Saves." Across the back doors, a verse had been inscribed saying: "Ye must be born again."

Peter and I watched with great interest as a young but rather scruffy couple got out of the van, opened the back doors, and began to unload music equipment. They set up amplifiers and loud speakers right there on the sidewalk, plugged in a microphone, and hooked it up to a battery located in the rear of the van. They went through this operation in a very efficient and experienced way. I could tell they had done this many times before.

When the equipment was ready, the young man stood at the edge of the sidewalk, opened up a large Bible, and began to speak through the microphone. From inside the restaurant, Peter and I couldn't make out what he was saying, but it was clear he was quoting scriptures. As he did this, the girl started handing out pamphlets to all the passersby.

Peter and I were fascinated by this performance. I couldn't help but notice, however, that nobody paid any attention to the couple. Their desired audience passed by with eyes averted. Some even refused to accept the pamphlets which the girl offered free of charge. Nobody stopped to listen. Most seemed intent on ignoring them, making it plain that they weren't interested.

I turned my attention back to Peter. "Do you mean to tell me that if we're really dedicated to our spiritual life, we'll do that sort of thing? Is that expected?"

"I certainly hope not. That would embarrass me to death."

"You have to admire their courage and sincerity, though."

"Maybe," Peter said. "But you can't give them high marks for wisdom or effectiveness."

I thought about that for a while. "So it's good to be sincere and dedicated, but if you're sincerely wrong or dedicated to the wrong methods, it can be quite harmful."

"I think a lot of goodness is wasted," said Peter. "Fine, dedicated energy is lost because it's used unwisely and for the wrong purposes."

"So even in pursuing God and His ways, you can waste a lot of time and energy if you don't do it wisely and with good insight?" I asked.

"Right. I don't want to waste my time and energy by pouring them into the wrong channels."

My attention was once again drawn to the young couple outside. Finally they had got the attention of a man who had stopped to talk to them. The three were engrossed in conversation. The dedicated young man was pointing with great energy to the Bible and seemed to be urgently emphasizing something in there.

As I watched, the conversation became more heated. Both men were raising their voices and arguing with each other. Neither one seemed to be listening to the other; both were intent only on making their own point. Finally, the passerby threw up his arms in frustration and stomped away, clearly unhappy and in an ill humor.

"Well!" I said, sitting back in my chair. "If he wanted to influence that man, he certainly went about it the wrong way."

Peter shook his head. "Not very wise. Not very wise at all. In fact, he may have done more harm than good."

"I bet they go to church, read their Bible, and pray. There must be more to it than that." I leaned across the table, gripping Peter by the arm rather urgently. "Peter, since last Sunday I feel my life has been changed. I'm committed to following Jesus Christ, but I want to be wise enough to know that my commitments are focused on the right objectives. I don't want to waste my time chasing empty dreams or dedicating myself to false causes. It is obviously important to be wise, but how do I know what's wise and how do I go about gaining wisdom?"

Peter leaned back and thought for a while. "You're right. If we don't go about this wisely, we could end up wasting our newfound spirituality pursuing nothing but fantasies. I think I know what to do. We need to go and talk to Hermes."

"Who in all the world is Hermes?"

"He's a man I knew at the church. Of all the people I've met, he seems to have things together. I've gone to him once or twice when I had a problem and he's always been able to give me good advice. If anyone can help us, he can. He seems to have an inner spiritual strength that's real. He understands the dynamics of spiritual experience and knows how to apply them to his own life. He told me that if I ever needed help to come and see him."

So the journey into wisdom began, although at the time we had no idea how exciting it would be. We agreed to seek Herme's guidance. We knew we couldn't just blunder forward blindly. We needed wise counsel.

The Importance of Wisdom

ONE

Hermes, the Wise Man

When Peter told me that Hermes was a wise man, I somehow pictured an old man with a long white beard, living in a cave up in the hills somewhere, or in a dilapidated cabin in the deep woods. I was therefore somewhat surprised when Peter took me to a new subdivision in a middle-class neighborhood. I was even more surprised when, in answer to our knock, the man who opened the door wasn't old, with grey hair and a long beard, but middle-aged, neatly dressed, and clean-shaven, with an enthusiastic, expectant face that had a big smile on it.

"Peter," he cried in an energetic voice. "Come in. I've just put the coffeepot on."

Hermes swung the door open and ushered us in. He was a big man with a dynamism that exuded confidence and strength. When Peter introduced us, we shook hands; his handshake was strong and warm.

Although I could see a comfortable sitting room in his house, he suggested we sit in the kitchen.

When the coffee was served and we were sitting sociably around the table, Hermes looked at Peter and asked, "Well, Peter, what can I do for you?"

Peter explained about our spiritual awakening. He said that only last Sunday we had both decided to commit ourselves to a more spiritual way of life, but we were uncertain about how to develop a relationship with God. We were confused about what was important and what should be avoided. Peter confessed that most of the people he'd met at church were very nice and sincere and wanted to do what was right, but even they sometimes seemed confused and uncertain about their spiritual journey.

In short, we hoped Hermes would be able to give us guidance.

"The only things we could think of," said Peter, "were to start going to the church, read the Bible, and pray. Is that correct, or is there more to it than that?"

Hermes listened intently. I then added to what Peter had said by telling him about the couple we had seen through the restaurant window.

"They appeared to be sincere and earnest," I said. "They clearly wanted to do something about their faith and share it with others, but they were so out of touch, and so careless about the impression they were giving. Their intentions were clearly good, but it was our opinion that their spiritual energy was being poured into the wrong channels, that much of it was going to waste. These good people were unaware that they were turning people off. Repelling them. Their efforts were having the very opposite effect of what they intended. We don't know anything about that couple, but we're convinced they were the type who go to church, read their Bibles, and pray. Despite doing these things, what they were doing was inappropriate and out of touch.

"Right now, I have a deep desire to get to know God and bring my soul into touch with Him, but I don't want this new spiritual life to be wasted by foolishly pouring my newfound devotion into the wrong channels. I want to do this right. I want to do this wisely. I want to get real returns by investing my faith and commitment into the right objectives and pursuing the right purposes."

Hermes sat quietly for a while, absorbing our concerns. He then responded with some confidence.

"First, let me tell you how glad I am that you've both had this spiritual awakening," he began. "This is a wonderful thing. I want you to know that you're not alone in this. The fact is that many people have such experiences in their lives. They become aware of a deep inner hunger and desire for God, a longing for a new and better way of life. Like you, they sense that their lives aren't going right and they need to seek another direction. While many people experience this, you're also correct in realizing that they often don't know what to do about it. Their spiritual desires are awakened, but they have no knowledge or understanding about what it will take to satisfy these desires."

"Is it quite common then," I said, "for people to come to a sense that they're out of touch with God, but have little understanding about how to improve their relationship with Him?" I realized that if this was true, I wasn't quite as different or strange as I thought.

"Yes," replied Hermes. "Most people sense a stirring in their hearts at some point in their lives. While these are very precious and valuable experiences, it's often like giving a person a million dollars. Everybody recognizes the value of the money, and having it opens up all kinds of possibilities. Some don't have much experience or insight about how to wisely control and channel this kind of money, however, so they spend it unwisely and foolishly. Soon its value is diminished, or even lost. Others seem to be a little wiser and know how to invest and cultivate the money so it grows and increases. In your new experience with God, you two have been given a treasure, and I'm glad you want to know how to invest it wisely, not letting it slip away through misdirection or carelessness.

"The second thing I would say to you is that I'm glad your spiritual hunger is leading you in the direction of God and Jesus Christ. While many religions and spiritual ideas attempt to respond to the hunger in the human heart, none can compare with Jesus Christ. The best way to channel your spiritual energy is to pursue Him and His way of life. The wisest way of life is to make Him your model and example. He said it Himself: *'I am the way and the truth and the life. No one comes to the Father except through me'* (John 14:6). So if you want to use your spiritual life wisely, not letting it be wasted in false values and false purposes, give great attention to Jesus Christ as He is revealed in the Bible. There has never been a wiser person. There has never been anyone who knew the way better. No one else who can lead us to God."

Wisdom Is a Journey

"The third thing is that I would urge you to go on a journey. You want to journey into this new spiritual land, but your lack of wisdom and understanding can cause you to move in the wrong direction, or become so frustrated with the mysteries you encounter that you give up, or settle down at a level of experience you know is incomplete. This spiritual awakening is just the start of a new and exciting journey that will lead you to rich and blessed experiences with God. But you'll need to have wisdom and understanding to steer this journey in the right direction. As journeys go, it won't be easy or short, but if you decide to embark on it, it will be of great value to you and bring your spiritual development to a rich and fulfilling outcome. It's a journey into wisdom."

"What kind of journey is that?" I asked, rather mystified.

"It is a journey down a river, the River of Wisdom," replied Hermes. "If you go on down the river, you will be taught what is wise, and what is not wise. You'll meet wise people who've invested their spirituality well, and you'll meet foolish people who have wasted it. You'll meet some teachers who can teach you the true values of life. A number of storytellers will be able to explain and illustrate both wisdom and foolishness. If you follow the river and don't get diverted, you'll be led to the Sea of Tranquility, which is a beautiful and satisfying place."

I realized that we were being challenged to undertake something that would call for considerable commitment and change the direction of our lives. I looked at Peter and could tell he wasn't convinced.

"But what about going to church, reading the Bible, and praying?" asked Peter.

"These are good and essential starting points," said Hermes. "But again, you need to participate in these things wisely. Praying has always been a vital part of any meaningful spiritual journey. You will be greatly handicapped if you don't learn how to pray. Understand that many people pray, but they don't know how to do it well and it becomes a very shallow and meaningless practice. To pray well, you need to learn and understand the spiritual dynamics of prayer, and that takes wisdom.

"I encourage you to read the Bible. It will guide you in your spiritual journey. Many read it, however, without much understanding, or else they read it and receive very little enlightenment from it. Again, inner wisdom and insight are needed.

"Committing yourself to the work and worship of a church is also vital, but you need wisdom as to how you can best serve and be involved. Ever-increasing involvement in the church doesn't necessarily improve your relationship with God. It depends on what you make out of it. That takes wisdom. People partic-ipate in many religious activities and spiritual means of grace with the hope and expectation that in doing them they will improve their relationship with God, but these activities can become empty exercises if they aren't used with wisdom and understanding."

"Okay, I can see that," said Peter. "Why do we need to go on a journey, however? It sounds like a major undertaking. Why can't you just tell us the truth now and save us the trouble?"

"Because wisdom and understanding are better learned from experience," said Hermes. "While I can certainly tell you about it, my telling will not have as deep or lasting an effect on you as experiencing it for yourself. You are correct in assuming that you should go about your spiritual journey wisely if it is to lead you to a rich and fulfilled life. Too many, in their search for a relationship with God, don't follow the River of Wisdom. They become lost or sidetracked and end up in spiritual conditions they never intended. The River of Wisdom will lead you to the Sea of Tranquility. I strongly recommend it. If you wish, I can take you to the river and show you where to start."

"What kind of journey will it be?" I asked.

Stages in the Journey

"There are four stages to the journey. In the first stage, you will meet teachers who impress upon you the importance of seeking wisdom. This is an essential stage, because many people feel no need or urgency to seek wisdom. In this stage, you will come to understand from the Bible just how vital wisdom is if your experience with God is to be fulfilling.

"The second stage will help you understand just what true wisdom is from the Bible's point of view.

"In the third stage, the river will pass through the mountains and you will encounter dangerous and difficult times, but you will also learn to understand how to seek and gain wisdom for yourself."

"The last stage will lead you to the Sea of Tranquility. There, you will meet with people who, like you, have found a measure of wisdom and try to put into practice the implications of good wisdom. If you reach the Sea of Tranquility, you will be urged to settle there and make it your home."

"It sounds interesting," I said. "But is it really necessary?"

"Many people don't think it's necessary. That's why the first stage is devoted to convincing you how essential wisdom is for the successful outcome of your Christian commitment. Your destination, the Sea of Tranquility, will be a way of life in which you reap the benefits of having wisely invested in the right values and pursued the right objectives and committed yourself to the true causes. It is a beautiful place. Although the journey will be difficult, it will be rewarding and well worth the effort."

I looked at Peter and again I could sense he was having doubts about this proposition.

"I don't see how wisdom is so important that we have to go to all this trouble to gain it," Peter said. "I went to church a lot when I was a child, and I didn't hear much about wisdom. I didn't hear the preachers address it, and it wasn't taught in church school. Wisdom didn't seem high on the church's agenda. If it's so important, why didn't they make more of it? I can understand that nobody is in favor of foolishness, but wisdom wasn't singled out in church, as I remember, as something you should seek, nor were we taught how to obtain it. And what about Jesus? He was certainly wise, but He didn't seem to make a great big issue out of it."

Hermes smiled at Peter. "You don't think wisdom was important to Jesus? As I mentioned, if you choose to go on this journey, you will meet up with storytellers. They will tell stories that illustrate to you what is wise and what is not wise. I'd like to tell you a story right now that will help you understand why wisdom was absolutely essential to Jesus. It was one of the vital qualities that made His life and ministry so rich and effective."

Hermes rose from the table and said, "Come, let's go to the sitting room. It is more comfortable there."

Topics for Discussion

1. Peter and Colin's conclusion as they discussed the young couple was that they were to be complimented on their sincerity, and yet much of their spiritual energy was going to waste. Do you agree with this conclusion? Can you think of other illustrations of good sincerity being directed to unwise causes or methods?

2. Do you agree with Hermes' statement that most people sense a spiritual stirring in their hearts at some point in their lives, a stirring which loses its effectiveness because they don't know what to do with it?

3. Discuss the idea that wisdom is usually gained not as an instantaneous endowment from God, but from a journey in the right direction taken over a long period of time. Is the gaining of wisdom an instantaneous endowment from God or a process?

Two

Jesus, the Model

Hermes led us into his sitting room, which had an atmosphere of comfort and warmth. As Peter and I settled into two easy chairs, Hermes began his story. I could tell right away that Hermes loved to tell stories and that he was a natural storyteller.

"It was every parent's nightmare. Their young son was lost in the big city. They searched everywhere and could not find Him. Mary and Joseph, who lived in the small village of Nazareth in Galilee, had made it a habit each year to attend the Passover Feast, which was celebrated at the temple in Jerusalem. The journey to Jerusalem was a community event. Friends and relatives joined together and made the pilgrimage as a group. It was a holiday with a religious purpose. It gave everyone a chance to get away from the mundane responsibilities of home and work, and in the company of others enjoy the journey.

"This was Jesus' first time making this exciting trip. He was twelve years old and full of anticipation about the holiday. Everything was new to Him. He had hardly ever been outside His home village of Nazareth. For Him, this was a journey into the wide world. Jerusalem was a wonder to His young eyes. The houses, the crowds, the congested streets, the noise, and the never-ending bustle of commerce excited His inquiring spirit.

"Then there was the great temple. The young Jesus was captivated by it. This massive structure lay within the city, and to His eager eyes it seemed overwhelmingly awesome and majestic. This first experience would never be forgotten. His spirit was stimulated by all this activity, His mind was challenged by the icons of His culture, His heart was moved as He worshiped God. Something within Him was mightily stirred by all of these experiences. He was awestruck by it. He felt part of it. He was comfortable here. This was where He belonged. This was where His destiny would lead Him."

"So it was that when the feast was over and all the celebrations were done, Mary and Joseph gathered with their friends and family and made their way back to Nazareth. The boy Jesus, still engrossed by the life and doings of the great temple, didn't accompany them. Because their group was large and there were many families and friends present, Joseph and Mary assumed Jesus was with His friends. They journeyed towards home for a whole day. It wasn't until they set up camp for the night that they realized that their precious boy wasn't with them. Worried and anxious, they made their way back to the city. They searched everywhere, checking with all of their contacts and making inquiries of the officials. Jesus was nowhere to be found.

"For three days, they searched the streets and public places of Jerusalem but were unable to find Him. With each failure, their stress and anxiety level rose. Their imagination began to paint all kinds of vivid and horrible pictures as they speculated where He was and what had happened to Him."

Peter, who seemed to know something of this story, interjected, "I think they must also have felt very guilty. After all, they were the parents of the Messiah. God had placed responsibility for this child on their shoulders."

"Absolutely," replied Hermes. "Their sense of guilt and anxiety grew heavier as the days went by. How could they have been so careless? Why had they not been more diligent and checked to see if Jesus was with them? It was their fault. They hadn't fulfilled their duty as parents. What if they never found Him? What if He was gone forever? Joseph and Mary were well aware of the massive responsibility and privilege God had laid on them. They remembered the excitement and promise of His birth, with the shepherds and angels and wise men. Had they, in their foolishness, placed the whole plan of God in jeopardy?

"By the third day of their search, they were desperate. Like all of us who have lost something, they began to look in places they had looked before and search in areas they knew He would not be. They even went back to the temple, and there, with stunned relief, they found Jesus. He was quite happily talking to the great teachers of the land. He was listening to them, asking questions, making comments.

"The teachers in turn were astonished at this young boy. How could He know so much? How could He have such depth of understanding? In all their wide experience, they had never encountered such a precocious child. His wisdom seemed far in advance of his age. The Bible describes the scene like this:

> *After three days they found him in the temple courts, sitting among the teachers, listening to them and asking them questions. Everyone who heard him was amazed at his understanding and his answers.* (Luke 2:46–47)

"Joseph and Mary were infinitely relieved, but they acted as if they were irritable and angry.

> *His mother said to him, 'Son, why have you treated us like this? Your father and I have been anxiously searching for you.'* (Luke 2:48).

"Jesus' answer was mystifying:

> *'Why were you searching for me?' he asked. 'Didn't you know I had to be in my Father's house?' But they did not understand what he was saying to them."* (Luke 2:49–50)

Jesus' Unusual Wisdom

"What is very evident from this story is that Jesus was endowed with an unusual quantity of wisdom and understanding. The teachers in the temple were amazed at His understanding and wisdom. In fact, when the Bible tries to describe Jesus during these years before His public ministry began, it seems that His outstanding quality was wisdom."

I thought about what Hermes was saying. "To pick wisdom as the outstanding quality in a child that young would seem very strange to us today. If we were to emphasize the outstanding qualities evident in the life of a young and promising child, we would point to intelligence, athletic abilities, creative technical accomplishments, or social skills. Wisdom would not likely be singled out. It doesn't seem to feature highly in our list of essential life skills."

"Yes!" responded Peter. "I think if we were asked, we would admit that wisdom is important, but it doesn't feature strongly in our thinking. It's like the power of electricity in our homes and businesses. We rely on it. We use it. It's vital to the function of our society, yet we hardly ever think about it. We just expect it to be there. But when we *lose* it, life is thrown into chaos. So, wisdom seems to be some great and important power that's there, but it's invisible. It's taken for granted."

"But in this attitude, the Bible would disagree with us," said Hermes. "The Bible is very aware of the presence and power of wisdom. It emphasizes wisdom as the outstanding quality found in the boy Jesus. The Bible obviously considers wisdom a necessary quality."

Peter, always looking for more confirmation said, "But that's only one Bible reference. It's not very much to go on."

"Oh, but there's more," said Hermes. "The Bible doesn't give us much information about Jesus' life before His public ministry, which began when he was about the age of thirty. However, the information the Bible does give us highlights the significance wisdom plays in Jesus' development. The Bible provides few details, but it gives us some summary statements of what took place during these vital developmental years. What does the Bible consider to be the chief characteristic in the boy Jesus? Consider these verses. After His birth, when Mary and Joseph returned to Nazareth from Bethlehem, the Bible says that *the child grew and became strong; he was filled with wisdom, and the grace of God was upon him*' (Luke 2:40). Then later on, when He was twelve years old and debating in the temple, His wisdom and understanding amazed the great theologians of the nation. After this incident, His parents took him back to Nazareth, and nothing else is said about the years Jesus spent there before his public ministry began on the banks of the Jordan. The Bible does, however, says that *Jesus grew in wisdom and stature, and in favor with God and man*' (Luke 2:52).

"There it is again," said Hermes. "He grew in *wisdom*. It wasn't spectacular. It was quiet and unobtrusive, but vitally important to the effectiveness and fruitfulness of His life and ministry. He grew in wisdom."

Peter nodded and seemed to agree. I was encouraged that he accepted what Hermes was saying.

The Importance of Wisdom to Jesus

Hermes continued, "When we think about it, of all the things the developing Son of God needed, the greatest was to develop wisdom. In order to be ready for His work, in order to guide His ministry, in order to effectively use His power and presence, He needed wisdom. He needed wisdom to understand the will of His Father, wisdom to determine the right values and reject secondary values, wisdom to understand and put into practice the principles and purposes of the Kingdom of God, wisdom to properly use His power, wisdom to choose the right disciples, wisdom to know how to heal the sick and whom to heal, wisdom to deal with the people He lived with. It took great wisdom to fully understand His relationship with God. It took wisdom to assess His powers and know how to use them correctly. It took wisdom to make full use of His opportunities."

"I think we take wisdom in Jesus for granted," Peter said. "We just assume He was very wise. What else would we expect?"

Hermes looked at Peter. "But try to imagine, Peter, the catastrophes that would have occurred if Jesus had lacked wisdom. What if He had promoted false values or made foolish errors? What if He had misused His powers or taught heresy? What if He had misunderstood what God the Father was saying to Him? What if He had listened to the devil, who tempted Him to use His powers and position for His own benefits, His own prestige and public stature? This lack of wisdom would have turned the most wonderful, fruitful, effective, and holy life ever lived into a colossal tragedy, unleashing upon mankind the most devastating errors and misconceptions. Wisdom was vital for the unfolding of Jesus' work and ministry. He absolutely needed wisdom to understand who He was, and what His unique standing was. He needed wisdom to understand the Father's will and hear the Father's voice. He needed wisdom to combat the errors and falsehoods of the day, keeping His values and priorities right."

All this was becoming clear to me. I could see that wisdom had been vital for Jesus. I could also see that if He'd lacked wisdom, the outcome of His life and ministry would have been different.

The outcome of my life will be very different if I lack wisdom, I thought.

Peter had likened the power and importance of wisdom to electricity in our homes and businesses. I thought it was even more basic than that.

"It's like the all-pervading power of gravity," I said. "It's invisible, yet it influences everything and affects everything. Everyone knows it's there. We act on it. We assume on it. All of life is organized around the fact that gravity is there. We scarcely give it any thought or attention. Yet if suddenly it wasn't there, it would be catastrophic."

"That's a good illustration," said Hermes, "except the Bible tends to make the power of wisdom more obvious than we do today. The wisdom of Jesus stands out even more prominently when you realize hardly anyone alive at the time of Jesus understood Him or agreed with the way He went about establishing the Kingdom of God. Everyone, including His own disciples, thought there was a more direct and practical way of introducing the Kingdom. No one thought the route of crucifixion and death was the way to go. Jesus must have been under great pressure to doubt HHHis wisdom and accept the more widely acclaimed view of the Kingdom. We should be eternally grateful that the Son of God, with so much power and authority resident in Him, was given enough wisdom to use it correctly and in harmony with the purposes of God.

"So you can see that if you go on this journey, you'll need to understand from the beginning that it's important for you. You won't take the journey seriously and will easily give up or get sidetracked unless you understand how vital it is for you to develop true wisdom in your life."

Peter seemed to be accepting this. "If Jesus, the Son of God, needed wisdom, how much more do we need it? We need to grow in wisdom so the grace of God can better express itself in us and through us. How foolish for us to neglect its development in our lives when the Son of God considered it so essential for His work and ministry! How foolish for us to blithely think wisdom isn't important for us to function effectively when it was seen as crucial for the successful fulfillment of the purposes of Jesus."

We were all quiet for a while, thinking deeply on what had been said.

Then Peter changed the subject. "In Christian circles, I've often heard people say, 'I want to be like Jesus.' This is commendable. But whatever graces and characteristics we conceive must be present if we are to be like Jesus, we must place wisdom high on that list."

Hermes agreed and replied, "No wonder the Bible says, *'Wisdom is supreme; therefore get wisdom. Though it cost all you have, get understanding'* (Proverbs 4:7)."

Wisdom Is Needed to Make Appropriate Choices

Peter and I sat quietly for a few minutes, trying to absorb this. Finally, I said to Peter, "I think entering this spiritual life is like entering a giant department store. In the store is a multitude of merchandise that is good, but we don't need it all. There are also some products that are bad for us and we shouldn't even consider buying them. Then there are some things we need, but even amongst the things we need are a wide variety of possibilities. We must choose carefully. We need to be wise shoppers. In pursuing this new spiritual life, there is a wide variety of possibilities, but we must not take for granted that everything available is good for us. In the midst of so many choices, we need wisdom to make the right choices."

"Yes!" agreed Peter. "We could squander a lot of time and energy following spurious or empty spiritual values, ultimately cluttering our lives with unnecessary spiritual junk. In the spiritual dimension, we really need to be wise enough to know what is genuinely valuable. Even in the spiritual world there are cheap, second-rate goods we don't really need. As you say, Colin, we need to be wise shoppers."

Hermes smiled at this. "You two are beginning to understand that wisdom isn't a luxury sought by the few, but a necessary ingredient for a successful and fulfilled spiritual life with God. So, what do you think? Do you think it's worthwhile to undertake the journey into wisdom?"

I was sure I wanted to do it, but Peter still seemed uncertain.

"Why not come with me to the beginning of the river and have a look at it," Hermes said. "If you don't want to venture any further, you don't need to. Even after you've started, you can stop anytime you wish. I have a friend who lives by the lake where the River of Wisdom begins. He has canoes and equipment to help on the journey. He knows the journey well and he can give you better guidance and direction than I can. Remember, the first phase of the journey is designed to convince you of the importance of wisdom. If you come to the end of the first phase and still aren't convinced, you need not go any further."

This seemed like a good suggestion, so Peter and I agreed to undertake this first step, without making any commitments beyond that.

Topics for Discussion

1. Peter said that wisdom is like electricity, a great power that is invisible and unseen. It's taken for granted. Do you agree that we pay little attention to the presence of wisdom? Discuss what you perceive to be the general attitude towards wisdom.

2. Hermes asked Peter to try to imagine the catastrophes that would have happened if Jesus had been unwise or lacked wisdom. Discuss the implication of Jesus having been unwise in the use of His powers.

THREE

The First Step

EARLY THE NEXT MORNING, WE DROVE WITH HERMES TO HIS FRIEND'S HOUSE. To get to the headwaters of the river, he took us out of town and into the hills. Hermes left the main road and started up side roads that weren't well-groomed. On this journey, Peter sat up front with his friend while I sat in the back. We soon got into an interesting conversation about the importance of wisdom.

"I wonder why so few people actually attempt the journey," Peter said thoughtfully. "I mean, a lot of people who go through life without any conscious attempt to go on a focused journey into wisdom."

"I suppose most people don't make the journey because they don't think it's that important," I replied.

Peter turned to Hermes. "You've helped me, Hermes, but I'm still not completely sure I really want to get into this. At least we still have time before making a commitment. As you say, we don't really begin until we get in the canoe and start down the river."

"And we could stop any time," I added. "That is, if we think we're wasting our time."

"Why do so few people think it's worth the effort?" asked Peter. "I mean, I think everyone would agree wisdom is a good thing. Nobody deliberately endorses foolishness. So why do so few of us really put effort into finding out what wisdom is by seeking it with clear purpose?"

Hermes responded, "Sure, everyone wants to be wise, but they don't understand that wisdom is something to be sought after and pursued. For example, everyone would like to play the piano well, but not everyone submits to the years of discipline it takes to master it."

Is Wisdom Natural?

"Perhaps people think wisdom comes naturally," said Peter thoughtfully. "I mean, you're either wise or you're not. Your level of wisdom is built into your genes. You were born to be wise or not. You have it or you don't have it, and there's not much you can do about it."

"You mean wisdom is like a person's intelligence level," I said. "You're born with a high intelligence and you have to live with that all your life. Just as some are more intelligent than others, some are wiser than others, but it's all fixed and predetermined."

Hermes replied carefully, "Well, I think it's true that wisdom comes to some easier than to others, and that some learn faster than others. But it's not fixed and unalterable. If your level of wisdom was predetermined, then the exhortations in the Bible to seek it, to ask for it, to desire it would all be meaningless. Wisdom is something we develop and grow into, and it takes effort and discipline to do that."

"So wisdom can be learned," I said. "You can improve and develop it. It's just that most people don't work at improving their wisdom."

"Right," replied Hermes.

Peter, who was always more careful than I and needed a little more convincing, said, by way of confession, "When I consider my own attitude towards wisdom, I realize that I don't think wisdom applies to me. I can see clearly how others could and should live more wisely, but it's not clear how I myself should be wiser, or even could be wiser."

I laughed at this. "You're right, Peter. I can easily see how others make bad decisions, follow wrong paths in life, and fail miserably in their interactions with other people. I can see the mistakes others make and the wrong values they embrace. I can agree wholeheartedly that other people certainly need to learn some basic lessons about wisdom. But me? I'm not very impressed with that. Wisdom is for others."

Peter smiled, but nodded his head in agreement. "That's it. I can see how others badly need wisdom, but I'm not so sure that I need it badly myself."

"In view of our own lack of sensitivity about wisdom, perhaps we're the very ones for whom this journey has real value," I said. "I think it's going to be a very personal inner journey—a journey of the mind and spirit that will improve our relationship with God and help us understand Him better. I think I need it, and I certainly want it."

"Well, I'm not going to commit myself until I get a better idea what this is all about," said Peter. "Until we get in the canoe and start paddling, I'll keep thinking about it."

Hermes looked to Peter. "Another way to look at this is to consider the colossal cost of not being wise. Look at the tragedies, mistakes, bad decisions, wrong directions, destroyed relationships, broken hearts, and disappointments that lack of wisdom have caused in the world."

Peter was quiet for a while and then laughed. "I'm thinking. The list seems endless. But you're right, Hermes, my friend, when you think of the horrendous cost of unwise decisions and attitudes, and how much pain and suffering could have been saved if we'd had a little more wisdom, then certainly wisdom comes out looking pretty good."

"I think when you've both completed the first phase of the journey, you'll be convinced about the importance of wisdom in your own life and in your relationship with God," Hermes said with confidence. "And I think you'll want to continue to pursue it and develop it in your own heart and life."

At this point, Hermes turned the car up a rough and bumpy track.

"This leads us to my friend's cabin," he said. "We'll soon be there."

Topics for Discussion

1. Peter opened the conversation by wondering why so few people actually attempt the journey into wisdom. How would you respond to the question?

2. Are some people born to be wise, while others are not? Can you develop greater wisdom?

3. Expand on Peter's statement, "I can see how others badly need wisdom, but I'm not so sure that I need it badly myself."

Four

The Beginning of Wisdom

THE CABIN WHERE HERMES' FRIEND LIVED CAME CLOSER THAN HERMES' HOUSE to my image of where a wise old man ought to live. It was built of rustic logs, nestled below some lofty trees. It was small and simple, yet had an atmosphere that was warm, inviting, and secure. It was situated about twenty yards back from the front of a lake. It was a beautiful, peaceful, and isolated place.

Even before Hermes had time to park the car, the door of the cabin opened and a smiling, weather-beaten man came outside. He was elderly but not old, with an honest and friendly face. He still had energy and life. With warm and open hospitality, he welcomed us into his home.

On entering the cabin, the first thing I noticed was a log fire burning happily in a stone fireplace. It added to the simple and relaxed atmosphere of the small room. The furnishings were rustic and simple. In fact, some of them looked as if they were homemade with material gleaned from the forest surrounding the cabin. The cabin itself provided all that was necessary for a simple life, but had

no extra comforts or luxuries. Hermes' friend seemed quite happy in these surroundings.

Hermes performed the introductions. His friend's name was Charles. Charles
had an unspoken dignity and confidence about him. He invited us to sit and
make ourselves comfortable while he cooked up some breakfast. When we were
all contentedly sipping our tea, which was very strong, and eating toast, Hermes
explained why we had come. Charles was immediately enthusiastic.

"Ah! You want to go on the journey down the River of Wisdom," he said. "It
will be one of the most interesting and valuable journeys in your life. I've helped
many people get started on that journey. Not all of them made it to the end, but
those who finished and arrived at the Sea of Tranquility never regret it."

In spite of this encouragement, Peter still expressed uncertainty. "We're still
just thinking about it. We aren't quite convinced."

"That's understandable," responded Charles. "I would urge you to get started
on the journey. Once you get going on the River of Wisdom and experience the
things it teaches, you won't doubt its value."

He paused for a while, as if he was trying to assess our state of mind.

"I imagine you're here because you want to handle life well and make it worthwhile," he continued. "You want to avoid harmful mistakes? You don't want to invest your lives in values and purposes that will ultimately prove false and empty?"

I replied to this. "Yes, all of that. We certainly want to be wise enough to
handle life correctly, but we also see this as a spiritual journey. We're just starting
our walk with God and we want to know how to do it right. We've both come
to the realization that we will find reality and true life in God, but we aren't clear
how best to do this."

Charles clapped his hands with excitement. "Oh yes! Yes! This is certainly a
spiritual journey, and if you've realized that, then you're ready for the first lesson
in learning true wisdom. It takes great wisdom to begin to understand how God
operates. It takes wisdom to be able to hear Him speak and understand His values and priorities.

"Why don't we take our tea and go out on to the veranda where you can view
the lake? You'll see where this whole thing starts, then you can decide if you want
to go or not. If you decide to go, I can equip you for the journey. But before you
get going, I want you to sit and listen to me, for I want to tell you where wisdom
really starts.

"While you're on the journey, you'll have to cope with the normal physical
demands of a canoe trip—there will be water, rapids, rocks, rain, and sunshine.

But while all of these are very real and important, I want you to understand that this is mostly a journey of your mind and heart. Wisdom is more than just getting the outward things right; wisdom lives and thrives in the heart and soul of each person. It has its roots in the deeper values and priorities of the soul. Your desire to know God better, to contact Him, and live in fellowship with Him is the basic and fundamental attitude in which true wisdom grows and flourishes. Come, let's go outside."

We took our teacups and followed him out to his veranda, which overlooked the lake. From here we could see the roughly constructed dock, with a variety of canoes and paddles lying on it. There was also a large shed, which I assumed held some of the equipment Charles was going to give us for the journey. The lake itself was long. The water was calm, smooth, and beautifully reflected the wooded hills that surrounded it. It was certainly a peaceful and relaxing scene and I could understand why Charles chose to live here.

When we were all comfortably settled in the deck chairs, Charles began to instruct us. Pointing to the lake, he said, "This is the lake where your journey will begin. I can supply you with canoes and all necessary camping equipment, but before you get started there's an essential lesson for you to learn if the journey is to be successful."

Where Wisdom Begins

The quiet, peaceful surroundings made me want to lie back and listen from a comfortable position, but I noticed Charles sitting on the edge of his seat, watching us with a great deal of earnestness. While he didn't speak loudly, the sincerity and depth of feeling in his voice conveyed that he was about to say something very important.

"King Solomon in the Bible wrote a book about wisdom," Charles began. "In the first few sentences of the book, he tells us that his purpose for writing is to help us all develop in wisdom. He says,

> *I want to make the simple-minded wise! I want to warn young men about some problems they will face. I want those already wise to become wiser and become leaders by exploring the depths of meaning in these nuggets of truth… How does a man become wise? The first step is to trust and reverence the Lord! Only fools refuse to be taught.* (Proverbs 1:4–7, TLB)

"The King James Version of the Bible translates that last verse a little differently: *'The fear of the Lord is the beginning of knowledge'* (Proverbs 1:7, KJV). This is the beginning, the first step. This is where true wisdom starts. It's wisdom 101. The Psalmist confirms this idea, for he says, *'The way to become wise is to fear the Lord. He gives sound judgment to all who obey His commands'* (Psalm 111:10, TLB).

"Fear of the Lord provides the soil and nourishment from which true wisdom grows and flourishes. It establishes in our minds and hearts the basic attitudes, outlooks, and principles that encourage wisdom to blossom. Fear of the Lord is the fundamental fertility in our mind which encourages wisdom to grow. If this soil is poor, the growth of wisdom will be weak and fragile. If, however, the soil is rich and well-watered, wisdom can grow healthy and strong. It can mature and give you a full and bountiful harvest."

I was a little perplexed with this. I said, "I don't know much about this since I wasn't raised in a religious home, but I heard that God is a God of love. Why then should we fear Him?"

"The word *fear* may have some negative connotations for you, but it's not used here in the sense that we are to be afraid of God, like a child is afraid of ghosts, or the bully who lives down the street. A better word in our culture would be *awe*. It means we have a deep sense of respect, honor, amazement, and wonder at what God is like. *Fear* expresses our recognition of the greatness and power of God. It is an atmosphere in our hearts that humbly and respectfully accepts the authority and superior wisdom of God and His will. When you fear the Lord, you are in awe of His greatness, majesty, power, and wisdom. When this is the atmosphere of your heart, you will develop a deep respect for His values, priorities, and wishes. It means you develop enough reverence for what He is, that you honor His opinions and believe in His instructions. Wisdom starts in our attitude towards God."

Peter said, "What you're saying, then, is that if we're going to grow in wisdom, the place to start is to develop a sense of reverent awe for who God is. When you have this fear of the Lord in your spirit, then you possess the soil in which wisdom grows. When this soil is plentiful in your heart, wisdom will begin to grow and flourish."

"Yes," said Charles, "that's exactly right."

"Isn't that much the same as the spirit we're supposed to have when we worship God?" asked Peter.

"Yes, and you can see how this works," emphasized Charles. "Because we have such a deep respect for God, we begin to accept His priorities and endorse

His values. We set the direction of our lives on the basis of His instructions and guidance. The development of this awesome relationship of respect and honor influences how we think. It changes the atmosphere and direction of our inner lives. We become increasingly aware of a whole new value system forming in our minds and hearts. Understanding and endorsing this value system is the beginning of true wisdom. Once you start making decisions and setting your course on the basis of these godly values and priorities, you become a wiser person."

The Importance of a Good Start

At this point, Charles paused and looked over to Hermes. He began to smile with a mischievous glint in his eye. "Our friend Hermes likes to play golf. Hermes would tell you that the most fundamental element in the game of golf is learning to perfect the swing. If you don't hit the ball correctly, the ball won't go in the desired direction, no matter how much you want it to. Every golfer wants to hit the ball accurately down the middle of the fairway, but as every golfer knows, what he wants and what actually happens are two very different things."

Hermes laughed. "What's challenging is that a very small misdirection at the point where the club hits the ball can translate into many yards of misdirection out where the ball is headed. I know that from hard experience. The way you hit that ball is essential. If you get it off to a wrong start, then the woods, the pond, and the rough grass are waiting for you. But if you get it off to a good start, your reward is having the satisfaction of seeing the ball sail down the middle of the fairway."

"Hermes' experience of that is rather scanty." Charles chuckled. "When we say that the fear of the Lord is the beginning of wisdom, we're saying this is the point of contact. This is the start. This is where the club impacts the ball. If you get this right, then you're going to move in the right direction. If you get this wrong, you're going in the wrong direction and correction after this is very difficult.

"We all want to make good and wise choices in life, but the outcomes of our decisions are often very different from what we want or plan. Like golfers, there was a fault in our swing which caused misdirection at the point of contact. The basic skill that guides us in making wise choices is cultivating the fear of the Lord."

This was all new to me. It was a pathway of thought I had never walked before. If I was to make any progress, I must cultivate this soil in my heart and mind. True wisdom would start with a reverent attitude towards God.

"I would never have arrived at that conclusion on my own," I said.

"It would be a new concept to most people," said Charles. "But you can see the sense in it when you stop and think. Wisdom springs from a correct relationship with God. When you accept God's value system and priorities, you're on your way to developing true wisdom. You'll begin to handle life differently. You'll relate to others differently, and in the long run you'll have chosen a path that leads to joy, fulfillment, and satisfaction."

True Wisdom Is in God

Charles concluded his little talk by saying, "Cultivating a right attitude towards God means accepting the fact that God knows a thing or two. In fact, He might even know more than we do. It means that we respect Him sufficiently to listen to His advice and follow His guidance." With a note of warning in his voice, Charles added, "Often His advice is quite different from the common advice we get from the philosophies that are popular in our culture and society."

"I can see that," I said. "But tell us how to go about developing this attitude towards God. God hasn't been very important to me, so I don't know how to cultivate this attitude."

"It takes time and effort to change the atmosphere of your mind and spirit," Charles said. "Most of us have been so engrossed in taking care of ourselves and our worldly affairs that this self-absorbed way of thinking is deeply engrained in our habits. To begin to change the pattern, we must make definite efforts to insert into our thinking thoughts about God that are reverent and worshipful.

"To begin with, we must make a point of taking time to focus our thoughts and desires on God and how great He is. Take time to meditate on the marvels of what God is and how He operates. He is great. He is powerful. He is majestic. Think of His power in creation, His love and care through Jesus Christ. Let thoughts of the greatness of God sink into your heart until you begin to sense the awesomeness of His being. Your own spirit will be humbled in His presence. Make this a practice. Make this a daily feast for your soul and you'll become more and more familiar with these feelings and be at home in God's presence. The more often your spirit is lifted up in worship and honor towards God, the easier it will become. Eventually, it will be the most natural atmosphere of your life and the normal dwelling place of your heart."

Charles gestured to the beauty around him. "That's one of the reasons I enjoy living here. In nature, I'm constantly reminded of the power and creative genius of God. It's easy to be awed by His beauty and power when you live in the midst of His creation."

Hermes entered the conversation at this point. "This is one way in which your ideas about going to church, praying, and reading the Bible can help. They're all instruments that help direct the mind and heart into a right relationship with God. Many find deliberate worship a great help in developing this atmosphere. In church, we participate in the sacraments and worship with others. They use the great hymns and sing from their hearts. They do this in public and private. Most will find it essential to take time alone and with others, when they can fashion a respectful image of God in their minds and concentrate on allowing their hearts to rise in worship and adoration to Him.

"Prayer and talking with God is another common method of developing a reverent attitude. In prayer we humble ourselves, recognize our need of Him, and acknowledge His power, love, and wisdom.

"Another important way of being reverent to Him is to always be ready and open to obey His guidance and follow His direction. Jesus put it quite simply when He said, *'If you love me, you will obey what I command'* (John 14:15). You can be sure that disobedience, neglect, and indifference to the ways of God will never create in our hearts a spirit of reverence.

"And read the Bible devotedly," continued Hermes. "It points to God and gives us information about what He's like and what His will and wishes are for all of us."

"That sounds good," I said, "but you can't be in church every day, nor can you kneel and pray all day."

"Train your mind to often think of Him in the course of the day," Charles said. "Refer the activities of the day to Him. Learn to praise Him and acknowledge His holiness and love in all the common, everyday incidents of life. Again the Bible says, *'In all your ways acknowledge him, and he will make your paths straight'* (Proverbs 3:6). It's just not sensible to imagine we can neglect Him, be indifferent to Him, disregard Him, even disobey Him and yet absorb all His wisdom and guidance.

"There are many ways of showing reverence, but however you do it, build this attitude of respect and honor towards God in your heart and spirit, for this is where wisdom germinates, grows, and flourishes. It will bring to your life a rich and fruitful harvest. One of my favorite verses from the Bible, which I would ask you to remember and keep always in your mind, comes from Proverbs: *'Wisdom is supreme; therefore get wisdom. Though it cost all you have, get understanding'* (Proverbs 4:7)."

Charles' words were very enlightening for me. "This is very surprising," I remarked. "I never thought the development of wisdom started here. But it seems to me the wisdom of God you're talking about is quite different from the common idea most of us have about wisdom."

"Yes," replied Charles. "On your journey, you'll spend some time with teachers, and one of them will give you a clear understanding of the difference between the wisdom of God and the common wisdom of man. I'll say no more about it now, but it's very important that you understand there is a difference. The time will come when you'll give a lot of thought and attention to that subject.

"Now, if you're ready, I think we should go down to the dock and prepare you for the start of your journey."

Both Peter and I agreed to this, so we followed Charles and Hermes down the pathway to the lake.

Topics for Discussion

1. Charles said that walking with God correctly will take great wisdom. Discuss.

2. The essential first step in developing wisdom is to learn the fear of the Lord. What is the fear of the Lord, and why is it essential in developing wisdom? Why do we tend to neglect this first step? How do you develop the fear of the Lord?

FIVE

The Journey Begins

IT WAS ONLY A SHORT DISTANCE FROM THE CABIN TO THE DOCK. I WAS EAGER now to get started on the journey. Charles pointed to a sturdy canoe that had obviously been constructed for durability rather than lightness and speed.

"I would advise you to take that large, strong canoe," Charles said. "You'll have a lot of luggage with you and there'll be some rough spots on the river where you'll need a strong craft."

While Charles and Hermes went into the nearby shed to gather the necessary equipment, Peter and I were left standing on the deck. In my eagerness to get going, I had forgotten about Peter's doubts. As we stood together, I realized he didn't share my eagerness.

"Are you sure you want to go on this journey?" I asked him.

"I still have a lot of questions that haven't been answered," he said. "What we've been told so far has been very helpful, but I need to learn more. I wish we could spend more time with Hermes and Charles to ask more questions and discuss the implications of what they've said. I hope we'll find more answers downriver."

Equipment for the Journey

When Hermes and Charles brought the equipment to the dock, Peter and I began to load it into the canoe. I noticed there was a tent, sleeping bags, camping gear, and cooking utensils along with dried food and wet weather gear.

"How do we pay for all this?" asked Peter

"Don't worry about that just now," replied Charles. "If you reach the Sea of Tranquility, I can pick it up from you there."

We both thanked him for his generosity.

When the canoe was loaded and ready for the journey, Charles said, "You won't need to camp out every night. In fact, many nights you'll have homes in which to stay. I think you have all of the equipment you need. Although all of it will be helpful, the canoe and paddles are absolutely essential. They're the top priority. You won't get far down the River of Wisdom without them. You notice the name of the canoe is called *Love*, and I've painted the names on the paddles—*Trust* and *Obey*. These aren't just sentimental names; they're given to make a point. Just as you won't make much progress down the River of Wisdom without a canoe or paddles, so the stalwart qualities of love, trust, and obedience are essential ingredients if you are to correctly develop your relationship with God. You said to me that while you wanted to walk with God, you're anxious to do it the right way. Well, the three qualities essential to success in a growing experience with God are love, trust, and obedience. You won't get very far with God if you neglect or lose these qualities."

This was more than I could absorb. "But what have they got to do with developing wisdom?"

"It's wiser to love than to hate or be hostile. It's always wise to obey God, and it's foolish to disobey Him. It's wise to trust and not to believe in your doubts all the time. A person who relies on love and is guided by trust and obedience will not go far wrong. To live wisely with God, you need to be motivated by love, quietly trusting in God and ready to obey Him whatever the cost. No successful relationship with God can last long without them."

I was a little concerned about this, as I didn't know much about loving God or trusting Him or obeying Him.

"Look, I'm quite new to this," I said to Charles. "I've never bothered much about God. I've never loved Him, nor have I had any desire to trust Him or obey Him. Where do love, trust, and obedience come from? If they're so important, how do I get them?"

Love, Trust, and Obey

"They grow in your heart as you get to know God," Charles assured me. "To know Him is to love Him. When you know Him better, you'll learn to trust Him and obey Him. As your relationship with God develops, so will your love, trust, and obedience. Do you remember when I said that the beginning of wisdom is to fear the Lord?"

"Yes," I said.

"Well, there's a strong connection between developing a spirit of reverent awe towards God and the growth of love, trust, and obedience. There is spiritual dynamism between all those qualities, so they merge into one another and co-operate. As your connectedness with God increases, so there will flow into your heart a stream of love, trust, and obedience. You don't create these things on your own; they come to you from God, but the channel between you and God must be open so His Spirit can flow into your spirit."

"But what has this got to do with wisdom?" I asked.

"Everything," replied Charles. He pointed to the canoe. "The canoe is central to the whole endeavor. It's called *Love*. God is love and those who follow Him and absorb His Spirit will sense love growing in their heart and life. You cannot stay close to God or follow Him without developing a spirit of love. When your relationship with God is dominated by love, you'll be less likely to make false decisions and choose erroneous paths. Our love for Him will cause us to adopt His values, accept His priorities, and obey His will. When you love Him, He becomes the center of your desires and purposes. We won't waste our lives seeking to achieve empty goals. Learning to love God and to love others is fundamental to the wise way of life God leads us into. When we're possessed by the spirit of love, we make decisions on the basis of love. We set loving goals and objectives for ourselves and others.

"This is also true in our relationships with other people. When we're guided by a spirit of love for others, we make better decisions and adopt better attitudes. When we set loving goals and priorities, the purposes and endeavors of our relationships will change. When love is being expressed, our relationships

31

are wiser and richer, stronger and healthier. The jealousies, hostilities, and resentments that so often feature in human relationships tend to destroy the spirit of wisdom, leading us into all kinds of foolish attitudes and decisions. When you hate someone, you don't usually make wise decisions regarding him or her. When you're dominated by jealousy towards someone, you often err in how you interact with them.

"Love is wise and builds rich and lasting friendships. A spirit of awe and reverence towards God will propel you down the pathway of loving relationships. When we are in awe of His love, we endorse His way of life. We make the expression of love the basis for our actions. When we do this, it's amazing how many barriers crumble, how much resentment melts, how many new friendships are molded, how many misunderstandings are solved. Love is a wise way to live. This is God's way. And God is anxious to fill our hearts with His Spirit of love. In fact, the Bible says, *'God has poured out his love into our hearts by the Holy Spirit, whom he has given us'* (Romans 5:5). So when you're paddling along, remember that the name of the boat you're travelling in is *Love*.

"Also remember that the paddles are called *Trust* and *Obey*. One of the qualities a spirit of awe towards God generates in our hearts is simple trust. It isn't always easy for us to trust that God knows best, that the plans He has for us will work out in the long run."

"I thought that I was always to trust myself," I said. "Since I was little, my parents encouraged me to trust in my own wisdom and to believe that the real way to happiness and success was the way that I, in my wisdom, thought best."

"It is hard for us to trust that God knows better than we do," Charles said. "His wisdom is far superior to ours. He knows how we should run our lives. The Bible warns us that our own wisdom is faulty and not to be trusted. The book of Proverbs affirms this when it says,

> *Trust in the Lord with all your heart and lean not on your own understanding; in all your ways acknowledge him, and he will make your paths straight. Do not be wise in your own eyes; fear the Lord and shun evil. This will bring health to your body and nourishment to your bones."* (Proverbs 3:5–8)

"I can see that." I pointed to the other paddle. "But obedience seems hard to me. I'm used to doing what I think is right and going the way I think I should go."

"Having a spirit of awe towards God induces in us a readiness to obey Him," Charles said. "Jesus was constantly insisting that the wise way of life is the way where we obey God. He said a wise man is one who *'hears these words of mine and puts them into practice'* (Matthew 7:24), while a foolish man is *'everyone who hears these words of mine and does not put them into practice'* (Matthew 7:26).

"Clearly Jesus understands wisdom as something more than knowing what to do. It's knowing it and then actually doing it. Wise men are those who do it; they *'shall enter the Kingdom of God'* (Matthew 7:21).

"So, you can see that there's a strong connection between a spirit of reverent awe towards God and the growth of love, trust, and obedience in our lives. An attitude of reverence towards God produces in us a realization that the wise way for us to live is to love Him and others, trust Him, and obey Him. Those who actually do the will of God are those who find life. Wise living starts with determining to do what God wants, and then doing it God's way. The hymn writer said it correctly:

Trust and obey,
For there's no other way
To be happy in Jesus
But to trust and obey.

But we never can prove
The delights of His love
Until all on the altar we lay;
For the favor He shows
And the joy He bestows
Are for them who will trust and obey.[1]

I turned to Peter, who had been quiet throughout this long interchange between Charles and myself.

"Whatever we do," I said, "we'd better not lose our boat or any of the paddles."

Charles nodded his agreement and added, "Take good care of them and they'll be good servants to you. Lose them or destroy them, and your journey into wisdom will falter. If you want to be real in your experience with God, be

---

1   John H. Sammis, *Sing to the Lord* (Kansas City, MO: Lillienas Publishing Company, 1993), 437.

wise and understand that without love, trust, and obedience, your growth in God will end up going astray."

Instructions for the Journey

By this time, we had loaded all of our gear into the canoe and were ready to begin our journey. I was anxious to get started and began to climb into the canoe. Charles, however, wasn't yet finished with us. He delayed me by holding on to my arm.

"Let me tell you one or two other things about the journey," he said. "First, the river isn't always easy to follow. Sometimes there are different channels to choose from, and it won't be clear which is the correct one. In fact, sometimes the erroneous channel will have all the appearances of being easier and simpler, and vice versa."

Charles lifted his arm and pointed towards the end of the lake. "Look where I'm pointing. In the distance, right at the end of the lake, as far as you can see, can you see the tip of a mountain?"

We followed his direction and could just see a mountain peak. It was so far away that it was very faint, but it must have been a high mountain for the top was white with snow.

"That is Far Mountain," said Charles. "It can always be seen from the River of Wisdom. At the bottom of that mountain is the Sea of Tranquility. In times of uncertainty, look for Far Mountain and follow it.

"Along the way, you will meet many different people. Some of these will be wise and others will be foolish. You can learn from them—from the wisdom of the wise, and from the mistakes of the foolish. Be observant.

"One of the important features of the journey is that you'll meet up with teachers and storytellers. Spend time with them and listen carefully to what they say. Part of living wisely is learning to listen. Listen well to these people. Their teaching will keep you aware of the truth. Their stories will illustrate the outcomes of wise and foolish living.

"You'll also come across some retreat centers and rest houses. It's important that you spend time in these places. In them, you'll be taught truths that are essential for you to know.

"Also remember what Hermes told you about there being four stages in this journey. The first stage will help you understand just how important wisdom is. The second stage is designed to help you understand what true wisdom is. The third stage will give you guidance as to how to achieve and develop wisdom for yourself. And the fourth stage, the Sea of Tranquility at the foot of Far Mountain, will give you practical advice about applying wisdom in your lives.

"There are no shortcuts or easier ways. You will need to pass through all of these stages. Many want to get to the Sea of Tranquility without going to the bother of the journey. It doesn't work that way. Making the full journey is essential. But I think you will find the journey exciting. Mostly it will be peaceful and quiet, but there will be times when it's rough and dangerous.

"When you reach the Sea of Tranquility, you'll see an island just off the shore. Make the island your headquarters as you explore and experience the benefits of living there.

"Best of all, my good friends, you can be assured that God is with you on this journey. His love, strength, and wisdom will guide you through all the twists and turns of the river. Rest in the assurance that He wants you to succeed, that His presence will never leave you.

"Now you're ready to go. When you paddle to the end of the lake, you'll find that the lake empties into the river. Most of the day is still ahead of you. I suggest that you stay with a farmer tonight. You'll easily see his house for it's built atop a hill along the riverbank. You can't miss it. Tell him we sent you and he'll welcome you. Goodbye and God bless you."

Peter and I embraced Charles and Hermes, thanking them for their help. We got into the canoe and, with the mixed feelings over what was to come—excitement at the adventure, sadness at leaving our friends, and apprehension at facing the unknown—Peter and I pushed off, paddling out into the lake.

Topics for Discussion

1. Colin asked two important questions in this chapter. Where does love, trust, and obedience come from? If they're so important, how does one get them? Respond to these.

2. Colin wondered why love, trust, and obedience are so important in the life of wisdom. How would you explain to him how these vital Christian qualities are an essential part of living a wise Christian life?

Six

The Wise Farmer

Peter sat in front of the canoe while I sat in the rear. Both of us paddled, but it was primarily my job to guide the canoe and keep its direction. There was very little wind, the water was smooth, and we were both eager to make progress, so we moved across the lake quickly.

Soon the dock where Hermes and Charles stood watching receded into the distance. It was a picturesque lake, surrounded by thickly wooded hills. The lake curved around the base of one of those hills, and as we travelled around it we looked back for one last view of Charles's cabin and the dock. We waved our paddles in the air as a final salute to Hermes and Charles. They waved back, and then we lost sight of them. We were now truly on our own.

We had no trouble finding the start of the River of Wisdom. You could hardly tell where the river began and the lake ended; the lake gently evolved into the river. But we knew we were entering the river when the current began to carry us along. We were at the head waters of the River of Wisdom. I looked up, spotted the peak of Far Mountain, and felt a surge of assurance that we were going in the right direction.

It was a warm and sunny day, and since we were moving with the current our progress was easy, allowing us to enjoy the scenery all the more. The river was not wide, but the water was deep and the current gentle. It made for a pleasant experience and I thought, *I'm enjoying this. If it's like this all the way, we'll have a good journey.* I wondered if Peter was enjoying this as much as I was.

"Peter, you've expressed doubts about the value of this expedition," I said. "Do you still wonder about it?'

"Yes," replied Peter. "For all the years I spent in the church, I didn't hear much about wisdom. You'd think if it is as important as Hermes and Charles say, it would have been discussed. Why was it not more prominent?"

I had no answer for this. "I remember in our discussions with Hermes and Charles, the power of wisdom was likened to the power of electricity and the force of gravity. They are not seen. We take them largely for granted, and yet they're immensely important to the way we organize our lives. In fact, they're so important that without them we would be thrown into confusion. It may well be the same with wisdom. Everybody recognizes it's immensely important, but it's not given much attention becaue it's invisible and unspectacular. It's largely taken for granted."

"But we shouldn't be taking it for granted! As I remember, in church nobody bothered with wisdom until a perplexing problem arose that they didn't know how to solve. Then they would pray for wisdom. Wisdom was neglected until there was a cry for help. But if I understand what Hermes and Charles said, we need to focus on it and positively, on purpose, seek it and try to develop it as a quality that guides us in our everyday lives."

"Yes. Most people treat wisdom like a spare tire," I said. "It's of no use except in emergencies. But it should be more like a steering wheel, used constantly to keep us going in the right direction."

Peter smiled. "That's a good way of putting it. The search for wisdom needs to be a constant and cultivated pattern in our daily lives. We should be constantly asking God for it and doing the things that help wisdom grow. It should be part of our lifestyle as followers of Jesus Christ."

"Well, they both emphasized that the first section of this journey is to convince us of the importance of wisdom and how vital it is if we are to properly develop our lives with God. Perhaps before we're finished this first section, you'll feel more assured."

"I hope so. If we don't, I'm not sure I'll bother going through with this."

We carried on in silence. The hills, the river, and the sky combined to form a very beautiful scene and I remembered Charles' talk about the fear of the Lord being the beginning of wisdom. He'd urged us to cultivate a spirit of reverent awe towards God. I wasn't in the habit of trying to develop such an atmosphere in my life. In fact, I was in the habit of living my days without giving God a thought. It occurred to me as we moved down the river that I could scarcely find a better time or place to make a start at teaching my mind to focus on God.

I tried to enjoy the beauty around me, letting my spirit relax in the majesty of it all. It absorbed me. I felt as if I was one with it. I marveled in its grandeur and realized the creator of all must indeed have a power and intelligence far beyond anything I could imagine. I began to sense His presence and wanted to thank and worship Him for the wonders He had created. I became conscious of a Presence that brought stillness, peace, and wonder to my soul. This inner spiritual experience was new to me, but I luxuriated in it. I realized I was worshiping God, that I wanted to praise and thank Him for who He was.

It seemed like a door opened in my spirit and for the first time I experienced the beginning of reverence for God. This living stream of well-being continued to flow through my soul for some time. I was at peace with myself, with the world around me and with God. I found this connection with God so fresh, clear, and strong; it was marvelous.

Neither Peter nor I were experienced canoeists, so after two or three hours we grew tired, even though the way was easy and pleasant. We were glad, therefore, when ahead of us we saw the woods begin to clear, revealing fertile farmland atop rolling green hills.

The Wise Man's House and the Foolish Man's House

Peter saw it first.

"Over there," he said, pointing. "There's a stone house up on the highest hill. I think that's the place Charles encouraged us to stay for the night."

The house was built of red sandstone and was well-situated on a hill above the river. It was surrounded by fertile fields of grain and some open range with grazing cattle and sheep. We decided this should be our destination for the day and pulled over towards the riverbank beneath the house.

"Look! There's another house on the other side of the river," I said to Peter.

This other house had a wooden frame and was situated on the low, flat ground stretching back from the river. This house looked new. In fact, some of the construction appeared to be still in progress. It was going to be a very nice dwelling place, but because it was placed in a vulnerable spot, I wondered what would happen if the river ever flooded.

I suppose they know what they're doing, I thought.

We pulled our canoe up the bank and tied it to a small tree. We then made our way up to the sturdy sandstone house. We were welcomed by the farmer, who lived there with his wife and two sons. They seemed a happy and contented family, and when they found out we had been sent by Hermes and Charles, they were even more welcoming.

Around the supper table, we complimented the farmer on his home, which he had built himself.

"It was a lot of hard work and expense" he explained. "We wanted to build on the hill to keep above the river in case of floods. Because of the solid rock up here, we had a hard time setting the foundation. Now that the hard work is over, we're glad we went to the extra work and expense. We feel very secure and safe."

We complimented him again on the outcome of his hard work and foresight.

"But what about your neighbor on the other side of the river?" I wondered. "He's building a wooden house, and it's situated right next to the river? If the river floods, won't he be in danger?"

"When he started to build the house, I went over and talked with him," said the farmer. "I pointed out that if he built there, he would be in danger of floods. He told me it was much cheaper to build the house there and that the river looked quite gentle. He didn't think it would flood. Besides, he was in a bit of a hurry and didn't want to bother transporting the building material from the river to higher ground."

We spent a very pleasant evening with the farmer and his family, but towards the end it began to rain. After we retired for the night, a fierce and dreadful storm developed. There was thunder and lightning. The rain poured down in sheets. The wind was fierce, and the anger of the storm continued most of the night. As I lay snuggly in bed, I was glad we weren't camping outside in a tent.

Towards morning, the storm had abated. As the sun rose, however, we became aware of a great deal of activity downstairs. People were speaking loudly in urgent, worried tones. Although it was still early, we hurried down to see what the problem was and found the farmer and his family quite agitated. When I asked what was going on, they pointed out the window.

"With that dreadful storm last night, the river has flooded," the farmer said. "It has overflowed its banks and I'm afraid our friend across the river has lost his house. We fear for his safety."

His two sons were pulling on oilskin coveralls.

"The boys are going to go over see what the situation is," explained the anxious farmer. "The river is quite wild right now and I'm not sure it's safe. But they insist on helping if they can."

Peter and I went over to the window and looked out. We were amazed at the change that had come over the scene. Yesterday it had been so peaceful and at rest. Today the river had swollen and its brown, muddy water had tripled in width. It was sullen and swift as it swept down its course. With shock, I realized that the house on the other side of the river wasn't there anymore. It had been washed away, unable to withstand the fury of the storm.

The farmer looked at us and said that we shouldn't continue on with our journey until the river had moderated some. He also told us the boys had gone down through the night and pulled our canoe further up the hill out of danger's way. Thank the Lord for their thoughtfulness.

We watched anxiously as the two boys got into a powerful motorboat and started out across the river. Our worries for them proved groundless as they had no trouble negotiating the swiftly flowing river. They passed over the spot where the house had been, slowed down and circled around once or twice. They then moved further along the forest's edge, searching for the neighbor and his family. Finally they docked the boat at the bottom of a wooded hill and got out. We watched as they disappeared into the trees.

"It won't take long for the river to calm down," the farmer told us. "You should be able to continue your journey by the afternoon. We'll do all we can to help our neighbors over there if we can find them. It looks like they've lost everything, and if they're safe they'll need all of the support they can get."

I was doubtful about continuing downstream in a small canoe while the river was so enraged, but the farmer was convinced this was just a flash flood. It would be over soon. True enough, as the morning wore on, the level of the river fell significantly until it was back within its banks. As the water receded from the opposite bank, we could see that the neighbor's home had been obliterated.

Towards lunchtime, the two boys came back and had with them the neighbor, his wife, and their small child. They were wet, cold, hungry, and terribly disturbed over what had happened. Our farmer friend had been on the phone informing authorities and other neighbors about the situation and we knew that help and assistance were on the way. Meanwhile, the farmer's wife prepared a hot meal for the destitute family. We did what we could to encourage them and understand their plight.

After the meal, we decided that there was nothing else we could do and that we should continue on with our journey.

The farmer came down to our canoe with us. "The next section of the river should give you no problems," he said. "It is gentle and deep. I'd advise you to stay the night with a widow named Phyllis, who has a small cottage near the river. You'll know it by its prominent red roof. She lives with her son, George, and is known for her wisdom and knowledge of the Bible. I know you still have a number of questions about the significance of wisdom and the value of your journey. I would encourage you to confide in her, for she's very understanding and will be able to answer your questions."

We thanked the farmer for his kindness and hospitality, then wished him well as he and others tried to help his friend who had lost his home in the flood.

Lessons from the House-Builders

As we were pushing off, the farmer called after us. "The experience you had last night should teach you something about the importance of wisdom. You should talk about it as you journey down the river. I'm sure Phyllis will discuss it with you when you get to her house."

I was surprised at how easy the river was after the fierce turmoil of the previous night. Peter and I quickly settled into a paddling rhythm and made good progress.

"I am sure that farmer was glad he went to the effort and expense of building his house on top of the hill, on a good and solid foundation," Peter commented.

"Yes," I answered, "and I'm equally sure his neighbor deeply regrets not taking a little more time planning and thinking ahead before he built his house."

"Right. Cheap and easy is rarely best."

"It seems wise to plan ahead before you plunge into a project like that. Perhaps the whole episode could teach us something about wisdom."

"Well," replied Peter, "it certainly teaches us that it's wise to make your decisions on the basis of long-range outcomes and not just on what happens to be cheap and easy at the moment."

"Yes, but it also teaches us that making short-sighted and unwise decisions can be costly. All you need to do is look at the dreadful loss and suffering the neighbor's unwise decisions have brought upon him and his family. The rewards of wisdom are great, but the costs of lack of wisdom can be devastating. I'm beginning to see just how important it is for us to gain wisdom."

Peter had no reply to this, but thoughtfully paddled on.

The journey that afternoon went well and our progress was good. As we traveled, I tried to renew my inner fellowship with God and develop again the sense of reverence and worship I had experienced the previous day. My spirit seemed hungry and anxious to renew this awareness of God, and I found that it was a little easier to guide my thoughts and spirit into the right atmosphere.

Practice makes perfection, I thought. It was a very satisfying and blessed time. I glanced ahead a few times, and in the distance I could see the top of Far Mountain. Its presence gave me a feeling of security and confidence that we were headed in the right direction.

It was fairly early when we came to the house with the red roof. Once again, we were warmly welcomed; this time, by a middle-aged widow. When she introduced herself as Phyllis, we knew we were in the right place.

Topics for Discussion

1. Peter pointed out that for all the years he spent in church, not much was said about wisdom. Has this been true of your experience in the church?

2. Do you think Colin is correct when he said most people think of wisdom more as a spare tire, rather than a steering wheel? Explain what you think these two concepts of wisdom really mean.

3. Colin used the beauty of nature to help him create a spirit of reverence towards God. Has nature ever inspired this sort of spirit in you? What other methods do you use to inspire reverence towards God in your soul?

4. Peter and Colin learned some lessons from their experience with the wise and foolish farmers. What were some of those lessons? Can you think of any additional lessons they may have learned?

SEVEN

Wisdom in Teachings of Jesus, Part One

I FOUND PHYLLIS TO BE A VERY COMFORTABLE AND ACCEPTING LADY, AND AS WE sat down to chat in her sitting room, we relaxed into an easy, open conversation in which we told her about our journey and the reasons for it. We gave her an account of our new spiritual experience and our desire to make our walk with God a real and fulfilling experience. Phyllis nodded agreement as we filled in the details. As we spoke, I was glad Peter felt so free to unburden himself of all his questions about the importance of wisdom and the need for this journey.

Phyllis listened to us quietly and carefully. Then she asked, "Is there any way in which I can help you?"

I looked at Peter, then did the speaking for him. "Peter, who knows more about the Bible and the church than I do, was grateful for what Hermes told us about how important wisdom was for Jesus' early development, but why, if wisdom is so important, does the church not make more of it? And why didn't Jesus say more about wisdom in His teachings?"

"Oh!" Phyllis exclaimed. "The need for wisdom was very important in the teachings of Jesus. You're saying to me that you want to develop a good relationship with God, and that's wonderful, but Jesus would emphasize that in order to do that correctly, you need wisdom. The more wisdom you have, the better you'll be able to understand His truth and apply it to your life and the development of your relationship with Him. Deeper wisdom can give you clearer insight into understanding His will, and guide you as you seek to put it into practice."

Phyllis looked at the clock on the wall and said, "We have time. Why don't we talk about this before I make supper? By that time, my son George will be home and he can help explain what I mean."

Wisdom Is Properly Applied Truth

We made ourselves comfortable and Phyllis began. "As a general statement, Jesus saw wisdom as more than mere intellectual knowledge. Wisdom to Him was an active word, more a verb than a noun. Wisdom means understanding right values and knowing how to apply them effectively to one's life and interaction with God. Jesus was constantly emphasizing that it wasn't enough to know about the truth or to know about God; you had to apply it and make it work in your life. He also indicated some of the dreadful outcomes that can result from lack of wisdom.

"Jesus not only lived a wise life, as Hermes pointed out to you. In His teaching, He also talked about the strong need for wisdom. Jesus urged His followers to be wise and pursue wisdom."

I spoke up at this point. "We're supposed to learn about wisdom from our experiences on this journey. I was wondering about the experience we had last night with the fierce storm and the two farmers. Is there a lesson we should take from that?"

"You experienced the terrible storm. You saw how one farmer was safe and secure through it, while the other farmer was devastated and suffered terrible loss. This experience will give you insight into a story Jesus told about wisdom."

Wise Living—the Sermon on the Mount

"In the early days of His ministry, after Jesus had established a group of devoted disciples and developed a good relationship with them, He wanted to give to them a concise summary of His teachings and an outline of the type of life

He wanted them to live. So he gathered them around Him and gave to them a condensed but clear statement of His moral and ethical teachings. This summary is commonly called the Sermon on the Mount, and it's recorded for us in Matthew 5–7.

"In this sermon, Jesus laid out the principles and priorities for His way of life. He described the fundamental personality characteristics and style of living we should strive for as His followers. As you read the Sermon on the Mount, you see that Jesus was advocating a lifestyle that, while very different from the normal pursuits of humanity, would bring us great joy and fulfillment. Underlying these spiritual principles is a kind of wisdom distinct from any other wisdom proposed by other spiritual leaders.

"Having presented us with a picture of how His followers should live, Jesus brought His sermon to a powerful conclusion by calling for a response. He wasn't just passing out information; He wanted a change in lifestyle. To illustrate what the wise and proper response should be to His teaching, Jesus told a story. The story indicates just how important wisdom was in His thinking." Phyllis looked at us and added, "And you really lived through that story last night.

"He told a story about a wise man and foolish man. Both of these men decided to build a house. That is a good and praiseworthy enterprise for both of them. But the wise man planned well and went to the expense and effort of building his house upon a solid foundation of rock, just like the farmer who accommodated you last night. He built his home on a solid foundation up on the hill. The foolish man took the less expensive route by building his house on a foundation of sand, just like the neighbor across the river who built his house on the flats. Building a house on the sand was easier and demanded a lot less work and expense, but sand isn't a stable foundation for a house. For the farmer's neighbor, building on the flood plain was very short-sighted. All went well for both of them until a great storm came."

I looked at Peter, and he smiled back at me. We could both see where this story was going.

"When the storm came, the houses of the wise man and foolish man faired quite differently. Jesus said of the wise man's house, *'And the rain came down, the streams rose, and the winds blew and beat against that house; yet it did not fall, because it had its foundation on the rock'* (Matthew 7:25). The house of the foolish man didn't survive so well. Jesus said of it, *'The rain came down, the streams rose, and the winds blew and beat against that house, and it fell with a great crash'* (Matthew 7:27).

45

"The objectives and purposes of both these men were the same. It was commendable that each of them wanted to build a house. They wanted to provide a safe dwelling place for the well-being and comfort of their families. But one ended in tragedy while the other ended in success. What made the difference between success and failure? One of them made a wise decision while the other made a foolish one.

"The wise man went about the job correctly. He understood the long-term implications of what he was doing. The foolish man, whose objective was the same, went about the job without seeking wise counsel and knowledge, disregarding the long-term implications of his decision. To the foolish man, the immediate economy and convenience were more important than future considerations. In spite of his good intentions, his lack of wisdom and foresight caused him to lose all his possessions when the storm came. He had hoped for the best and wasn't prepared when the best didn't happen."

Phyllis paused here to make sure we were following her. When we made no comment, she continued. "The difference between success and failure was wisdom. For us, very often the difference between fulfilling our purpose and not fulfilling our purpose lies in wisdom, or lack of it. The difference between a satisfying and effective life and an ineffective, unsatisfying life is determined by the wisdom of the decisions we make."

"You know," said Peter, "when I think about it, it's true that the farmer who lost everything in the flood didn't seem to be a bad man. While he was clearly devastated over his loss, he hadn't really done anything evil or wrong. He treasured his family and his home like most other men. His problem was not his sinfulness; his problem was his lack of wisdom."

"It seems that even good men can be foolish," I said. "They still have to suffer the results of their foolishness."

Phyllis nodded. "You just made an important statement, Colin. The harsh realities of foolishness affect us whether we are good or bad. Jesus makes it clear that wisdom is more than having good intentions and fine ideas. Wisdom is even more than knowledge. Wisdom is understanding the right values and priorities and then knowing how to translate them into real-life decisions. Jesus said that *everyone who hears these words of mine and puts them into practice is like a wise man who built his house on the rock'* (Matthew 7:24). On the other hand, Jesus also said that *everyone who hears these words of mine and does not put them into practice is like a foolish man who built his house on sand'* (Matthew 7:26). Wisdom can be the difference between those who live life successfully and those who don't.

"Like these two men setting out to build a house, most of us set out in life with the strong intention to be successful and live a full, satisfying, and happy life. Wise people, however, get to know and understand what it takes to achieve this kind of living and then seek to implement it. Foolish people, in spite of their good intentions and strong wishes, neglect or ignore the principles that are necessary to make such a life come to pass.

"Unutterable loss litters the human landscape because we neglect wisdom and don't apply its principles. Many of us suffer failure and loss in our personal lives because we make decisions that are unwise and follow guidance that leads us astray. Our intentions are no doubt good. We want a successful life and desire the very best for our own lives and the lives of our family, yet in spite of good intentions and nice dreams, we end up missing the full life we hope will be ours because we move ahead without paying attention to wisdom."

Here, Phyllis spoke directly to Peter. "Of course wisdom is important. It's vital for the outcomes of your life. Never underestimate how important wisdom is."

Wisdom Is Listening to God and Responding

I looked at Phyllis. "I can see that this is true for life in general, but we're also seeking to develop a satisfying relationship with God, and I believe wisdom is necessary to enter into, and grow in, that kind of relationship."

"That's right, Colin," said Phyllis. "Both of you sincerely want to know God better and make your fellowship with Him real and fruitful. That's wonderful, but many people have had the same desires awakened in their heart and haven't known what to do about it. They end up with something much less than what was promised and what they anticipated. As Jesus said, a wise man is one who *'hears these words of mine and puts them into practice'* (Matthew 7:24).

"Wisdom is a combination of listening and responding, hearing and doing. Wisdom is important because it goes beyond knowing. It goes beyond good intentions and fine aspirations. Wisdom is the quality that gives us insight into how to implement godly principles and turn them into reality. Wisdom is able to see what is necessary if we are to translate aspirations into practical reality. Jesus said quite clearly, *'Not everyone who says to me, "Lord, Lord," will enter into the kingdom of heaven, but only he who does the will of my Father who is in heaven'* (Matthew 7:21). It takes wisdom to know the will of the Father and it takes wisdom to know how to go about fulfilling it."

I could tell that this conversation was having a deep effect on Peter. He never took his eyes off Phyllis. He now spoke up and revealed to me the direction of his thoughts.

"Since Colin and I started this journey," he said, "I've been troubled trying to reconcile the importance that you, Charles, and Hermes place on wisdom. I keep asking myself, if it's so important, why didn't I hear more about it from the people who should have known? But I'm beginning to see that in life, the fundamental guideposts are placed by wisdom. Ignoring where they point or refusing to follow their guidance can be tragic. We may be sincere and our intentions may be fine, but when we try to implement and achieve them without wisdom, we can fail badly.

"I knew of people in the religious circles I was in who had inspiring visions and great spiritual enthusiasm. They wanted to pursue a high quality of life. I'm sure that in their heart and soul they wanted to achieve this, but their visions and dreams lay unfulfilled, not because of poor wishes or intentions, but because of lack of wisdom. They ignored the guideposts and ended up in the wrong place. This suggests that, while pursuing our purposes and wishes for life, if we make unwise choices and go in the wrong direction, we'll end up at the wrong destination."

Phyllis nodded. "You're getting the right idea, Peter. The only thing I would change in your statement is that these wise guideposts were placed there by God, for the benefit of us all. We all want to experience and achieve a happy, successful, and fulfilling life. That's not the question. The issue is, are we being wise enough to do the things, adopt the attitudes, make the necessary decisions, and follow the priorities that will actually produce that kind of life? Since God knows exactly what it takes for you to experience a full and fulfilled life, His guideposts are the ones to follow. It's not enough to have good desires; you have to know the way in which those desires can be satisfied, and that takes wisdom. The pursuit of wisdom should be a continuing search for those who want to live close to God. That's why we're told in the book of Proverbs, *'Have two goals: wisdom—that is, knowing and doing right—and common sense. Don't let them slip away'* (Proverbs 3:21, TLB).

"I'm beginning to understand," Peter said with some enthusiasm. "Jesus wanted us to grasp that the wise way of life was the way He proclaimed. Real wisdom, He said, was in hearing His words and doing them. It isn't wise to disobey God. It isn't wise to neglect God's values, disregard His word, or pursue objectives that are contrary to His will. It *is* wise to embrace and commit to God's way of life."

Wisdom Is Getting First Things First

"So, those church people Peter worries about who know all about the Bible and yet don't handle life any better than everyone else," I interjected, "are like that not because they lack sincerity or desire, but because they aren't wise enough to truly understand what God is saying and put it into practice?"

"Yes," Phyllis replied. "Jesus talked about people who *'strain out a gnat but swallow a camel'* (Matt. 23:24). This emphasis on minor things isn't wise; it saps spiritual energy and wastes good enthusiasm. Wisdom guides us to see what's really important and helps us discipline ourselves so that the important things get sufficient time and attention."

Phyllis paused to see if we had any more comments before continuing. "Throughout his ministry, Jesus continually referred to wise and foolish people. He made it clear that the pursuit of wisdom was essential for a good outcome in our lives and experience with God. Good intentions are fine, but good intentions with unwise implementation and direction can end in failure. Don't underestimate the importance of wisdom."

At the end of this admonition, we were interrupted by Phyllis's son coming in from work. Phyllis proudly introduced us to George. He was a fine, vibrant young man with a large frame and strong body. He was clearly one who worked hard outdoors and had developed a healthy lifestyle. When he shook hands with us, his grip was confident. He looked us right in the eyes and said with genuine feeling, "It's good to have you here."

Phyllis explained to George about our journey and why we were there. She told him that we had been talking about the importance of wisdom in the life and teachings of Jesus. He nodded in agreement.

"I have to go and make supper now," said Phyllis. "I'd like George to tell the story of the ten girls. It's another example from Jesus' teaching about foolish people and wise people."

I expressed to Phyllis our deep appreciation for her hospitality, but indicated to her that time was passing and the day was getting late for travel. If it was alright, we would set up camp on her property and sleep there for the night. Phyllis was more than willing to accommodate us.

I then explained that we needed to set up camp before dark, because neither Peter nor I were experienced at camping. This was our first night of camping and all the equipment we'd received from Charles was new to us. We needed light to see what we were doing.

George immediately offered his help. "I know just the place for you to camp for the night. I've done some camping myself. Why don't you let me show you the spot? I'll help you set up camp."

This offer was much appreciated, so while Phyllis went about preparing supper we followed George to a level spot down by the river and started, under his guidance, setting up our camp. With George's help, we soon learned how to operate our camping equipment. We even built a good fire. Since there was still some time before supper, George used the time to tell us the story from Jesus' teaching about the ten girls.

Topics for Discussion

1. In emphasizing the importance of wisdom in the teachings of Jesus, Phyllis said, that the more wisdom you have, the better you can understand His truth and apply it to your life. What are the two main elements found in true wisdom?

2. Discuss the two statements made by Peter and Colin as they talked about the wise and foolish men illustrated at the end of Jesus' Sermon on the Mount. Peter said of the foolish man that his problem wasn't his sinfulness but lack of wisdom. Colin said that even good men can be foolish; they still have to suffer the results of their foolishness.

3. Jesus said that a wise man is one who hears His words and does them. Phyllis said that wisdom guides us to see what's really important, helping us discipline ourselves so that the important things get sufficient time and attention. Compare these two statements about wisdom. How do they support one another?

Eight

Wisdom in the Teachings of Jesus, Part Two

George began, "Jesus said there were ten young girls, five of whom were wise and five of whom were foolish. The girls were happy and excited. They had been invited to a wedding and had been given important and responsible roles to play in the celebration. It was the custom and culture at that time for the bridegroom to arrive with great fanfare at the home of the bride, and that's where the celebration took place. When the bridegroom arrived, he was accompanied by a happy, noisy, rejoicing group of friends and relatives.

"It was the duty of the ten girls to meet this group and welcome them into the bride's home. When everybody was in, the door would be shut and the extensive celebrations begun. The ten girls were to help make sure everything went well.

"The girls were excited that they had been chosen. Part of their responsibility was to carry lamps. The lamps would be used to show the bridegroom into the house and then to give added light when the celebrations began. Jesus said of the ten girls,

*Five of them were foolish and five were wise. The foolish ones took
their lamps but did not take any oil with them. The wise, however,
took oil in jars along with their lamps.* (Matthew 25:2–4)

"There was lots of fussing as the girls went out to await the arrival of the
bridegroom and his party, but unfortunately a problem arose—the bridegroom
was delayed and didn't arrive when he was expected. The delay was very extensive, and while the girls waited for him their excitement began to fade. Weariness
set in and eventually they all fell asleep. It had been a long day. There had been so
much to take care of, with many detailed preparations. They were all fast asleep
when the cry finally came that the bridegroom, at last, was arriving.

"The ten girls aroused themselves and with renewed excitement prepared
their lamps so they could welcome the bridegroom and accompany him, with
honor and joy, into the home of the bride. The five foolish girls, however, were
dismayed when they discovered that in the course of the delay their lamps had
run out of oil. Their lack of foresight placed them and their hosts in an embarrassing position. In their panic, the foolish girls asked the wise girls, who had
anticipated such a possibility and brought extra oil, if they could borrow some
oil from them. But the wise girls indicated that they would now need all the oil
they had. So the foolish girls ran off to get more oil, but when they were away, the
bridegroom arrived and was welcomed into the home of the bride and the door
was closed and locked so no one could crash the party. The wedding celebration
began, but the foolish girls missed it."

The Foolish Girls Missed the Celebration

Since my Bible background had been rather neglected, this was a new story to me
and I was fascinated by it. Even Peter, who had probably heard it before, listened
intently as George continued.

"While the wise girls were inside enjoying the celebration and fulfilling
their purpose, the foolish girls were left outside. This was a frustrating loss for
them. Wisdom, on the other hand, brings the reward of being able to fulfill your
purpose."

"Just like the two farmers and their houses," I said.

"Yes," said George. "It was clear all of the girls, wise and foolish, had the
best of intentions. Nobody planned to miss out on the wedding feast. They all
intended to be there. Their purpose and intentions could not be criticized. They

were sincere about attempting to meet their responsibilities and honor the bride-groom and assist in the celebration. The foolish girls, however, weren't prepared for the delay. This lack of foresight—wishful thinking not based on reality—caused them to miss the wedding feast.

"So, lack of wisdom can cause us to miss out in so much of the richness, blessing, and success God has planned for us. We all intend to live a quality of life that will fulfills our purpose and satisfies our destiny. While we all want to experience happiness in life, not all of us do. Very often, the thing that causes us to miss out on the realities of life is lack of wisdom—unwise decisions, unwise attitudes, unwise values and priorities. In the case of these girls, most of their unwise choices were made because they didn't think ahead. They thought the wedding would work out for them the way they wanted it to without any inter-vening problems. Oh, how important wisdom is."

Wisdom Cannot Be Borrowed

"You may have some comments," said George, "but first let me point out one more thing. It's worthwhile to notice that although the foolish girls asked the wise girls for some of their oil, they didn't get it. Although we can ask a wise person for advice, we cannot take or borrow their wisdom and make it ours. We cannot borrow wisdom from someone else. We need to provide our own wisdom. Wisdom is an innate quality which each person possesses on his of her own. The development of wisdom is our own personal responsibility. Others can try to help, and may gladly give us advice and direction, but ultimately the responsibility belongs to us.

"The lesson from this parable is clear. Wisdom brings great rewards. Foolish-ness has its own rewards of frustration and loss. *'Wisdom is supreme; therefore get wisdom. Though it cost all you have, get understanding.'* (Proverbs 4:7)."

When George was finished, we sat quietly around the fire for a few minutes, absorbing the meaning of what he had said.

Finally, Peter spoke up. "When I think of the two men who built their hous-es, one was rewarded with a secure and contented life while the other found only loss and failure. It's the same with the ten girls. Five met their expectations while the other five missed out, and wisdom made the difference. Wisdom is so im-portant. Being unwise can lead to all kinds of disappointments and catastrophes, while being wise leads to a rich, full life. I certainly want to be wise in my rela-tionships with God and other people. I'm beginning to see that wisdom is vital."

"I'm glad you understand," said George. "The teaching of Jesus is clear that attaining wisdom is a key factor in the outcomes of our lives in general, and our spiritual lives in particular."

"I can also see that the principles of wisdom Jesus proclaimed for His culture and age are really eternally true for all cultures and all ages," I said.

George agreed. "Although Jesus lived a long time ago, and expressed Himself in the language and illustrations of another culture, His message is true for all time. Wisdom is necessary for all people in every race, male and female, old and young, if they are to make full use of their opportunities and handle their problems successfully. If you want to be in the flow of wisdom, then you certainly need to experience God and live for God in a real and meaningful way, for true wisdom comes from God.

"Today, as in Jesus' day, wisdom brings fulfillment and richness to life. Lack of wisdom brings failure, distress, and emptiness. Godly wisdom gives us insight into how God wants us to live guiding us in how we can do it. Wisdom, in all times and places, tells us what's important and shows us how to implement these important values into our everyday decision-making. Wisdom gives us basic guidance to steer us through life's difficulties. One of the great responsibilities Jesus lays upon us is to seek to be wise and develop wise attitudes and values."

At that moment, Phyllis came out and announced that the meal was ready. We all moved into the dining room where she had laid out a very satisfying and enjoyable meal. We continued talking as we sat around the table.

Wisdom Is Still Necessary Today

"I can see from the life and teachings of Jesus that He considered wisdom to be a vital part of successful living, essential for any progressive experience with God," I said. "But I wonder if wisdom is as necessary for us today as it was for those in Jesus' time. I mean, today we have so much more knowledge. Through technology and scientific discovery, we have access to vast amounts of information. In the light of all these resources, do we still need wisdom as much as less informed people did in other cultures and ages?"

Phyllis had obviously given this matter a lot of thought, for she answered without hesitation. She spoke like a teacher who had often lectured on this subject.

"In our present advanced technological age, we may be tempted to think the need for wisdom has diminished," she said. "As we try to handle life in our modern culture, the danger is that the eternal and ancient worth of wisdom may be eclipsed by our advanced communication and information systems. For modern people, the idea of wisdom may seem a little quaint and antiquated. We've developed such technological skills that a whole world of knowledge is available to us at our fingertips. With such easy access to information, we could quite easily wonder, who needs wisdom?"

I could tell that Phyllis was very much at home talking about this, so I pursued the subject. "But we now have access to specialists and scientists who have discovered answers to many of our problems. Instead of needing personal wisdom, we can consult them and find the answers we need."

"You're right, Colin," she said, surprising me. "Technology not only provides us with great amounts of information, but also puts us in touch with answers to our problems. We live in an advanced civilization. Science has solved all kinds of problems. We have technology, skills, machines, and specialists. We have developed great faith in them. We think there must be technological or scientific solutions out there for all our problems. No matter the difficulty, we expect to find a device, drug, specialist, or government program to take care of it. We think the answer is found in technology and knowledge rather than within ourselves. If we don't find the help we need in our systems, we become frustrated, thinking that technology needs to improve or the government needs to come up with a better program."

It seemed to me Phyllis had restated my point very well.

"We can be so enamored by our access to knowledge and information that we forget the simple reality that information isn't wisdom, that knowledge has to be applied," she continued. "Technology provides us with great tools, but it doesn't make us wise. Some of us will use the tools unwisely, and others will use them wisely. Some people will take information and apply it wisely to the business of living. Others will take the information and use it unwisely. Still others will neglect it or not use it at all. With so many powerful gadgets in our hands, there is an increasing demand for us to know better how to use all of this knowledge wisely, for our benefit and the benefit of others, and not to ignore it or use it unwisely to our own destruction."

George nodded in agreement with all his mother was saying. "We live in a day of specialists," he added. "Medical specialists, family specialists, automobile specialists, computer specialists, psychiatric specialists. With so many specialists around us, we think they will know how to deal with our problems. If we have a situation we cannot handle, we contact a specialist to fix it for us, or else tell us what to do in order to have it fixed. So who needs wisdom? We can rely on them! We're in danger of not developing the spirit of wisdom within ourselves, rather looking outside ourselves and depending on the wisdom others. We rely on all of these outside systems to take care of us and enhance our lives, satisfying our needs. Our faith in technology may be badly misplaced."

"Despite our information and technology," I said, "there still seems to be an epidemic of broken homes, empty lives, confused people, and endless hostility, division, and violence. The basic problems of humanity continue on. The human heart is still angry, greedy, hostile, and divided. Our lives today may be more comfortable and convenient than in previous generations, but we still hunger for something better, something more real. The human heart still seeks God and yearns for fellowship with Him. Our sciences cannot provide that. In my search for a good relationship with God, I cannot turn to technology."

"You're right," said Phyllis. "Improved technology and better education has improved our standard of living, and has been helpful in many ways, but none of it has solved our inner problems. Jesus' message is still as needed today, perhaps even more than ever before: *'Wisdom is supreme; therefore get wisdom. Though it cost all you have, get understanding'* (Proverbs 4:7)."

Wisdom in the Church

"What's your opinion of the status of wisdom in the thinking and operation of the church?" Peter asked. "Since starting this journey, I've been trying to understand why the church doesn't talk more about the importance of acquiring wisdom."

Phyllis thought about this for a while. "Peter, everyone, inside or outside the church, will acknowledge that wisdom is good. We all approve of it. No one approves of foolishness. In fact, people hope they'll be wise even though they don't understand what that means.

"You keep worrying about the church, Peter. You may be underestimating it. While wisdom may not be well articulated or defined by the church, there is still a lot of wisdom and good understanding circulated in the church. God's truth and way of life, which is the center of wisdom, are encouraged in the church. You probably have more true wisdom coming from the church than from any other organization in society. The church understands that true wisdom comes from the truth of God.

"But I do agree that wisdom is often assumed, taken for granted, rather than articulated and defined. It's something we hope for rather than a specific goal we are to pursue and develop. We vaguely hope we can call on wisdom when the need arises rather than seeking to develop a wise lifestyle. It would help people if we ceased to see wisdom as a vague, invisible spirit that mysteriously floats around in our minds. We should view wisdom as a special guest, with a name, whom we welcome into our minds and honor as a permanent and significant member of our family. Wisdom needs to be a real, structural presence in us. Without clearly articulating the quality of wisdom, there will be no end to the confusion, misunderstanding, and misdirection that robs us of the riches wisdom provides."

Wisdom and Christian Theology

Peter nodded in agreement. "Alright, I think we're together there, but I have another question. I've heard that God's salvation is a gift we receive, that it has nothing to do with our own works, efforts, or wisdom. If we just believe, God's abundance will flow into our lives. Is that true?"

"It's true that the gift of salvation is something we receive by faith," Phyllis replied thoughtfully. "It has very little to do with our own wisdom or efforts. But after you receive the gift, it takes wisdom to open it, understand what it's for, and use it in your daily life.

"Imagine, for example, an elderly man getting a new computer for Christmas. It's a gift. It's an expression of the love and care of his family. They want their dad to keep up with modern developments. Once he receives the gift, however, he must learn to operate it. It doesn't take any wisdom to receive the gift, but it takes considerable skill, wisdom, and ability to put it to good use. If he's wise, he'll learn to operate a computer and benefit from it. If he's not wise, the valuable gift will remain largely unused. If he develops only an elementary skill, then the value of the computer will be limited. Depending on the level of skill he develops, the computer can open up for him new worlds that would otherwise be closed.

"Salvation is a free gift from a loving and forgiving God, but we have to apply wisdom to understand how the grace of God works in our hearts and operates in our lives. It takes wisdom to let the real value of the gift unfold itself into the new and beautiful life only following Christ can grant us. This wisdom must be sought, developed, and cultivated if it is to grow in our hearts. That's why Jesus said that a wise man is one *who hears these words of mine and puts them into practice*' (Matthew 7:24)."

George intervened, saying, "I sometimes think about this while I'm out on the farm or working in the woods. God provides the raw materials. He provides the soil. He provides the rain, the sun, and the warmth to make things grow. All of that abundance is given by God, but I have to take them and apply my skill and wisdom as a farmer to make something out of them. I acknowledge the value of God's gracious gifts. If there was no sunshine or rain, if there were only rocks and no soil, I could do nothing by way of producing a farm."

"So faith and wisdom aren't contradictory," Peter said. "To realize the growth of God's life in our hearts, we need to combine them and balance them."

"When I work on the farm, I do it because I have faith that God will provide the rain, sunshine, and soil that will support the seed," George pointed out. "If I don't believe God would provide these things, there would be no purpose in me going out to work. I believe God has put a system together. I believe I have to co-operate with the system. To do that, I need to be wise enough to understand the system and how it works. I'm smart enough to know that in this northern climate I cannot plant palm trees and expect them to grow. Nor do I expect to harvest apples in January. If all I did was sit at home and pray and have faith, not cooperating with what God has provided, my farm would be useless and I wouldn't reap a harvest. The wiser I am as a farmer, the better the crops I will harvest.

"God has provided all that is necessary for an abundant and victorious life, but I must learn how to cooperate with the system. That's where I need wisdom. I need both faith in the system and wisdom to know how it works. James said it clearly:

> *What good is it, my brothers, if a man claims to have faith but has not deeds? Can such faith save him? Suppose a brother or sister is without clothes and daily food. If one of you says to him, 'Go, I wish you well; keep warm and well fed,' but does nothing about his physical needs, what good is it? In the same way, faith by itself, if it is not accompanied by action, is dead.* (James 2:14–17)

"Wisdom is hearing and applying," George concluded.

Peter seemed to understand this and accept it, but he continued to debate. "From my time in church, I was also told that if I wasn't experiencing the blessings I was promised from God, if I wasn't living the way a Christian should live, the problem was not so much a lack of wisdom but a lack of commitment. I wasn't receiving the blessing because I wasn't as dedicated to God as I should be."

I realized that this part of the discussion was for Peter's benefit. Not being part of the church all my life had left me uncomprehending about the problems of the church, but to Peter it was obviously a major concern.

Phyllis picked up the argument. "Yes, Peter, commitment and dedication are important elements in developing a fruitful inner spiritual life. What we haven't always done, however, is use our earnestness wisely. We have taken our commitment and spent it on secondary issues. It's like a rat running on a spinning wheel. A lot of energy is expended for little purpose.

"But I think there is a stronger sense of commitment in the church than we give it credit for. What the church often lacks is the wisdom to understand how to apply that commitment meaningfully. Christians have a depth of willingness that has remained untapped because they're confused about what they're supposed to be willing to do."

Phyllis shook her head sadly. "I'm afraid that good dedication is sometimes squandered because it's misapplied. Many committed people become discouraged, giving up in their search because they're searching in the wrong place. To use George's illustration, they try to grow palm trees in a cold climate, or harvest apples in January. The fault is not in their earnestness, but their lack of wisdom.

"In our Christian culture," Phyllis gently continued, "the presence of the grace of God doesn't mean we automatically know how to receive, implement, and apply this grace in our lives. We aren't awakened to the fact that wisdom is to be sought after and acquired. Wisdom shouldn't be left to chance, but should be pursued. Wisdom should be developed as an important feature in a Christian's growth and maturity. Effort should be made amongst us to grow in wisdom."

My Summary

"I'm don't know much about these theological issues," I said. "Let me see if I understand this correctly. The power of God is made abundantly available to us, but to be useful that power must be harnessed and channeled into the issues of life, and knowing how to harness and channel God's power requires wisdom. In the same way, God has made great grace available to us. We don't deserve this gift, nor have we earned it. It is free. But the ability to recognize grace and know how to apply it in our lives takes wisdom. Likewise, if truth is to bring light to our lives, it must be able to shine. The light comes entirely from God. It has nothing to do with us. The ability to receive the light and shine it into the confusions and uncertainties of our lives, however, takes wisdom. Everyone understands that the love of God is abundant and available, but wisdom is needed for us to know how to accept this love and express it to others. We also believe that God wishes to communicate with us, but we need to understanding His way of doing this before we can reap the harvest of God's guidance. Wisdom is the vital function that helps us make contact between the vast resources of God and the needs of our own hearts."

I had warmed up to the subject, surprising myself.

"So, that night when Peter and I found God and started on the path of following Him," I continued, "I didn't know anything about wisdom, grace, or obedience. I just received from God His loving forgiveness and salvation. This was given to me by faith. But it didn't stop there. That was just the beginning of a process. Now I must work out the dynamics of how God's riches can be appropriated in my own life. That's where I need wisdom.

"You mean," said Peter, who had been listening carefully, "if we're going to make progress and develop, we'll need more than faith. We'll need wise obedience to God!"

"That's what I think," I said. "When we set out on this journey, I didn't know anything about all this. I think we're being taught that we need to be wise in order to make the grace of God effective and powerful in our lives. We really do need to be like the man who listened and obeyed, wisely building his house upon the rock, or like the wise girls who knew how to supply themselves with enough oil to meet their needs. It is wise to listen to Jesus and then be wise enough to know how to put what He says into practice."

Phyllis's Summary

Phyllis clapped her hands with enthusiasm. Turning to Peter, she said, "I understand you have been brought up in religious circles, so I suggest to you that wisdom is a treasure that's been largely lost or neglected. It's a virtue we really need to set about recovering and bringing back into prominence. We need to get people to understand that wisdom is vital to their progress and fruitfulness as Christians. People should be strongly encouraged to seek and develop it. Wisdom should be moved to center stage."

In her gentle way, Phyllis seemed to come alive. Passion burned in her eyes. "Would a renewed interest in wisdom help us develop more fruitful and abundant Christian lives?" she asked. "Would a wiser use of the gifts and graces of God make these gifts more effective? Would a wiser approach to serving Him make our service more rewarding? As we seek to live for Him and apply the truths of the Gospel, would more wisdom not make all of this of greater value? Does the neglect of wisdom impoverish us? Do we fall short of the power and grace of God because we don't wisely understand how to apply His promises in our lives? Are the fruits of the Spirit dry and unsweetened in our lives because we don't possess the wisdom to nourish and ripen them? Has the joy and wonder of our growth been stunted because we don't understand how to nourish the Spirit of Christ within us? Do we often miss out on God's will and direction because we aren't schooled in wisdom enough to understand and interpret His voice and leading? Has our growth in grace languished because we aren't wise enough to apply His values and priorities? Have we been sidetracked by becoming engrossed in side issues, not developing the wisdom to see and appreciate what's really important? Perhaps we've allowed our neglect of wisdom to impoverish our whole walk with God. We could be so much better and effective if we become wise enough to know what God is saying and understand how He operates."

"Well, that has been very helpful," said Peter in a rather subdued voice. "I can see that wisdom was very important in Jesus' life and teaching. The valuable role wisdom plays in our spiritual development isn't well recognized. Thank you for your patience in explaining all this. But could I call on your patience even more? I still have one or two other questions. I still don't see much evidence of wisdom being proclaimed loudly in the early Christian church. Did the apostles preach about wisdom? Did they teach the early Christians about the importance of wisdom?"

Phyllis smiled. "I think we've had enough heavy talk for now. Let's enjoy the rest of the meal and then have a restful night. Tomorrow you'll carry on with your journey and come to a training center which is run by a friend of ours named Craig. He loves to teach small groups and he'll help you understand that the apostles did indeed say a lot about wisdom. But enough of that just now. Let's enjoy the meal."

Topics for Discussion

1. What were some of the characteristics of the foolish girls? What were some of the consequences of their foolishness?

2. Why do modern technology and science not make wisdom obsolete?

3. Phyllis urges Peter not to undersell the church when it comes to wisdom, but she conceded that wisdom is often taken for granted rather than articulated and defined. It isn't often seen as a specific quality that's essential if we are to successfully enlarge our experience with God. Do you agree with Phyllis? Expand on your answer from your own experience in the church.

4. Discuss Peter's statement that he was told that if his experience with God wasn't working out, the problem may not have been a lack of wisdom but a lack of commitment.

5. Discuss the implications of Peter's statement that they got started on their journey by faith, but if they were going to make progress and develop, it would require wise obedience to God.

NINE

The Swamp

WE SPENT A VERY NICE EVENING WITH PHYLLIS AND GEORGE AND HAD THE additional satisfaction of knowing we were making good progress on our journey into wisdom.

As we retired to our campsite for the night, I remembered that I was trying to cultivate a spirit of reverence and respect towards God. I took time to go outside by myself and sit by the river, trying to appreciate and worship Him. It was a beautiful and silent evening and I once again felt a spirit of thankfulness creep into my soul. I retired for the night with a spirit of peace and gratitude towards God filling my mind. I slept well.

Although we rose early the next morning, we found that George had already left for his day's work on the farm and Phyllis had prepared a hearty breakfast. As we ate, she sat down and told us a little of what to expect as we continued down the river.

More Instructions for the Journey

"Today you'll encounter the Swamp of Confusion," she explained. "In the swamp, the river breaks up into many channels and it's difficult to know which is the correct course. The secret is to keep the top of Far Mountain in view. Follow that and you'll soon get through the swamp and stay on course. If you take your eye off Far Mountain, you'll likely get confused and follow channels that look easy but which will lead you in the wrong direction.

"Once you're through the swamp, you'll come across a village. I would stop there and call in at the resource center. Craig, the man in charge there, will be able to supply you with any additional equipment you need. He's spent his life on the river and can give you good advice. He's also a good Bible teacher. If you ask him, he'll help you understand more about the importance of wisdom in the Bible. He'll be glad to spend time with you. Remember that at this stage of the journey, the emphasis is on convincing you about the importance of wisdom. This first stage of the journey is long but vital. If you aren't convinced that wisdom is important, the difficulties you encounter further down the river will discourage you and you'll question if the journey is worth the effort.

"Craig will give you insight into the importance of wisdom in the teachings of the apostles and the early Christian church." She paused, looking at Peter. "I think you'll find what he has to say very helpful, Peter. It should finally convince you of the importance of wisdom, not only in the life and teachings of Jesus but also in the life and teachings of His early apostles."

We thanked Phyllis for her help and hospitality, then loaded up our canoe. This time, we set off with me upfront and Peter in the rear, doing the guiding. As I looked ahead, in the distance I could see the snow-covered peak of Far Mountain. It seemed a little clearer and nearer here than when we had first set out. I was encouraged to think we were making progress.

At first, we had an enjoyable time. The gentle river flowed through some very beautiful country. There were low-lying hills covered with a verdant forest. The way was relaxing and easy and we made good progress. As we paddled along, I once again felt my spirit reach out and commune with God.

After a while, however, the country began to flatten out and the river broadened. We noticed weeds floating in the water, and downriver we could see the stagnant water being invaded by tall bulrushes. We realized we were entering the Swamp of Confusion.

"It looks like we're coming to the swamp," I called over my shoulder. "Since you're guiding the canoe, remember to keep your eye on Far Mountain. As long as we're pointing toward it, we won't get lost."

Soon the bulrushes gathered around us, and in their thick growth we lost all sense of direction. A channel wound its way through them, but the river had stilled itself. The water was shallow and murky. There seemed to be no current at all and our paddles stirred up the soft mud. The bulrushes, with long thick leaves and brown seed boxes, pressed in around us.

Company Along the Way

Suddenly Peter cried out, "Look! There's another canoe ahead of us."

I looked in the direction he was pointing. Sure enough, partly hidden in the rushes was another canoe. It didn't seem to be going anywhere, but resting still on the water. As we drew near, I could see there were two people in the canoe—a young couple, and they looked quite perplexed.

Peter guided our canoe to the side of theirs, and we greeted each other.

"We're heading down the river," I said. "We hope to reach the Sea of Tranquility."

"Yes," said the young man. "We're on the same journey, but right now we don't know which way to go. You can't see anything among these reeds. There are three ways forward here, and we're just debating which one to take."

"I was telling him to take the central channel," said the young woman. "Why don't you follow us? It's the largest and it's reasonably clear of bulrushes. The channel to the right isn't quite as broad, while the one to the left is quite choked with weeds, and very narrow."

"Good idea," said Peter. "That way, if we get lost, we'll be lost together and we can help each other."

"But we were instructed to take our directions from Far Mountain, not to follow the easiest-looking channel," I said. "I think I can see Far Mountain and it lies down this choked channel to the left."

"That can't be right," argued the young woman. "Look at it. It's far too narrow and full of weeds. I'm not certain we'd be able to get through. Obviously far more people take the central channel, because the way has been cleared."

"But the instructions were quite clear. If we choose only the easy channels, we'll get lost." I pointed to Far Mountain. "The correct way may not be the easy way. If we're going to reach the Sea of Tranquility, we take our directions from Far Mountain."

"Well, the mountain is a long way off," she said. "Right now I'm tired and just want to get out of this messy swamp. This looks the best way to go."

She seemed so sure of herself. Peter and her companion nodded their heads in agreement.

I looked at the central channel again, and it did indeed look much easier. If everybody else wanted to go this way, who was I to argue? It appeared the decision was made. I shrugged my shoulders. The young couple began to lead the way along the easy channel and we followed.

At first it looked like a good decision and we made encouraging progress, but I lost sight of Far Mountain and felt uncomfortable about our direction. After a while, the channel between the bulrushes narrowed until there was scarcely room to push the canoes through. Finally the channel disappeared altogether and we got bogged down in dense weeds. Obviously this had been the wrong way and we would have to go back.

As we paddled back the way we had come, Peter said apologetically to me, "I was wrong. We should have followed the instructions. We must use Far Mountain as our guide or we'll never get through this confusion."

On the way back, other possible channels kept opening to us and the young couple, in perplexity, wondered if we shouldn't try some of them. But Peter and I were now determined. We would go back to where we had left the proper direction. We would follow Far Mountain, even if the way seemed difficult and narrow.

The young couple wasn't convinced.

"There must be a better and simpler way," she insisted.

So it was that when we returned to spot where the channels had first divided, they decided that the right hand channel still looked better and easier. No matter what Far Mountain seemed to indicate, they decided to try the more convenient and easy way.

Peter was as determined as I was. He guided us into the channel from which we could see Far Mountain in the distance, leaving the young couple behind.

The way wasn't easy. The water seemed thick and heavy with weeds. Our paddles kept getting tangled in underwater roots. It took all our strength to push through the ever-present bulrushes. Soon we were both tired and weary, but we kept on. Even through the reeds and bulrushes, we got glimpses of Far Mountain. It seemed to beckon us. This was the right way to go, we were sure of it.

As we pushed our paddles into the thick and murky water, I was reminded of the names Charles had given the paddles—*Trust* and *Obey*. I felt assured that we were obeying what we had been told in spite of difficulties. I trusted we were making progress in the right direction even though the way seemed very demanding.

I'm learning another principle in developing a right relationship with God, I thought.

After a long and exhausting struggle, the weeds thinned out and the channel got easier to navigate. Sure enough, the water began to deepen and the bulrushes thinned out. With great relief, we paddled out of the bulrushes and saw the bright clean flow of the river ahead of us. We had made it through the Swamp of Confusion and felt triumphant.

We never did meet up with the young couple who kept looking for an easier way. For all we knew, they were still lost in the Swamp of Confusion.

Lessons from the Swamp

Peter and I paddled to the bank to take a rest and have some refreshment. As we rested, we discussed the meaning of our experience in the Swamp of Confusion.

"I'm sure glad we're out of that place," Peter said.

"Yes," I agreed. "We could have gotten ourselves lost quite easily, and that would have destroyed our journey."

"The danger of the swamp was that it presented all kinds of alternate routes. Many of those routes seemed easier than the true route, but following them would have sidetracked us. We could have easily lost our way."

"I think one of the lessons we need to learn from the swamp is that the way to wisdom isn't always easy. If our main priority is to choose the way of personal ease, comfort, and convenience, we'll be continually following paths that lead us astray."

"In difficult times, does the way to wisdom sometimes call for discipline and perseverance?" Peter asked.

"Yes," I replied. "More than that, we need to keep our eyes on Far Mountain."

"That certainly gave us our direction," Peter said. "But why is Far Mountain so important?"

"Because it's our destination. At the foot of Far Mountain lies the Sea of Tranquility. All our instructors have told us to get our directions from Far Mountain. Part of growing in wisdom is knowing where you want to go in life and what you want to become. You need a clear picture of these important, long-range objectives, and then you need to keep them in mind as you make decisions."

"The important thing is to keep your objectives in mind and do the things that help you reach them," Peter said. "This sometimes means making hard decisions and denying yourself easy alternate routes. They may appear convenient, but they lead us in the wrong direction. I think the young couple wasn't as determined to get to the mountain as we were."

"Their desire was weak enough that they were prepared to give it up in favor of easier paths," I said. "Our desire to reach our objective must be strong enough that it keeps us motivated and determined, even when it comes with personal sacrifice. Overriding purpose gives you guidance when difficult or confusing decisions have to be made. Certainly if your main purpose is to satisfy your own convenience, the way of wisdom isn't for you. The way of wisdom sometimes calls for discipline and sacrifice."

Peter smiled. "You mean there's short-term pain for long-term gain."

"Choosing long-term objectives will be very important. You and I have set out to find a better way to walk with God and fellowship with Him. Our objectives are to get to know Him better, and to live the life He has in mind for us."

"Of course," said Peter. "But it is by no means easy. I remember a saying of Jesus I had to memorize in Sunday school. It went something like this:

> *Enter through the narrow gate. For wide is the gate and broad is the road that leads to destruction, and many enter through it. But small is the gate and narrow the road that leads to life, and only a few find it."* (Matthew 7:13–14)

"Clearly, Jesus didn't think the easy way was always the right way. Another lesson we should learn from the swamp is that it's wise to be careful from whom we take advice. The young couple was very nice and I liked them, but they clearly had a different set of objectives than we had. We shouldn't have listened to them or followed them."

"But they said they wanted to arrive at wisdom, just like we do," objected Peter.

"Yes! But not if it was going to prove too difficult, painful, or inconvenient. We're going to have to accept the fact that if we want to gain wisdom, we'll have to make difficult decisions along the way. We need to be careful to follow the guidance of those who understand where we want to go and approve of our commitment to it. Those who have other objectives or are consumed with their own interests aren't likely to give us good advice. We cannot listen to all the voices that speak to us."

Peter then made a very important remark. "It will call for wisdom to know from whom we should take advice. There's lots of advice around, but as you said, not all of it is good." Peter smiled. "Another thing I had to do in Sunday school was memorize the first Psalm. I didn't comprehend at the time, but now it makes sense. The first two verses go like this:

> *Oh, the joys of those who do not follow evil men's advice, who do not hang around with sinners, scoffing at the things of God: But they delight in doing every thing God wants them to, and day and night are always meditating on his laws and thinking about ways to follow him more closely."* (Psalm 1:1–2, TLB)

I laughed and congratulated Peter on his good memory.

We loaded up the canoe and started out again feeling, better for having come to new conclusions. We realized how easily we could have lost our way.

Topics for Discussion

1. What lessons were learned in the swamp? Can you give examples from your own life when you've been lost in a "swamp"?

Ten

The Resource Center

After the confusion of the swamp, we found the journey pleasant and not too demanding. The afternoon passed quickly. Peter continued to guide the canoe, so I was the one who first caught sight of the village. It was built on the left bank of the river. The village was modest, with only a few houses, but it was still a welcome sight as we were hungry and tired.

I pointed to the village. "That must be the village Phyllis told us about, the one where we can find the resource center."

There was a convenient dock for us to disembark. As we looked about, there was only one street in the village, with a few older houses on each side. As we secured our canoe, a man came down to welcome us. We explained that we were travelers and had been advised to stop here and visit Craig at the resource center.

The man's face lit up with recognition. "Come, I'll take you to his house. He'll be glad to see you. He always welcomes visitors."

With friendly and easy chatter, the man led us up the street, stopping occasionally to introduce us to the few people who happened to be passing by. Craig's house was the last house in the village. It was a simple dwelling but well-maintained. Behind it was a large building that looked like a workshop.

Our friend led us up the pathway to the house and knocked on the door. The man who answered the call was elderly with grey hair and a wrinkled face. Yet his dark eyes seemed alive and alert.

"Come in, come in," his deep voice said to us. It was full life and energy.

The man who met us at the dock seemed to assume responsibility for us and explained to Craig who we were and what our purpose was. Happy to welcome us, Craig took us into his sitting room, where he invited us to make ourselves comfortable. We talked for a while until our friend, feeling his responsibilities were taken care of, excused himself and left.

Craig was interested in our journey, and we told him about our spiritual awakening. He listened carefully to our whole story.

"We understand this first section of the journey is to convince us just how important wisdom is," Peter said. "Having listened to our instructors so far, I can see wisdom was indeed vital for the successful outcomes of Jesus' life and teaching. But Phyllis indicated you are knowledgeable about the teachings of the early church and can show us how important wisdom was to the early Christians. She said you're a good Bible scholar and can teach on this matter."

Craig smiled at this. "I'm no great Bible scholar. Nevertheless, I'm glad you've come. It just happens that there will be a small group of us meeting tomorrow morning and this is what we'll be talking about. I hope you can join us."

We both indicated we would be very happy to do that.

"In that case, please stay with me tonight," Craig said. "We can have supper together and spend the evening in conversation."

We were delighted with this arrangement, so Craig led us into his kitchen. Since he lived alone, we could all help prepare the meal. As we worked busily under Craig's direction, he told us that he had been married and had three children. All of his children were now adults and had left home to get on with their own lives. His beloved wife, the love of his life, had died three years ago.

"It was a dreadful shock," he said. "We were so close. I've tried to fill the void by operating this small resource center. I enjoy it, but it's not at all demanding. I've also started Bible study classes to teach young people like you the importance, meaning, and principles of biblical wisdom. People keep coming to me for advice, and I enjoy helping as many as I can. The group who's coming tomorrow is from the surrounding area. There will be about six of them. Most of them attend church, and like you they seek to be wiser in their spiritual lives, learning to invest their spiritual energy in the most meaningful way."

As we sat around the table eating, Peter said, "I know everyone would say that wisdom is important. Certainly those we have met so far on the journey have impressed this upon us. I understand now that wisdom was important for Jesus, but I wonder about His early followers and disciples. Was wisdom important for them?"

"I think tomorrow's class may help you with that," said Craig. "I'll be talking about the importance of wisdom in the teachings of the original apostles. However, if you like, after we've cleared up I can tell you the story of Stephen. He was one of the very first Christians and his story illustrates how the early church viewed wisdom."

When the meal was finished and everything was cleared up, Craig made coffee and we sat down in the living room.

The Story of Stephen

"After Jesus' death and resurrection," Craig began, "the message and spirit of Jesus Christ was absorbed by the apostles and the other members of the early Christian church. With great effectiveness, it was promoted throughout Jerusalem and all of Palestine, and then in the Middle East and Europe. Because these early disciples had been so close to Jesus, they accurately reflected His priorities and values. In response to your uncertainty, Peter, we need to ask if wisdom was one of the values and priorities amongst those first Christians.

"The growth and sudden development of the Christian church inevitably created some administrative and internal problems, and it took great wisdom to deal with them. Lack of wisdom in handling some these problems could have significantly crippled the forward march of the young church. The need for wisdom amongst the leaders and spokespersons for the church became obvious. A good illustration of the primacy of wisdom is seen in the story of Stephen.

"Stephen was a young man who lived in Jerusalem when the events of Jesus' crucifixion took place. Since all of Jerusalem was alive with stories and rumors about Jesus, Stephen, like most people in the city, showed a great deal of interest in Jesus and His teachings. One day, Stephen's curiosity got the better of him and he went to the temple to see and hear the prophet for himself. He came away deeply impressed. The aura that Stephen sensed around Jesus was quite different from those of the other teachers and rabbis he'd heard. Jesus had a spirit of authority, and His teachings seemed fresh and new.

"Stephen went again to hear Jesus, but this time he mixed and mingled with the man's followers. They were very sincere and passionate about their leader, although they obviously couldn't stretch their minds to understand all that He was saying.

"Stephen had never actually seen this prophet perform a miracle, but he'd heard many stories. Jesus' disciples maintained that the miracles gave authenticity to what their teacher was saying. To Stephen, everything about this man was both captivating and disturbing. Like many others in Palestine, he began to seriously consider whether or not this man could be the long-promised messiah.

"The dream, that Jesus was indeed the messiah, seemed to be quite decisively destroyed on the terrible day when Jesus was crucified. No messiah would let himself be crucified. It was devastating to Stephen that all the hopes and expectations that had built up around this man should be so quickly and completely destroyed. He had almost been ready to believe in Him. Now all was lost. Jesus was dead and buried. It was finished. Jesus' disciples were scattered and demoralized. With the crucifixion over, Stephen knew he had to try to forget the whole episode, but still he couldn't dismiss the sense of deep disappointment and broken hopes that the death of Jesus brought upon him.

"Not quite," said Craig with a gentle nod of his head. "Surreptitious stories began to circulate that the disciples of Jesus were claiming He had risen from the dead. Stephen had a hard time believing this. Since he knew some of the disciples, he sought them out. They were reluctant to say too much out of fear that they too might arouse the wrath of those who had crucified Jesus. But little by little, Stephen pieced together the story. The tomb had been closed by rolling a great stone over the mouth of the cave. It was then sealed and guarded by Roman soldiers. When the followers visited the tomb on Sunday morning, they discovered the seal had been broken, the soldiers weren't present, and the great stone had been rolled away. The grave was empty. Jesus' grave clothes were lying on the ground. Some of the disciples said they saw angels in and around the tomb.

"Amazingly, on various occasions, Jesus then appeared to some of them. Stories quietly abounded. Stephen could clearly sense that these followers were themselves amazed and excited. They didn't look like men who had manufactured a story just to justify their commitment to a lost cause. The excitement in their voices and their shinning eyes announced the truth of the claim. They seemed unwilling, however, to make any public proclamation.

"A few weeks later, during the festival day of Pentecost, the secrecy was shattered and the followers of Jesus burst out in public with the stunning message that Jesus of Nazareth, who had been cruelly crucified and buried, had victoriously risen from the dead.

"As Stephen heard the story, the disciples had a vivid experience that transformed them from being secretive and timid believers into dynamic public proclaimers. It has been described this way:

> *When the day of Pentecost came, they were all together in one place. Suddenly a sound like the blowing of a violent wind came from heaven and filled the whole house where they were sitting. They saw what seemed to be tongues of fire that separated and came to rest on each of them. All of them were filled with the Holy Spirit and began to speak in other tongues as the Spirit enabled them.* " (Acts 2:1–4)

This was new to me, and I was fascinated.

"In the power of this new anointing from God, the apostles and early disciples went out into public to proclaim in no uncertain terms that Jesus of Nazareth had indeed risen from the dead," Craig continued. "They said that Jesus was none other than the promised messiah. The disciplines' power and conviction was such that their message sank into the hearts of many who heard them and a whole multitude of people cried out in repentance and believed in Jesus. The number of people who became believers that day was a stunning three thousand. That was only the start. Day by day, great numbers of people accepted the message and believed in Jesus.

"The original followers had been few, but now literally thousands were turning to the cause. Stephen was amazed at the power and dynamism being exhibited by the apostles and other leaders of the new movement. Soon all Jerusalem was alive with the new faith, and it was spreading beyond Jerusalem. It was like a great tidal wave of religious fervor. Everybody was talking about it."

This was the first time I'd ever heard about the start of the Christian church after Jesus' death. I watched Peter, knowing he must have heard this story before, but he too was captivated.

"In addition to these happenings, stories about miracles began to circulate again," Craig said. "Only now it wasn't Jesus performing the miracles, but His disciples. Stephen wondered, could it possibly be true?"

Stephen Becomes a Christian

"Stephen then remembered the great day when he had finally decided to believe in Jesus and accept Him as his master and messiah. That decision was decisive. His heart was changed. He was a believer in the power and resurrection of Jesus Christ. He accepted His teachings. He tried to live his life in harmony with what Jesus had taught.

"The excitement of being part of this new movement gripped Stephen. The power and energy of the message, the change it was bringing into people's lives, the hope and joy it seemed to generate, the remarkable miracles the disciples were performing in the name of Jesus all seemed to indicate a power and authenticity that could only be explained as the presence and activity of God. Stephen had never seen anything like it, and he gave himself to Jesus wholeheartedly, and to spreading and developing the movement."

Stephen Becomes a Leader

"Perhaps it was because of his youth and energy, and because he'd already had contact with the disciples, but Stephen came to the attention of the leading apostles. They engaged him as an assistant in their ever-mushrooming responsibilities in the new church.

"With great enthusiasm, Stephen committed himself to the work and message of the Christian movement. These early Christians were an exuberant and joyful group. Such was the depth of their conviction and faith, and so great was the evidence of God's power amongst them, that their numbers continued to grow very rapidly.

"While Stephen threw himself into the work and ministry of the new church, he couldn't hope to keep in touch with all the rapid developments that were taking place. In addition to his work with the apostles, he became engaged with a smaller group of believers with whom he met, worshiped, and fellowshipped on a regular basis.

"The apostles circulated amongst the growing groups of Christian believers and provided them with teaching and information about the exciting developments taking place in Jerusalem and beyond. Stephen was glad for the leadership these men were giving to the early church and maintained his pledge to help them in any way he could. He sometimes accompanied the apostles as they visited the various groups. Soon the apostles' trust in Stephen enabled them to give him charge over some of the teaching and administrative matters that arose. These were busy, involved, and fulfilling days for Stephen.

"As he circulated in the Christian groups, under the guidance of the apostles, Stephen became aware of a developing problem. Many of the first Christians met together for meals and fellowship. Food was brought in for these occasions and distributed among all the members. As the numbers increased, however, this became a major administrative problem. The Bible describes it like this:

> *In those days when the number of disciples was increasing, the Grecian Jews among them complained against the Hebraic Jews because their widows were being overlooked in the daily distribution of food.*" (Acts 6:1)

Stephen Was Appointed Because of His Wisdom

"And this," said Craig, "is where the matter of wisdom emerges as a vital element in the early church. The apostles, along with the other leaders of the new movement, met to discuss the problem. Stephen was honored to be one of this group. These Christian leaders realized that if the matter wasn't dealt with, it could easily sow seeds of hostility and division. Since the apostles' time and energy were already stretched to capacity, they decided that other leaders should be elected to handle this problem, and those leaders would supervise the distribution of the food.

"Because of the sensitive nature of the problem, and its potential for significant disruption to the spirit and dynamism of the Christian movement, they realized that trustworthy and respected men were needed. These were the disciples' instructions: '*Brothers, choose seven men from among you who are known to be full of the Spirit and wisdom. We will turn this responsibility over to them*' (Acts 6:3). Stephen was surprised to be elected as one of these seven men. He understood that they had been chosen because they exhibited two qualities—they were full of the Spirit and wisdom. It was clear that the quality looked for in the very first elected leaders of the Christian church was the spirit of wisdom. Even in the midst of all the excitement and wonder of these early days, wisdom emerged as a significant value."

Craig sat back. "So you see, the story of Stephen illustrates how important wisdom was in the practical administration of the early Christian movement.

Men of wisdom were sought after and prized. They were placed in positions of responsibility and leadership. Whether stated or not, the possession of wisdom by our leaders, in all walks of life, both inside and outside the church, has always been very important.

"One doesn't need to look far to see how easily lack of wisdom can allow issues to deteriorate into squabbles and hostile disagreements. These disputes can rob people of their fellowship and dynamism, distracting them from their purpose. Many a fine cause has lost its initial enthusiasm and vision due to this tension. There are many examples in the history of Christian churches of delicate problems that were unwisely handled and developed into major dissention."

The Wisdom of the Apostles

"While we recognize that the spirit of wisdom in the heart and character of Stephen and those first elected leaders was necessary, we also need to acknowledge that the apostles themselves were wise on this occasion. The Bible states,

> *So the Twelve gathered all the disciples together and said, 'It would not be right for us to neglect the ministry of the word of God in order to wait on tables. Brothers, choose seven men from among you who are known to be full of the Spirit and wisdom. We will turn this responsibility over to them and will give our attention to prayer and the ministry of the word.'"* (Acts 6:2–4)

At this point, Craig turned to us. "Why do you think this decision showed wisdom on the part of the apostles?"

I responded, although I thought Peter may have been better qualified to answer the question. "The apostles were wise enough to insist that their focus, attention, and energy be given to the top priorities of their ministry—prayer and preaching. They wouldn't allow themselves to be diverted from their fundamental responsibilities."

"A good answer," said Craig. "An essential ingredient of wisdom is the ability to recognize the things that are important and then organize life so that these priorities are given appropriate time and attention. It's not wise, for example, to neglect God while busily pursuing your own affairs. It's not wise to neglect those you love in your home and family in order to take care of outside interests.

It's not wise to become so absorbed in worldly affairs that you must forsake the needs of your spirit and soul. Good wisdom saved the early church from making critical errors in its fragile early years."

I interrupted Craig, saying, "That sounds similar to the advice we were given by Charles. He told us to keep our eye on Far Mountain, that it would give us direction and save us from being diverted into side channels. It's the marker that guides us to our desired destination."

"Exactly," replied Craig. "You establish your priorities and then direct the affairs of your life so that you are moving towards their fulfillment. Good objectives and priorities are the fundamental values you want to reach and possess. You make all decisions with these in mind."

Wisdom Was Prominent in the Early Church

Craig brought his story to a conclusion. "As the Christian church continued to expand and mature, the need for God-given wisdom continued to be an important emphasis both in the teaching and practice of the church. The early church seemed to understand that there was a connection between the work and ministry of the Holy Spirit and the spirit of wisdom. Under the guidance of the Holy Spirit, wisdom remained an essential element in the church. The need for wisdom was built into the consciousness of early Christians.

"When we meet with the class tomorrow, we'll talk about wisdom in the writings of Paul the Apostle, and you'll see how greatly he prized wisdom. He wanted urgently for his new converts to be blessed with wisdom."

Both Peter and I had been enthralled by the story of Stephen. We could see why Craig had taken the time to tell the story. It illustrated the emergence of wisdom as an important factor in the establishment and smooth operation of the early Christian church.

Peter sat especially quietly, deep in thought after the story.

"This is just an introduction to what I'll talk about tomorrow. It'll give you a bit of background as we look into the writings of the early apostles. Why not give it some thought?"

We retired for the night. Both of us were now looking forward to the next day's class.

Topics of Discussion

1. Stephen was elected to office by the early church because he was full of the Holy Spirit and wisdom. Are those still essential for church leaders today? What other qualities would we look for in church leaders?

2. The apostles made a wise decision when they decided not to give up prayer and the preaching of the word in order to serve tables. Outline what you see as the essential ingredients that made this a wise decision.

ELEVEN

Wisdom in the New Testament

AFTER BREAKFAST, THE STUDY GROUP BEGAN TO ASSEMBLE. THERE WERE EIGHT OF us altogether: three couples with Peter and me. The couples were all young and married. They belonged to the church Craig attended and most of them were, like us, new Christians who didn't know much about the Christian experience but were eager to learn.

What a good thing Craig is doing in taking these young people under his wing and mentoring them, I thought.

The young people, in turn, seemed to deeply respect Craig and looked to him for guidance.

Once Craig had introduced us all, we sat down and prayed together. He then explained the questions Peter and I had raised about wisdom. Today, he wished to talk about the significance of wisdom in the writings of the apostles, especially the Apostle Paul. He wanted us to particularly notice three aspects in which wisdom is emphasized in Paul's epistles. These three aspects were wisdom in Paul's prayer life, wisdom as one of the gifts of the Spirit, and wisdom as it came from the heart of Jesus Christ.

Wisdom in the Prayers of Paul

To begin, Craig opened his Bible. "When you examine the Apostle Paul's prayers for his Christian converts, you can see how important wisdom was in his estimation. Paul understood that these people were new Christians who had very little background or understanding of the Christian way of life. They had been raised as pagans and they lived in a pagan society, surrounded by pagan ideas and practices. Christianity was contrary to their customs and culture.

"Paul was able to teach them the elementary truths about Jesus and the way of salvation, but since he was called to be a Christian missionary, he was also anxious to reach new people with the Gospel. As soon as he was satisfied that a group was strong enough in their faith, Paul felt the urge to move on.

"Paul did, however, do everything he could to help young believers continue to grow and develop into mature followers of Jesus. For their guidance, he sent teachers to give them further instruction. He appointed leaders among them to organize their local churches. He wrote them letters in which he gave further advice. In addition to all that, as part of his continuing ministry, he prayed for them. In each of his epistles, Paul assures his readers that he's praying on their behalf.

"It's enlightening to notice the content of Paul's prayers. One of the things he constantly prayed for was that these new and growing Christians would be given wisdom. Paul understood that receiving wisdom was a vital element in their spiritual growth. If these people developed a wise insight into what God was like and how He operated, all kinds of spiritual richness would flourish in their lives. On the other hand, he understood that lack of wisdom could result in errors, misunderstandings, disappointments, and conflicts. So Paul didn't pray that they become rich and prosperous businessmen, or successful and powerful politicians. He prayed for something much more important; he prayed that they become wise in the ways of God."

Now we're getting to the heart of it, I thought as Craig spoke. *This is why I came on this journey. I wanted to become wise in the ways of God.*

"Now let's look at some of the specific concerns Paul had as he prayed for his young church converts."

81

The Ephesian Prayer

"Paul prayed for the Christians in Ephesus by assuring them,

> *I have not stopped giving thanks for you, remembering you in my prayers. I keep asking that the God of our Lord Jesus Christ, the glorious Father, may give you the Spirit of wisdom and revelation, so that you may know him better."* (Ephesians 1:16–17)

This quotation struck me very forcefully.

"I'm so glad to hear that," I exclaimed with enthusiasm. "We set out on this journey so we could get to know God better, and here the Apostle makes a clear connection between wisdom and getting to know God. His prayer has been my prayer. I pray that I'll be given the spirit of wisdom so I can know Him better."

"Yes," Craig concurred. "Paul makes a clear connection between wisdom and Christian growth. Those early Christians needed Paul to pray about many things, but at the top of the Apostle's list is the prayer that they be given the Spirit of wisdom. They needed wisdom so they could learn how to know God better. They needed wisdom to understand how the Christian spirit worked in their everyday lives. They needed wisdom to know how the Spirit of Christ within them could be applied to the daily decisions they made in a pagan culture. They needed understanding to experience how the energies and power of God's love could be released in their lives. And they needed to be willing to wisely seek ever new and greater insights.

"A rich and wonderful life was available to them now that they were followers of Jesus Christ. New power from God flowed into their lives, transforming everything. They needed wisdom to know how best to appropriate this grace from God. They needed wisdom to know how to properly channel God's life into the habits and practices of daily fellowship with Him. Paul wanted them to understand that the level of fruitfulness they experienced as Christians was largely determined by their level of wisdom."

One of the young men raised his hand. "Does that mean the function of wisdom is like a tool that helps us get the job done better?"

"I've never thought of it like that," said Craig slowly, "but, yes, when you think about it, the two could be compared. If you can imagine a carpenter trying to do intricate work on a piece of wood with poor tools, or no tools at all, then you understand he would never be able to produce the fine piece of art he wants to produce. Every carpenter knows that good, well-maintained tools are essential to doing good work. Wisdom shows us how to take the raw material of our experience with God and shape our unwieldy and ignorant personalities into the beauty and likeness of Jesus Christ. This can't happen satisfactorily if our tools are faulty or blunt. Good wisdom is to our spirit like good tools are to a carpenter."

I felt encouraged, for it seemed to confirm that in my desire to know God better, my journey down the River of Wisdom was indeed the correct thing to do.

The Colossian Prayer

"In fact, the same expectation is expressed by Paul in his prayer for the Colossian Christians," continued Craig. "He prayed,

> *For this reason, since the day we heard about you, we have not stopped praying for you and asking God to fill you with the knowledge of his will through all spiritual wisdom and understanding.* (Colossians 1:9)

"Paul again prays that these people receive spiritual wisdom and understanding. He goes on to explain that spiritual wisdom is the key to opening for them all manner of blessings, spiritual richness, and fulfillment. In Colossians 1:10–12, he outlines the blessings which this spiritual wisdom can unlock. The outcome of following the spiritual wisdom of Jesus Christ is that they

> *may live a life worthy of the Lord and may please him in every way: bearing fruit in every good work, growing in the knowledge of God, being strengthened with all power according to his glorious might so that you may have great endurance and patience, and joyfully giving thanks to the Father, who has qualified you to share in the inheritance of the saints in the kingdom of light.* (Colossians 1:10–12)

"That's quite a list of blessings, but Paul knew and understood that wisdom would help those Christians understand God and know better how to enter into the richness and fullness of loving God and following Christ. Lack of wisdom would cause them to neglect, misdirect, and misuse the great energies of God in their lives."

Craig looked out over all of the class, pausing for emphasis. "For them and for us, the silent, unobtrusive power of wisdom is essential to grasping the abundance of life in Christ. A rich, wonderful, and exciting spiritual life is available for us, but in order to enter into it and possess it for ourselves, we need to develop wisdom in the ways of God and be willing to apply it."

The Philippian Prayer

"Look at another prayer of Paul's, this one recorded in the book of Philippians," continued Craig. "It follows the same theme:

> *And this is my prayer: that your love may abound more and more in knowledge and depth of insight, so that you may be able to discern what is best and may be pure and blameless until the day of Christ, filled with the fruit of righteousness that comes through Jesus Christ—to the glory and praise of God.* (Philippians 1:9–11)

"The spirit of wisdom gives us valuable depth of insight. We need good wisdom to be able to discern what is best and pure. Paul was trying to impress upon these early followers of the Lord that their growth, fruitfulness, and victory will be largely dependent on how wisely they learn to respond to truth and the activity of the Holy Spirit in their lives. He understood that if they neglected the matter of being wise, much of their sincere efforts would be spoiled, the sweet fruit wouldn't mature, and they wouldn't experience the victory that knowing God should bring to their lives.

"The Apostle was well aware that one's life in Christ is abundant and fruitful. In order to experience this abundance, Christians need to learn how to appropriate the truths of the Gospel and apply the principles and priorities of the Spirit of Christ to their daily lives. A lack of wisdom leads to unrealized abundance. Without wisdom, we fail to reap the great harvest made available to us, leaving us weak and underdeveloped in our walk with God."

We Should Pray for Wisdom

Craig looked at all of us, and was quiet for a while. The silence allowed the meaning of what he had said to impress upon our minds.

"It is vital that we join the Apostle and begin to pray for wisdom," he continued. "Paul was a great man of prayer and would have prayed for many things, but wisdom was among his top priorities. We, like Paul, have many things that we bring to God in prayer, but wisdom must be high on the list so that the life He has planned for us can become a reality. This prayer for wisdom should also be extended to others, including our leaders."

"I'm glad you said that," commented Peter. "I have to confess that I've never prayed much for wisdom."

One of the ladies present added to what Peter had said: "I haven't prayed much for wisdom, either. The only time I've heard others pray for wisdom was when they were facing some difficulty that perplexed them. When they didn't know what to do, they prayed for wisdom."

Peter pointed to me. "We were discussing this before and Colin had a good illustration. He said wisdom shouldn't be considered a spare tire, for use only in emergencies. It should be more like a steering wheel, in constant use to keep us on the right road."

Craig laughed at this. "Certainly it's good to pray for wisdom when we're faced with a difficult problem, but we need wisdom through everything we handle in life. Only praying for wisdom when you face a crisis is like using it as a spare tire. The prayer for wisdom should be a habit we include regularly in our prayers. Paul wasn't just praying for himself here, he was praying for others. It is a great kindness for you to include wisdom in your prayers for others. Those of you raising children should certainly pray that they be given wisdom as they make essential life decisions."

Another thought occurred to me. "The fact that Paul prayed for wisdom not only means that it's important, but that he believed God would answer that prayer and give us more wisdom."

"Yes," Craig said. "God wants to answer our prayers and help us grow in wisdom. It means wisdom can develop in our hearts. You can grow in wisdom. You can get better at it. No matter how wise you think you are, you can improve. When it comes to wisdom, nobody's perfect. If you're unwise and have done unwise things, don't despair. If you pray about it, God will help you to improve. Indeed, He's anxious to help you handle life more effectively. So pray for wisdom, because God answers this prayer."

Another gentleman in the class put up his hand. "I wonder if the prayer for wisdom is particularly relevant for us today. Because of the pressures of my life, I become confused about how to balance my spiritual values with the physical and worldly necessities of living. I don't know how to discipline my physical legitimate needs so that I can enjoy both a full life here on earth and also satisfy my need for fellowship and intimacy with God."

"One of the things wisdom does," replied Craig, "is help us find a balance between the requirements of life in this world with the inner needs of the soul. The demands of the world seem very urgent, while the needs of the soul can be easily neglected. Living life to the full, so each dimension is taken care of, calls for great understanding and wisdom. Maintaining this balance isn't easy. In order to function with balance and effectiveness, we need the quiet, steady strength of wisdom. We need to act on what we know. That's why Jesus said that *wisdom is proved right by her actions* (Matthew 11:19)."

"This is good," a young man said. "It seems to me that God has provided for us a bountiful harvest of spiritual reality, but without wisdom guiding our labor the harvest can be largely unreaped. We can even foolishly neglect the harvest while we become engrossed in less important matters."

Another of the ladies present now spoke up. "I see it more like an orchard. The orchards of God hang heavy with fruit, but without the good sense of wisdom the fruit is largely unpicked and unseen, because we're foolishly unaware that it's even there. Or perhaps we neglect it while we dig around looking for weeds."

"This is good," said Craig. "Harvests and orchards are very common metaphors in the Bible. It's tragic when rich fruit doesn't ripen, when harvests go to waste. These are the results of not wisely cooperating with the systems God has put in place to make these riches available to us. In fact, one of the great activities of the Holy Spirit is to produce within our hearts the beautiful fruits of the spirit."

"What are the fruits of the Spirit?" I asked.

"They are listed for us in Paul's letter to the Galatians," said Craig. Turning in his Bible, he read, *'But the fruit of the Spirit is love, joy, peace, patience, kindness, goodness, faithfulness, gentleness and self control. Against such things there is no law'* (Galatians 5:22–23). When you cooperate with the systems of God, you reap this rich and blessed harvest. It's a beautiful way to live.

"The work of the Holy Spirit in a person's heart not only brings these wise fruits, but Paul also talks about the gifts of the Holy Spirit. This leads into the second aspect of wisdom Paul emphasizes in his writings—wisdom in the gifts of the Spirit."

The Gifts of the Spirit

Craig began to turn the pages of his Bible. "In writing to the young church in Corinth, Paul outlined a list of special gifts given by the Holy Spirit that would empower them to more effectively serve God. He named nine gifts in this list:

Now to each one the manifestation of the Spirit is given for the common good. To one there is given through the Spirit the message of wisdom, to another the message of knowledge by means of the same Spirit, to another faith by the same Spirit, to another gifts of healing by that one Spirit, to another miraculous powers, to another prophecy, to another distinguishing between spirits, to another speaking in different kinds of tongues, and to still another the interpretation of tongues. All these are the work of one and the same Spirit, and he gives them to each one, just as he determines. (1 Corinthians 12:7–11)

"I don't want to go into everything Paul meant by the gifts of the Spirit," said Craig. "It's simply important for us to take note that wisdom is named as one of these gifts. Therefore, wisdom is something God wants to impart to the church to make it more effective in its service to Him. It's a desirable and important quality for Christians to possess.

"More than that, as you read about the gifts of the Spirit you notice that wisdom is mentioned first. One of the great activities of the Holy Spirit is to impart wisdom, so we can live wisely and serve effectively in this world. Since the gift is called "a message of wisdom," this means we can enrich and guide others by our God-given wisdom. The Holy Spirit is anxious to impart to us the spirit of wisdom so we can serve Him more effectively and be a blessing and enrichment to others. Wisdom will enlighten us, so we can deepen our fellowship with Him."

Craig paused in his lesson and leaned forward. "When we think of the Holy Spirit and His work in our lives, we often think of the power and effectiveness He brings. This is correct. However, power without wisdom can be dangerous. Sincerity without wisdom can be wasted. Enthusiasm without wisdom can lead us astray. No wonder Paul urges those same Corinthian Christians, *'Brothers, stop thinking like children. In regard to evil be infants, but in your thinking be adults'* (1 Corinthians 14:20).

As Craig spoke, my mind went back to the young couple Peter and I had seen outside the restaurant.

How beneficial this discussion would have been to them, I thought. *They were so dedicated and so earnest, yet so unwise and ineffective in the expression of their devotion.*

"In the early church, the Holy Spirit seemed to be very active and present," Craig said. "Great and miraculous things were accomplished for God. But Paul is trying to teach them that much effort can be wasted if the energy is expended unwisely. The power and presence of the Holy Spirit is a wonderful and necessary gift not only for the church community, but also for the personal development and guidance of individual Christians in their experience with God. But an unwise, immature response to this power can lead to fanatical excess or lazy indifference.

"Sincerity is a great Christian virtue, but unwise sincerity can create great misunderstanding and hurtfulness. Enthusiasm is a strong energy producer for the work of God, but enthusiasm without discipline and direction can be misdirected into wastefulness and folly. One of the essential and primary gifts the Holy Spirit brings into the life of the individual is wisdom. We neglect wisdom to our peril. We need to be more like Stephen and be filled with the Spirit and wisdom. Paul reaffirms this in writing to the Ephesians:

> *Be very careful, then, how you live—not as unwise but as wise, making the most of every opportunity, because the days are evil. Therefore do not be foolish, but understand what the Lord's will is."*
> (Ephesians 5:15–17)

One of the men interrupted. "I'm a volunteer firefighter. I know from experience that fire can be either a great benefit or a destructive force. Fire has brought warmth, light, energy, and health to our lives. If all the benefits of fire were to be suddenly withdrawn from the world, our lives would come to a premature end. Fire is essential for life here on earth. But I've seen houses consumed by out-of-control fires. I've seen forests destroyed by wildfire. I've seen beautiful grasslands scorched by windblown prairie fires. Fire can be a blessing or a curse, depending on whether or not it's controlled and channeled. I imagine it's much the same with the spiritual energies in our lives. If they're used wisely, they are a great benefit. If not, they can cause much disruption."

Craig nodded his agreement. "The energies released in our lives by our new commitments to God can be channeled into great blessing and produce wonderful fruitfulness and fulfillment. But if they run out of control, they can cause great damage. Wisdom guides us to discipline, focus, and control our energies so they can be channeled into fulfilling the correct purposes."

Wisdom and the Riches of Christ

"Now, let's look at a third aspect of wisdom in Paul's writing. He makes it clear that if we are to experience the riches of God, we must understand that they come from the heart of Jesus Christ. And it takes wisdom for us to understand just how these riches of wisdom work for us. Paul says that and while Jesus Christ has made all of these riches available to us, the key to unlocking them is wisdom. He writes to the Christians in Colossae,

> *My purpose is that they may be encouraged in heart and united in love, so that they may have the full riches of complete understanding, in order that they may know the mystery of God, namely, Christ, in whom are hidden all of the treasures of wisdom and knowledge.* (Colossians 2:2–3)

"The treasures of wisdom and knowledge are hidden in Jesus Christ. True wisdom points us to Jesus Christ. Jesus Christ points us to true wisdom.

"Not everybody has grasped the concept that there's a dimension to human existence in which life is found in fellowship with Jesus Christ. It takes spiritual understanding to see beyond the physical and material aspects of life and experience the wonders of spiritual realities. For those who grasp this, there are great riches hidden in Christ, but we need the wisdom of God to know how to unlock them.

"Jesus wasn't shy about pointing to Himself and His way of life as the source of true and abundant living. He said, *'I have come that they might have life, and have it to the full'* (John 10:10), and *'I am the way the truth and the life. No man comes to the Father except through me'* (John 14:6). He claimed, *'I am the bread of life. He who comes to me will never go hungry, and he who believes in me will never be thirsty'* (John 6:35). These are amazing claims. But Jesus is saying that if we want real and abundant life, if we want to experience fulfillment and joy, we must find it in Him, in what He represents. The Christ-centered life is the wise life. It is great wisdom to believe in Jesus Christ and to adjust our lives to conform to His Spirit and will."

The Doxology

"Paul cries out in the book of Romans, *'Oh, the depth of the riches of the wisdom and knowledge of God!'* (Romans 11:33) The riches of God are deep, and it takes considerable wisdom to dig into them and bring them to the surface so they can be experienced. In a similar vein, in 1 Corinthians, speaking about the wisdom of the Spirit, Paul says,

> *We have not received the spirit of the world but the Spirit who is from God, that we may understand what God has freely given us.*
> (1 Corinthians 2:12)

"It has all been given to us, but we need the wisdom of the Spirit to understand and experience what has been so freely made available."

The Wisdom of Christ Within Us

"In another important verse, Paul declares, *'It is because of him that you are in Christ Jesus, who has become for us wisdom from God—that is, our righteousness, holiness and redemption'* (1 Corinthians 1:30). The Spirit of Christ, living in our hearts, enlightens us as to how we appropriate for ourselves the wonderful blessings of righteousness, holiness, and redemption. But these are experienced in their fullness as we live in fellowship with Him, because the Spirit of Christ in us provides the wisdom to unlock all these treasures. As we get to know Christ and let His Spirit control our lives, we gain the wisdom to know how to experience the blessings of God. The wise life is the Christ-centered life. It is unwise, indeed, to lose all this richness by giving unbalanced attention to lesser priorities."

Craig raised his voice slightly for emphasis. "Paul makes it clear that when the principles and machinery of the spiritual life are working effectively, one of the basic principles at work is wisdom. When wisdom is absent, the spiritual machinery of our lives just doesn't function correctly. Our problem isn't a lack of knowledge, but a lack of wisdom in knowing how to apply that knowledge to our everyday lives."

Someone said, "I believe what you're saying, but could you give us an example?"

"Better still, I want you all to think of some aspect of your own spiritual life that isn't working as effectively as it should," Craig said. "I think you'll see a lack of wisdom in how you're going about it."

There was silence while we all hesitated to respond. Finally, the firefighter answered. "I don't seem to have the peace I should. I know God has promised that the peace of God will guard your hearts and minds, but guilt still haunts me.

I know the truth about the forgiving love of God, but I can't seem to appropriate that promise into peace and contentment. I know I have repented and trust in God and I believe in His loving forgiveness, but still there are times when I'm disturbed about my past and the things I've done. It robs me of peace."

"What about prayer?" the same man's wife asked. "God has made such wonderful promises about prayer. I know prayer should be a wonderful and exciting part of my fellowship with God, but so often I find it too formal. I don't seem to get answers for many things I pray for. My prayer life should be a source of great inspiration and fellowship, but often it's not."

Others jumped into the chorus of confession that their Christian lives didn't seem to function with all the riches and power that had been promised.

"What about the power of the Holy Spirit?" a young man asked. "I know from the Bible that we're promised great things through the power of the indwelling Holy Spirit. With the active presence of the Holy Spirit filling our lives, God could do great things with us. He promises power to overcome, fruitfulness in service, the constant and abiding comfort of His presence in our hearts. Why then do I remain so weak? Why are my efforts for Him so unavailing? How can it be that so much power is available to us from the Holy Spirit and yet my life and service is so ineffective?"

"And then there's purity," said a woman. "I know we're supposed to be pure in heart. I know that the blood of Jesus Christ is supposed to cleanse us from all sin, but why do I still have impurities in my heart? At times, I get hostile and jealous and proud. I know Jesus said, *'Blessed are the pure in heart, for they will see God'* (Matthew 5:8). But I don't always experience this."

"Alright! Alright!" Craig laughed, putting his hand up to stop us. "You can see that all of us have parts of our Christian lives that don't work the way they should. We could all do better. We are falling short because we've failed to understand and apply the grace God has made available to us. There could be any number of reasons for our spiritual faults. It could be an unwillingness to cooperate with what God wants to do. It could be lack of faith. But it could also be lack of wisdom. We don't do things right, or we do things in a misguided way. We don't understand the principles of God, of how He wants to work. We therefore fall short of the richness available for us. We need wisdom. We need to *seek* wisdom. We need to *pray* for wisdom. Our weaknesses are due to not applying the principles by which God works in our lives.

"Take prayer, for example. It could be such a powerful force in our lives, yet many people fall short of the promise in this area because they don't understand the principles and conditions by which God operates in answering prayer. No wonder we're told above all to seek wisdom.

"It's amazing how easy it is for false ideas about God and the way He works to become deeply engrained in our thinking. We jump to wrong conclusions and assume on misplaced principles. We place great faith in erroneous methods and yet wonder why God isn't more active in our lives. Instead of being wise, we continue to champion these methods and rely on them. Or else we become so comfortable in our wrong ways that we're unwilling to change. Perhaps the time has come for us to humbly acknowledge that parts of our lives aren't working and ask God for wisdom and insight into how to be more effective."

Be a Seeker after Wisdom

Craig rose, walked over, and stood behind Peter and me. He placed his hand on our shoulders. "To our visiting friends, let me say that one of the wisest things we can do is be seekers after wisdom. Have no doubt that your journey into wisdom is important.

"To all of us, let me say that one of the greatest functions of our lives is to become men and women of wisdom. Clearly, the Apostle Paul saw wisdom as a vital quality that needed to be present in the lives of early Christians if they were to function effectively and experience the full benefits of salvation in Jesus Christ. One of the greatest requests we can make of God is to request wisdom. No wonder Paul urged the early Christians,

> *Be very careful, then, how you live—not as unwise but as wise, making the most of every opportunity, because the days are evil. Therefore do not be foolish, but understand what the Lord's will is.*
> (Ephesians 5:15–17)

"We need to join the Apostle Paul and acknowledge our need for wisdom. We need to seek wisdom and insight into how He works, wisdom to understand the mind of God, wisdom to pursue His will for our lives, wisdom to be wise enough to understand His guidance and will, wisdom to know His values and priorities and pursue them, wisdom to know how to operate better and more efficiently in the spiritual world. And once you know, ask for grace and help to be willing to implement them in your lives. This is a prayer, indeed, and God has made a wonderful promise to us that this prayer will be answered."

After this, Craig returned to his seat, indicating that the session was over.

"You must understand," he said, "that there's much more in the New Testament about wisdom. I won't cover everything. Remember, you're only at the first stage in this journey. The next stage will teach you what wisdom is. But what you've heard today should help you settle in your mind that spiritual wisdom was indeed an important issue to the early church.

"I'd like us now to break. When we come back, I want to point out that wisdom was also important for success and leadership in the Old Testament."

Topics for Discussion

1. Expand on the concept that good wisdom is to our spirit like good tools are to a carpenter.

2. Discuss the difference between praying for wisdom as a regular, habitual request and praying for wisdom when we face perplexing situations.

3. Power without wisdom is dangerous. Sincerity without wisdom can be wasted. Enthusiasm without wisdom can lead us astray. Discuss.

4. Like the members of the class, think of some aspects of your walk with God that don't function properly. Is part of the problem a lack of wisdom in how you're going about it?

Twelve

Wisdom in the Old Testament

During the break, we were able to enjoy some refreshments and get to know the other people in the class. We had many friendly questions and exchanged personal information. Both Peter and I enjoyed the warm fellowship we sensed from the group.

Towards the end of the break, however, one of the couples singled us out and talked to us about our journey. We told them we were still in the early stages and that we understood there were four stages to the journey. The first, the stage we were in, was to help us gain an appreciation for the importance of wisdom. This was vital, for it seemed that we hadn't understood the importance of wisdom, or made any effort to develop or attain it.

"I'm quite convinced now," I said. "I look forward to getting to the second stage."

The couple, whose names were Lloyd and Elizabeth, continued to ask questions and seemed very interested in the journey. While we answered as best we could, we weren't always able to give them all the information they sought.

Finally, Craig called us together for the next session.

Looking at Peter and me, Craig said, "Your journey so far has focused on the importance of wisdom in as revealed in the New Testament. Right now, I want you to know that wisdom was also important in the Old Testament. The Old Testament writers often allude to wisdom. In fact, the whole books of Proverbs and Ecclesiastes are devoted to urging us to pursue wisdom. The author of Proverbs, King Solomon, wrote,

> *I want to make the simple-minded wise! I want to warn young men about some problems they will face. I want those already wise to become the wiser and become leaders by exploring the depth of meaning in these nuggets of truth.* (Proverbs 1:3–6, TLB)

"This morning's session on the Apostle Paul was rather heavy, so to lighten things up, I'd like to tell you a story from the Old Testament that illustrates just how important God considers wisdom to be."

We were all pleased with this suggestion and settled back to listen to the story.

Solomon Chooses Wisdom

"It was night across the land of Israel. The nation was at ease and slept securely. All was quiet except for a restless groaning coming from the royal tent of the young king, Solomon. Solomon had left his capital city of Jerusalem to visit the famous religious shrine in Gibeon in order to pay homage to God. But one night, as he was attending to these religious duties, Solomon's sleep was disturbed by a vivid dream. In the dream, God spoke to him, making a most unusual offer. Solomon had of course had dreams before, but never a dream like this. He was convinced God really was communicating with him, and not only that but He was also expecting a response.

"Solomon was in his early twenties and very inexperienced. Kingship had been thrust upon his young shoulders by his father, King David, who on his deathbed had declared that Solomon was to succeed him. Ready or not, Solomon found himself on the throne of Israel with all of the authority, power, and wealth that position brought with it. But along with these assets, he also felt the heavy weight of responsibility. He was now king, and he wanted to be a good king. He wanted the nation to prosper and grow under his leadership. His father had been an outstanding king in Israel, but David had been a warrior. During David's reign, Israel had been constantly at war, seeking to establish itself in a dominant position among the nations that surrounded it. Solomon, on the other hand, was not a warrior. He wanted peace and security. He hoped prosperity and justice would prevail. But how could an inexperienced young man lead the nation through this transition?

"In these early, uncertain days, Solomon had the dream. Its outcome was to launch Solomon on a path that would lead him and his nation into the most fruitful and prosperous time in all of Israel's history.

"In the dream, God made a breathtaking offer. God said, *'Ask for whatever you want me to give you'* (1 Kings 3:5). There were no conditions or limitations attached. For a young king just starting out, many possible responses must have passed through his mind: *I'll ask for wealth, so I can bring prosperity to the nation and to myself. With wealth, I can be a blessing to the people. I would have resources to build a great temple to God and a palace for myself. I could strengthen the fortifications of the city and afford a powerful army.* Although wealth would have been very tempting, Solomon decided to ask for something else. *I could ask for power. If I have power, my throne would be unchallenged. Great prestige and authority would come to the nation. My power would bring security and peace to the people.* But Solomon rejected the desire for power. He continued to think of other possibilities. *I'll ask for health and long life. I need energy and vitality to fulfill all of my duties. I need many years to accomplish what I want to accomplish. There's so much to be done that it cannot be done in a few short years.* But Solomon didn't ask for a long healthy life. Of all of the things he could have asked for, of all the things that were important for a young king to have, Solomon laid them all aside and decided on a surprising request: wisdom."

As I listened to this story, I wondered why, of all things, Solomon would ask for wisdom.

Craig continued, "In the dream, Solomon explained his needs to God. He said,

> *Now, O Lord my God, you have made your servant king in place of my father David. But I am only a little child and do not know how to carry out my duties. Your servant is here among the people you have chosen, a great people, too numerous to count or number. So give your servant a discerning heart to govern your people and to distinguish between right and wrong. For who is able to govern this great people of yours?* (1 Kings 3:7–9)

"So young Solomon, in the flush of his new power and authority, asked for wisdom. Above all else, he wanted wisdom to govern his people well and have insight so he would know the difference between right and wrong. He wanted wisdom to make the right decisions, support the correct values, and lead the country in a fruitful direction."

God Approves of Wisdom

"God's response to Solomon's choice of wisdom was very positive. The Bible records,

> *The Lord was pleased that Solomon had asked for this. So God said to him, 'Since you have asked for this and not for long life or wealth for yourself, nor have asked for the death of your enemies but for discernment in administering justice, I will do what you have asked. I will give you a wise and discerning heart, so that there will never have been anyone like you, nor will there ever be.'*
> (1 Kings 3:10–12)

"In fact, God was so pleased with Solomon's decision that He assured Solomon,

> *Moreover, I will give you what you have not asked for—both riches and honor—so that in your lifetime you will have no equal among kings. And if you walk in my ways and obey my statutes and commands as David your father did, I will give you a long life.* (1 Kings 3:13–14)

"It may only have been a dream, but when Solomon awoke he realized it had profound significance. He returned to Jerusalem, believing he'd had an important interaction with God that would establish the direction for his reign. In Jerusalem, he was determined to be a wise and discerning ruler. And God kept His promise. The reign of King Solomon became a time of unprecedented prosperity, peace, and security for the nation of Israel. At no other time in the nation's history would it rise to the same heights of power and honor it achieved under the direction of Solomon."

Wisdom, the Primary Value

"It's impossible to guess what the reign of Solomon would have been like if he had never received this divine endowment of wisdom. Nor do we know what would have happened if he hadn't chosen wisdom but opted for power, money, personal honor, or pleasure. But we do know that from the seeds of wisdom given to him by God that night, there grew and flourished a great kingdom, and that kingdom also accumulated all the other trappings of power, wealth, and success. Solomon became rich and powerful, gaining great honor and stature amongst the nations of the world. Israel's flowering during this era developed out of the fertile heart and mind of a man who chose and prized wisdom."

Craig now began to draw the lessons from the story. "Wisdom emerges as an important and vital quality. In fact, in the value system of God, wisdom is of greater worth than wealth, power, or health. God was pleased with Solomon's choice. It's not that wealth and power weren't important to a young king. Indeed, the accumulation of wealth and power was necessary in the big picture of Solomon's success as a ruler. Wisdom, however, was the catalyst from which the other qualities sprang.

"Many have been given wealth and power but lacked the wisdom to use them well. Because of their unwise decisions and values, they watched these benefits deteriorate into trouble, confusion, and conflict. Wealth and power without wisdom can be catastrophic. Many have succeeded in becoming wealthy only to degenerate into greedy self-indulgence. Many have sought for and gained power only to have it corrupt them. Many have been given authority and used it to glorify themselves and destroy and impoverish others. Money and power without wisdom can be incredibly dangerous, as the history of mankind has amply demonstrated. Power and wealth in the hands of unwise, selfish people can cause untold misery and destruction."

Someone interrupted by saying, "But it's not the wealth and power that's bad. It's what you do with them."

"Wealth can be good or bad depending on the wisdom and character of the one who has it," Craig agreed. "Power and authority can be used constructively or destructively. Wisdom emerges as the dominant virtue. It directs and guides the other assets. God prizes wisdom more than wealth. God honors wisdom more than authority or position. The inherent power of wisdom directs us to use the assets of life effectively."

Craig looked carefully around the class. "We have been given gifts and assets. Some of us have received more than others, but all have been given a measure of possible opportunities. The way we respond to these opportunities is determined not so much by our wealth or position, but by our wisdom. The crucial issue isn't how many assets we have, but rather how we use those assets. Appreciating what we have and applying it constructively is the job of wisdom."

Lloyd, our new friend with whom we had talked during the break, raised his hand. "I know you're talking about the Old Testament, but isn't this just what Jesus taught when he told us about the three servants who each received sums of money from their master? Two of the servants took the gift and worked hard, increasing its value, while the third just hid his in the ground. When the master came back to find out how well they had done with their gifts, the issue wasn't the value of the gift but what they had done with it. The servants who had wisely used the gift to increase its value were rewarded, but the third servant was punished. The judgment was based on what he had done with what he received."

"You're right," agreed Craig. "When it comes to assets and opportunities, we're all at different levels. What's important is what we do with the opportunities we have. Using them effectively and well becomes an issue of wisdom.

"Solomon was presented with rich and unusual opportunities in life. He was also wise enough to take those opportunities and make something even greater out of them. Many others, presented with the same opportunities but lacking wisdom, have at best fallen short of their expectations, and at worst turned life into a catastrophe for themselves and others. The determining ingredient is wisdom."

Power and Wealth Without Wisdom

Craig paused here and changed the subject of his talk. "Great tragedy came to Israel when Solomon died. His son was a man by the name of Rehoboam. Rehoboam was presented with even greater opportunities than Solomon had received on the death of David. Rehoboam inherited from his father a kingdom of fabulous wealth, power, and honor. He became the ruler of a rich, influential, and secure nation. Rehoboam had it all, but he lacked the wisdom of his father. He became greedy. He used his authority foolishly. He had little respect for the wise and balanced decisions his father had made. Because of lack of wisdom, an unparalleled opportunity became a catastrophic failure.

"The trouble started right at the beginning of Rehoboam's reign. A delegation from the people came to him with a request. They asked him to ease their burdens and be kinder to them, less demanding than his father had been. Faced with this precedent-setting decision, Rehoboam turned for advice first to the experienced and seasoned elders who had served under his father. Their advice was to listen to the request of the people and give them a respectful and cooperative response: *'If today you will be a servant to these people and serve them and give them a favorable answer, they will always be your servants'* (1 Kings 12:7). This was good and wise advice. If Rehoboam had implemented it, he would have gained much support and respect.

"But Rehoboam then consulted with the young men who had grown up with him. They gave very different advice.

> *The young men who had grown up with him replied, 'Tell these people who have said to you, "Your father put a heavy yoke on us, but make our yoke lighter"—tell them, "My little finger is thicker than my father's waist. My father laid on you a heavy yoke; I will make it even heavier. My father scourged you with whips; I will scourge you with scorpions."'* (1 Kings 12:10–11)

This was poor advice and exhibited an unwise, disrespectful, and selfish attitude towards the people. Rehoboam, however, listened to the unwise advice of the young men and boorishly rejected the advice of his mature elders. He showed disdain for the request of the people and decided to oppress them so that he could squeeze more money out of them for his own profit, wealth, and pleasure.

"This unwise decision caused discontent and rebellion amongst the people. Whole sections of the nation decided to reject Rehoboam's authority. Confusion, bloodshed, and rebellion followed. The nation became divided. Rehoboam's power and authority diminished rapidly. How different the history of Israel might have been had Rehoboam shown a little wisdom at this critical juncture. Instead of failure and rebellion, he could have experienced even greater honor, power, and respect than his father. But the wealth and authority he inherited soured and disintegrated for lack of wisdom. From wisdom flows power, wealth, and success. The opposite brings disintegration, failure, division, and bloodshed. No wonder God places wisdom so high in His list of values.

"In many ways, the stories of Solomon and Rehoboam reflect the history of the human race. The story would have been different if there had been more wisdom in the hearts of the men and women who held power and authority. What wars might have been avoided? What rebellions and conflicts might we have missed? What misery, poverty, bloodshed, and pain could have been alleviated? Untold damage and suffering litters the history of mankind because wisdom hasn't been prized, used, or respected. On the other hand, amazing benefits and growth have come to mankind from those who had wisdom and foresight.

"The Bible is full of stories of people who acted wisely and brought blessing and grace to others. There are also stories of people who acted unwisely and brought ruin and destruction. In this, the Bible reflects the realities of life as it is lived even in the twenty-first century. Those who are wise over the years build satisfying and fulfilling lives. Those who use their opportunities unwisely end up with emptiness and disappointment."

When Craig had finished this session, I turned to Peter. "Well, my friend, are you now sure that wisdom is important?"

Peter smiled. "There can be little doubt about it. Even a stubborn person like I am could hardly deny the importance of wisdom after all we've heard."

"The presence or absence of wisdom certainly seems to be the crucial factor in many outcomes," I said. "The Bible is clear that wisdom is vital. For you and me, as we seek to know God better and live for Him, we need wisdom to understand how to go about it, to have insight into His will and His truth, and to know how to apply those truths to the issues of our lives."

"Yes, I can see that," agreed Peter. "I'm anxious to move on to the next stage of the journey and find out just what wisdom is and how we discover and develop it."

I felt the same sense of anticipation. It was time to move on. "Let's talk to Craig and ask for his guidance in progressing to the next stage of our journey."

The Next Stage

We approached Craig, who was deep in conversation with Lloyd and Elizabeth, the couple who had talked to us during the previous break. At our approach, they allowed us to join them.

"Craig, thank you very much for the help and teaching you've given us," I said. "Both Peter and I have found great encouragement. We feel we're ready to move on to the next stage of our journey. Do you have any advice or guidance for us?"

Craig seemed very pleased with this. "I, too, think you're ready to move on, but I have a suggestion. Lloyd and Elizabeth are also interested in taking the rest of the journey into wisdom. I would suggest that you consider joining forces. As a team, you could help and support one another. I would suggest that you stay another night with me and then leave in the morning. This would give Lloyd and Elizabeth time to get things together and join you in your venture."

I had felt an immediate kinship with Lloyd and Elizabeth when we'd talked earlier. I found the thought of their company exciting and pleasing. Lloyd seemed a strong, silent type while Elizabeth was more talkative and vivacious. They would certainly add variety and interest to the journey.

I looked at Peter. He, too, seemed happy to accept this suggestion. I then turned to Lloyd and Elizabeth and shook their hands.

"We would be very happy to have you join us," I said. "It will give us strength and encouragement on the journey ahead."

"Great!" exclaimed Craig. "Why don't we meet at the dock after breakfast tomorrow? This will give you time to prepare, and I can give you some advice as you move on to the next phase."

Topics for Discussion

1. Review the options Solomon was faced with, then discuss the statement, "In the value system of God, wisdom is of greater worth than wealth, power, or health."

2. Appreciating what we have and applying it constructively to life is the job of wisdom. Discuss.

SECTION TWO

What Is Wisdom?

Thirteen

The Lake of Mammon

After breakfast the next morning, Craig walked with us down to the dock. Lloyd and Elizabeth were already there with their canoe packed and ready to go. After exchanging pleasantries, I turned to Craig and said, "You were going to tell us about the journey ahead."

"You are now at the end of the first stage of the journey," Craig said. "The emphasis in this second stage is to give you a good understanding of what true wisdom really is, especially wisdom as understood and taught in the Bible. While pursuing Biblical wisdom, you'll meet up with some who will try to convince you that others types of wisdom are more important, that you should give up your journey to Far Mountain in favor of other routes. Some of these people will be very convincing. You must remember to keep Far Mountain in view and follow its direction and not be tempted to follow other routes. If you allow yourselves to be distracted, you won't arrive at your desired destination and you'll miss the Sea of Tranquility."

"You'll come to a pivotal point which is called the College of Wisdom. It will be important that you stop at the college, for there you will be taught from the Bible about the wisdom that comes to us from God. Whatever you do, don't miss the college. It's vital to your understanding of wisdom. Now, off with you and I wish you the very best. Let's pray together before you go."

We all bowed our heads and Craig prayed. He prayed that we would stay faithful to the journey, follow the guidance of Far Mountain, and arrive safely at the Sea of Tranquility. He prayed that we would resist the temptations that would come to us, and be wise enough to reject those who would seek to divert us from the true route. He prayed that we would be strong enough to overcome dangers on the river. He then committed us into God's hands.

Craig stood on the deck and waved goodbye to us as we pushed off. We were glad to be accompanied by our new companions, Lloyd and Elizabeth.

The river here was very gentle and we were able to canoe side by side, carrying on a conversation.

"Tell us about your journey thus far," Lloyd said.

So we explained to him about our spiritual awakening, which to us no longer seemed recent. All the details poured out of us.

"Quite a journey," said Lloyd when we finished. "I'm looking forward to what lies ahead of us now."

We all agreed with him and for a time paddled along in silence. Then Elizabeth, who had been humming under her breath as she paddled, began to sing quietly. She had a clear and soothing voice. Soon Lloyd and Peter, who both seemed to know the hymns, joined in. I longed to be part of this, but I didn't know the words or the tunes. I listened with appreciation. They sang hymns of worship and adoration towards God, and as they sang I felt my own spirit rise on the wings of praise and thankfulness towards God. Great waves of joy and peace rolled over my soul. It was a beautiful experience, bringing gladness to my heart and strength to my soul.

I'm learning better how to revere God and feel His presence, I thought. *It comes to me more readily now and I'm more comfortable with His nearness. If the beginning of wisdom is an atmosphere of awesome reverence towards God, I must be getting closer.*

I was glad Lloyd and Elizabeth were with us. As I suspected, Lloyd's quiet strength and Elizabeth's vivaciousness added to the life of our group.

The singing and meditations came to an end when we noticed an obstruction across the river just ahead. It was like a fence that crossed the river, with only one opening in the center for boats to pass through. Someone had anchored a floating platform to guard the opening. In order to get through, we'd have to pass close by this platform. On the platform stood a man, who was clearly waiting to talk to us.

We negotiated our canoes up to the edge of the platform.

"Good morning to you all," said the man in a loud and cheerful voice. A broad smile was fixed to his face. We were uncertain as to his purpose, but we politely returned the greeting.

An Alternative to the Sea of Tranquility

"I expect you good folks are on the journey to the Sea of Tranquility down by Far Mountain," he said.

"Yes," I said rather tentatively, for something about the man didn't seem quite genuine. The enthusiasm in his voice didn't ring true and his smile seemed artificial. He reminded me of a salesman trying to sell me something he knew wasn't worth the asking price.

He pointed down the river towards Far Mountain, whose peak could be seen clearly, though it was still far away. "That's a long distance," he said, "and the river becomes very wild and dangerous as you pass through the mountains."

"That may be true," I answered, "but we're determined to make the journey into wisdom and find the Sea of Tranquility at the bottom of the mountain."

In response to this, the man clapped his hands with energy. "I have the very thing for you. I know how to get wisdom, but my way is much shorter and easier. You don't need to undertake the hazardous and demanding journey to Far Mountain."

I was suspicious of this man and wondered why he was talking to us like this. I looked at the others and could tell by their faces that they, too, were unconvinced.

"What do you mean an easier way?" I asked.

He kneeled down at the edge of the platform, leaning over our canoes. "Listen to me carefully. You don't need to go to all this trouble and effort to gain wisdom. Just around the next corner, you'll come to a lake. I'd like you to pause and look around that lake, for there are a lot of people living there. I want you to see how prosperous they are. They're living successful lives and are surrounded by all the comforts and pleasures money can buy. You talk about wisdom? They have it all. They have everything they need and all their desires are met. Take my advice:

be wise, be smart. I'd settle down on that lake. Let your journey end there. You'll become successful. You'll have lots of money. You'll be able to buy anything you want. Everything that's necessary for human happiness is there and within your reach. You would be wise to stop at the Lake of Mammon. It's a popular place."

I thanked the man for his guidance but didn't feel within myself any desire to accept his advice. Peter and I pushed off from the platform and headed down the river with Lloyd and Elizabeth right behind us.

"So, what do you think about that?" I asked Peter.

"Not much. It sounds like one of the alternative diversions our guides have been telling us about."

Lloyd and Elizabeth came alongside us, so we included them in the conversation. Lloyd, who seemed well-educated and had a thoughtful and philosophical turn of mind, said, "The man said the name of the lake was Mammon. Do you know the meaning of the word mammon?" Without waiting for an answer, he continued. "Jesus used it when He was warning us not to make a god out of gaining money and riches. He said,

> *No man can serve two masters: for either he will hate the one, and*
> *love the other; or else he will hold to the one, and despise the other.*
> *Ye cannot serve God and mammon.* (Matthew 6:24, KJV)

"He was warning us about making a god out of riches, making it so important that our dominant devotion would be the making of money. Mammon is the god of material gain."

"So Jesus is telling us that it isn't wise to make a god out of money and riches?" I asked.

"I think so," said Lloyd. "The important part of what you said is the word 'god.' We don't want to place the acquisition of riches on a pedestal so that it takes the place of God in our lives, overpowering all our other priorities. Jesus warned us that acquiring wealth can become such an important issue that it begins to dominate us. Money is important, but not that important."

"Yes, that sounds right," I said, thoughtfully. "Money is important to us, but not all-important. After all, I don't think Jesus would want us to be foolish with money, or careless in the way we handle it. He's not saying it has no value, but rather that its value must be kept in its place and not allowed to consume us."

"I don't think we should jump to conclusions," Elisabeth said. "Let's wait until we see this lake and meet some of the people and talk with them. After all, this lake isn't a diversion from our journey; it's part of the journey. That means part of learning wisdom is learning how to develop a proper attitude about money. Let's wait until we experience the Lake of Mammon before deciding on it."

The Lake of Mammon

This seemed like good sense, so we paddled on, anxiously trying to look around the next bend of the river. We worked the canoes around the corner and were absolutely stunned when we emerged into the Lake of Mammon. The territory we had passed through up until now had been sparsely populated and surrounded by hills and forests, but when we emerged onto the Lake of Mammon, we were amazed to find ourselves in a bustling community. Houses, hotels, and grandiose buildings lined the shores of the lake. The lake itself was busy with a confusion of boats. Those boats were mostly luxurious pleasure craft. Our poor little canoes were clearly out of place. The houses we could see were large and distinguished, the hotels affluent and expensive. And there were people everywhere—some were busy, others lay on the beaches enjoying the sunshine, while still others were in the water swimming. Many milled around casinos and restaurants, and even out here on the lake the sound of loud music reached us. Everyone seemed intent on some activity or another. The contrast between this place and the quiet and open country we had become used to was startling.

We stared at all this in amazed silence for a while. Peter expressed all of our thoughts when he said, "Well, this is different."

It was different, indeed.

The People of Mammon Lake

A high-powered speedboat raced up the lake in our direction. It created a great wash that would have risked capsizing our canoes, but fortunately the thoughtful occupants of the boat saw the danger and gently came alongside us and stopped. The occupants were clearly as curious about us as we were of them. Small, man-powered canoes filled with basic camping gear weren't a common sight around here.

"Hello!" said one of the men in the boat. "Where are you going in your canoes?"

I spoke up for our group. "We're travelling down the River of Wisdom and want to arrive at the Sea of Tranquility."

The spokesperson on the speedboat nodded and turned, smiling at his companions. "I can remember being on that journey, but when I got here, I thought this was far enough. There's enough wisdom here for me." The others nodded and agreed with him. "You really don't need to go any further. Look at us. We've obviously got on well. We have everything we need. Let this be your destination. You have arrived."

"You think you don't need to go any further?" I asked. "You really have enough wisdom here?"

"Well, look around you. You can see that we're all well-off. We're prospering and have everything we need. We've been wise enough to gain all of this, isn't that wisdom enough?"

"But we seek a wisdom that touches the soul. We want to be wise enough to know God better and understand His will and His way of life."

The man in the boat once again looked at his companions with a knowing smile on his face. "Well, perhaps God helped by providing all this for us."

"Perhaps," I said doubtfully.

Before the conversation could continue, another luxurious boat sped up to us and stopped on the other side of the canoes. There we were, sandwiched between these two opulent pleasure crafts. The new boat was even larger than the first.

The occupants of the two boats now ignored us, but eyed each other with a critical, envious eye.

Finally, a lady from the new boat shouted over to the people on the other boat. "How do you like our new boat? It's such an improvement over our last one. We just love it."

She's enjoying her sense of superiority, I thought.

"It looks lovely," said the original spokesperson. "We're thinking of getting rid of this old one and trading it in for a better model."

The lady nodded but made no comment. Instead she looked at us in the canoes. Having examined us, she decided we weren't of much importance. She waved over to the other boat again. "Well, I just wanted you to see our new boat. We must be going now."

With that, she nodded to her driver and the powerful boat took off up the lake with a roar of powerful engines.

The people in the first boat watched the progress of the other boat as it made its way up the lake. The encounter seemed to drain them of all interest in us, and they decided it was time for them to move on. Before they did, they gave us a piece of advice: "We would advise you to stay here. You could have a good life. We have everything you could ever want."

With those parting words, they sailed off, leaving us alone to get on with our journey.

We continued slowly up the Mammon Lake, fascinated by the extravagance we saw all around us. Strangely enough, I didn't feel inferior. Elizabeth, however, seemed to be having a harder time of it.

"They have so much," she said wistfully. She turned to look at Lloyd. "Imagine living in a house like that, and having a swimming pool in the yard and a boat at the dock. How grand it must be!"

Lloyd thought carefully before replying, as was his way. "Yes, perhaps, but did those people in the boat appear any happier than we are? They tried to hide it, but I think they were a little distressed when their friend showed off her better boat. They didn't seem to be satisfied with what they had."

"I picked up the same thing," said Peter. "In fact, I suggest that satisfaction will always be a bit out of reach here. I think if you were to ask what it would take to make them happy, they'd say, 'Just a little more, just a little more.' But they never have enough to satisfy their souls."

Lloyd nodded his agreement. "They've become so engrossed in their material affairs that they've lost all sense of spirituality. Let's get off this lake and then sit down to discuss this. I think there are lessons to be learned here."

We agreed with Lloyd, and with extra effort began to paddle towards the end of the Lake of Mammon. Elizabeth however, continued to look around her with longing in her eyes.

If she was in charge, I think we would stay here, I thought.

Disillusionment in the Lake of Mammon

When we reached the end of the lake and entered the river again, we came across another boat—a large yacht. It was stationary in the water and had only a single male occupant. The front of the yacht faced back towards the lake, but the man was sitting at the back, looking downriver. When he saw us and understood where we were going, he immediately struck up a conversation.

"Are you going further down the River of Wisdom?" he asked.

I sensed a touch of longing in his voice as he spoke. "Yes," I said.

He motioned back toward the lake. "Don't you want to stay here?"

"Why should we?" I asked in return.

This response seemed to catch him by surprise. "If you stay, you can accumulate wealth. You can buy anything you want. You can live in ease and luxury."

I challenged him, "Then why are you looking down the river with such longing in your eyes?"

He sighed, then slowly and sadly shook his head. "Because I'm not satisfied with all this. I have everything I want and more, but in my heart I'm empty. I long for something more."

I understood the hunger in this man's soul and felt my own heart reach out to him. "Why don't you join us then?"

"And leave all of this behind?" he asked. "I know I won't find what I long for here, but I love the things I have and cannot agree to leave them." The man suddenly made an unexpected suggestion. "If you're not in a hurry, why don't you come aboard and have lunch with me? Afterward, you can carry on with your journey."

He said this with such earnestness that I knew he wanted to talk to us. On behalf of the group, I accepted his generous invitation. We all clambered aboard his yacht.

For lunch, we sat outside on the deck of the yacht. The man seemed hungry for information about our journey and the purpose of it. I gave him an outline of all that had happened from the time of our spiritual awakening.

"You know," he said, "I made that journey, too. I remember it quite vividly."

"Then why did you stop here?" I asked.

"When I got to this lake and met the people, they convinced me that this was a good place to stop, that there was no need to go on. Things were good enough here. Here you can get money. You can buy things. You can become rich and get everything you ever wanted. Why go on? So I stayed."

"And did things work out for you?" Elizabeth asked.

"I certainly became rich and got all I wanted. At first it was exciting and satisfying to get so many things. But once the initial excitement passed, I began to feel rather dissatisfied. I thought it was just a phase. I thought if I could just get more money and more things, I would be satisfied. But instead of diminishing, my inner dissatisfaction grew. Lately I've been thinking that maybe I didn't do the right thing. Perhaps I should have continued on with the journey. The lake is certainly pleasant, but the lifestyle is so empty and vain."

The man spoke with such longing that I renewed my earlier invitation. "Come with us. Join us in our journey."

"When you came up in your canoes, I was just thinking about what it would be like to go down the River of Wisdom. I'm sure there's more to life than what's offered here."

"Then come with us," I repeated.

I sensed a deep sadness come over the man. "But I have so much now. How can I leave all of this? It has become too valuable to me. I know I should move on, but I can't give it all up." He looked up. "But I don't want to discourage you folks. You're doing the right thing. You were wise not to let the temptations of this lake deter you. Keep going and don't get distracted, for no matter how appealing it may seem, if you devote your life to the culture of this lake, it leads to emptiness of the soul."

I wanted to stay and try to persuade this man who was so divided in his heart, but I knew he'd been trying to make this decision for a long time, and in spite of his spiritual emptiness his mind was made up. He would stay here and deny himself the spiritual satisfaction of a closer walk with God.

With sad hearts, we left him. He sat in his expensive yacht and watched us paddle down the river until we turned a bend and lost sight of him.

Lessons from the Lake of Mammon

Once we were well free of the Lake of Mammon, I suggested to the rest of the party that we pull over to the bank, brew up some coffee, and discuss the meaning of what we had experienced.

When the coffee was ready, I opened the discussion. "I think Elizabeth said a very important thing back there, that this lake wasn't a diversion that lead us off onto the wrong route. It was part of the route we were supposed to follow. That means we have something to learn from this. If we're going to live wisely, we need to develop the right attitude towards money and material possessions. Money and possessions are an important part of life. We cannot do without them. The secret is to know how to use them properly."

"Yes, I agree," said Peter. "God doesn't want us to be foolish with money, nor does He want us to be careless and indifferent about it. It's an important factor in our lives. We just have to learn to keep it in its place."

Peter and I were in agreement, so I continued. "I remember hearing a saying once that the trouble with money is that it costs too much. What I observed back at the lake is that those people were no longer wise about the value of their money. They didn't control it; it controlled them. They seemed to have become so consumed in their affluence that it was the overpowering value in their lives. They really thought, since they had so much, that they ought to be happy and satisfied. But they weren't. They thought the hunger in their soul had to be satisfied and the best way to do that was to get more and more stuff. They placed too much faith in material things."

Peter and I seemed to be of one mind. "Material things are important to life, but they aren't designed to satisfy the soul or meet our spiritual needs. True wisdom has to take all of life into consideration, not just our physical existence. We have a soul. There is a God. There is existence beyond the body. It's foolish to live as if these spiritual matters aren't important or don't exist."

This was a fairly long speech for Peter, but he seemed to state the case accurately.

Until now, Lloyd and Elizabeth hadn't taken part in the discussion, but Lloyd now spoke from his knowledge of Scripture. "There's a verse in the Bible that says,

> *People who want to get rich fall into temptation and a trap and into many foolish and harmful desires that plunge men into ruin and destruction. For the love of money is a root of all kinds of evil. Some people, eager for money, have wandered from the faith and pierced themselves with many griefs.* (1 Timothy 6:9–10)

"I sensed the people we met on the Lake of Mammon fell into this trap. They had so many false ideas about what money could achieve. They thought their own personal value was based on how much money they had. Those ones with the better boat felt they were superior to the others. They certainly considered us, in our little canoes, to be of no significant value. On the lake, status, rank, value is determined by how much you have, and the more you have the higher your rank. This is an unwise and false value system."

"Also," added Peter, "they seemed so consumed in their quest for material things that they lost interest in and desire for any other aspects of life. They held the false notion that satisfaction and happiness come from what you possess. So if you aren't happy, the answer is to become richer and get more possessions."

"That's what I sensed in them, too," said Lloyd. "Then again, their love for money seemed to have spawned in their hearts all kinds of bad values. They were jealous of each other. They were competing with one another to see who could get the best boats, the best houses, and so on. You could see covetousness in them, not to mention pride and greed and superiority and false humility. They were, as the scripture said, piercing themselves with many griefs. I think we had to pass through here to learn that an essential part of wisdom is knowing how to deal with money and possession correctly. I expect we'll hear much more about this when we get to the College of Wisdom."

I then noticed that Elizabeth hadn't said a word. In fact, she didn't seem comfortable with the way the discussion was going. I wondered just how she felt about leaving behind the Lake of Mammon and all of its luxuries. Although she seemed uncomfortable with our opinions, she didn't venture one of her own.

I had one other comment to make. "You notice that there were a lot of people back there. It's a very popular spot. I think many of them were on the same journey we're on, but like our friend in the yacht, they decided that life here was wisdom enough for them. The number of people who have decided to stay indicates that this is a very common problem."

Lloyd immediately added to this, saying, "Jesus said,

> *Do not store up for yourselves treasures on earth, where moth and rust destroy, and where thieves break in and steal. But store up for yourselves treasures in heaven, where moth and rust do not destroy, and where thieves do not break in and steal. For where your treasure is, there your heart will be also.* (Matthew 6:19–21)

"It's important to understand," Lloyd continued, "that our hearts will follow our treasures, rather than our treasures following our hearts. He said, *'Where your treasure is, there your heart will be also.'* These people were rich, and they allowed their hearts to follow their riches. They no longer saw significant value in the care of their souls. Their hearts were set not on serving God or doing His will, but on extending their own kingdoms and furthering their own material benefits."

"That's good," said Peter. "Your heart follows your treasure, so you had better make sure you treasure and value the things of God before the things of the earth."

We were ready to move on, so we packed up and pushed our canoes into the river, paddling on down the River of Wisdom.

Topics for Discussion

1. The journeyers were constantly told to keep their eye on Far Mountain, and be guided by it. What do you think Far Mountain is, or what does it represent?

2. Discuss the importance and meaning of Elizabeth's statement about the Lake of Mammon, that it's not a diversion from the journey but rather part of the journey.

3. What do you perceive was the greatest spiritual problem for the people who chose to live on the Lake of Mammon?

Fourteen

The Joy

We didn't encounter any more major population centers. Towards evening, we came across an island in the middle of the river and decided to set up camp and spend the night there. It was relaxing to build a fire and sit around it eating, talking, and laughing. We all seemed to enjoy the evening, except for Elizabeth, who still seemed rather withdrawn.

When everyone had retired to their tents, I stayed up to spend some time by myself. When the fire died out, it was completely dark. I went down to the riverside and sat on the grassy bank. It was a beautiful moment. There were no clouds in the sky and it was a moonless night. I had never seen the stars so bright and plentiful. They crowded the night sky. The outline of the river could be seen even in the dark and the gentle sound of water lapping against rocks only added to the stillness. I was alone with nature, and with God.

I began to sense an awareness that a presence surrounded me. The presence was not only around me, but actually within me. My soul was enveloped in a great sense of peace and joy. I sensed I was at one with God and His creation. What I felt was exquisitely beautiful. I was overwhelmed by the wonder and greatness of God, and yet deeply humbled that I should be privileged to sit in His presence in this beautiful place. My heart was possessed, overflowing. The joy was so intense that it was almost painful. I was in touch with God and I loved it.

The majesty and power of His presence was so overwhelming that I bowed my head low in awesome reverence. I worshiped. I adored. I loved. Such joy seemed indescribable. I felt like I was experiencing an inexpressible and glorious joy.

I wanted this presence to sink deeper into my heart. I wanted to be possessed by it all the time. This was greater than I was. I wondered about wisdom. I sensed I was in the presence of infinite wisdom. He knew. He understood. He was aware of everything. I knew that the more I was possessed by this Spirit, the wiser I would be. If the fear of the Lord was the beginning of wisdom, then I knew the Spirit of God would guide me and give me insights I'd never had before. There was a vividness about the truth and a greatness about God that was very real.

The words of a hymn I had heard the others sing as we paddled along came to me and expressed my experience, I was "lost in wonder, love, and praise."

I didn't know how long this experience lasted, but gradually I became aware of the cold chill of night. Their air was damp and I had to move to the warmth of the tent. But as I made my way to my tent, I knew that new wisdom was beginning to fill my mind. My mind was larger now. My heart had grown. New values were overtaking my soul. My decision-making would be done on a different basis than before. My motivations were changing. I would be guided by my new love for Him. More and more, His will would be my will, what He loved is what I would love, His ways would be my ways.

The wisdom of the Lord was beginning to dawn on my soul. It was such a night. I will never forget it.

Topics for Discussion

1. Discuss the spirit of joy. Where does it come from? How do you cultivate it? Is it dependent on favorable circumstances? What causes it? What destroys it? Do you ever experience it?

FIFTEEN

The College
of Wisdom

IT WAS RATHER LATE IN THE MORNING WHEN WE SET OFF. WE MADE A LEISURELY breakfast, dismantled the camp, and loaded the canoes. Once we were on the water, I thought, *It's good to be on our way again.*

We steadily paddled until late in the afternoon. I was thankful we were back into quiet wilderness again. Even the farms were few. As I paddled, I tried to let my soul enjoy the beauty around me and create again the consciousness of God's presence and nearness.

One thing I noticed was that Elizabeth wasn't singing today. She seemed to be absorbed in deep thought. After my experience with God the previous night, I was more sensitive to the fact that she was struggling with inner conflicts. I felt I could understand and have insights to help her resolve the problems that were weighing her down.

We were still moving in the right direction, because I could see Far Mountain ahead of us. It filled me with assurance that we were getting closer to our destination; the mountain didn't seem to so far away now.

It was with some relief, however, when we arrived at what we took to be the College of Wisdom, which Craig had described for us. We expected to spend some time here, and I hoped in the course of my stay to gain a better understanding of what wisdom really was.

We beached our canoes and walked up the pathway to the building. It was a large brick building with many windows. Spaced out around the building were a number of smaller cabins. Back in the trees were more elaborate houses, which I took to be the living quarters for the teachers and staff.

We entered the brick building and were welcomed by a secretary, who gave us the keys to some empty cabins and instructed us to make ourselves at home.

"Supper," she said, "will be served in the main building in about an hour's time."

Peter and I shared a cabin and soon settled in. Since we expected to stay for a day or two, we brought most of our gear up from the canoe.

At the designated time, we went over to the dining room. Tables were set out with about twenty people of various ages standing around them. One rather heavyset man in thick tweed trousers and a woolen shirt came over to us and introduced himself as Andrew. I realized right away from his accent that he was of Scottish descent. He had a deep rich voice that would, I thought, be a pleasure to listen to.

As it turned out, Andrew was the main teacher at the college. He took the liberty of introducing us to the rest of the students. Some of them, like us, were staying overnight in the cabins, but others were day students. The meal was pleasant and the company interesting and stimulating.

After the meal, Andrew suggested the four of us get some coffee and meet with him in one of the small lounges for a short conversation. We responded positively to this, so, coffee cups in hand, we followed him into a small comfortable lounge.

When we were set, Andrew began abruptly and without introduction. "What we'll be doing in class tomorrow is talk about what wisdom is and describe it. We'll do this mostly from material taken from the book of James in the New Testament. I thought it might be good for you to meet with me this evening so I could give you some background information about James and why he wrote the book. It'll help you understand better just where James is coming from, why he has such deep understanding of what wisdom is and why wisdom was so important to him.

"Most Bible scholars believe that the James who wrote the book was actually the brother of our Lord. On that basis, I want you to use your imagination and think about what it would have been like to be brought up as the little brother of Jesus. James spent all those years living in the same house as Jesus, watching, listening, and interacting with Him in all the affairs of life. You can understand from this that James developed a deep appreciation for the wisdom and character of Jesus.

"When Jesus began His public ministry, James didn't understand or appreciate all that Jesus was doing. But after His death and resurrection, Jesus made a special resurrection appearance to James. This transformed him and he became a respected follower of Jesus."

These were all new accounts to me and I was having trouble wrapping my mind around them.

Elizabeth interrupted by asking, "You mean that Jesus actually appeared to James after His resurrection?"

"Yes," said Andrew. "The Apostle Paul, in writing to the church in Corinth, summarized some of the resurrection appearances of Jesus. He wrote,

> *After that, he appeared to more than five hundred of the brothers*
> *at the same time, most of whom are still living, though some have*
> *fallen asleep. Then he appeared to James, then to all the apostles...*
> (1 Corinthians 15:6–7)

"This was a life-changing experience for James; it strengthened the foundation of his belief. His mother, now that Jesus was gone, felt free to share with him for the first time the accounts of Jesus' birth. James heard the incredible stories about the shepherds, the angels, and the virgin birth. James was amazed, but he now believed. He must have wondered, *How could I have lived so close to Him for all of these years and never understood who He was?*"

James Becomes a Leader of the Christian Movement

"After the resurrection, James associated himself with the disciples of Jesus. This group of believers began to grow and spread, and James became one of their leaders and a well-respected authority in the new Christian movement. As the apostles scattered and traveled abroad, James became the leader of the mother church in Jerusalem. His family association with Jesus gave him a unique position amongst the followers. He loved to remember and relate tales of what it had been like when Jesus was at home with him. He could now understand why Jesus had seemed so different.

"When James came to write a letter to the new Christians of the day, it's not surprising that he emphasized the matter of wisdom. He had lived with it, observed it, and absorbed it. Jesus, as he remembered Him, had been so wise. James had had the privilege of watching this wisdom develop. He had seen it in action. He'd observed it in a way that no one else could have. Jesus had been his brother. James had seen His wisdom operate behind closed doors. He had seen it function within the closeness of the family.

"Jesus had always seemed to know what was right and wrong. He seemed to completely understand the most important values and priorities and let these principles guide His life. With growing enlightenment, James realized that Jesus had exhibited great wisdom growing up. James had had the privilege of being the beneficiary of it."

"So," Lloyd said, "because James saw how important wisdom was in the formation of Jesus' personality, and the impact it had on His ministry, he wanted us to understand that the possession of it is also important for us."

Andrew nodded. "Since it was so vital to Jesus' growth and development, he emphasized how vital it should be for them. In his writing, he wanted them to understand what wisdom was, and how practical and useful the spirit of wisdom could be. He wanted them to clearly understand that if they were to become like Jesus, part of that lifestyle would demand that they become men and women of wisdom. Wisdom is an essential part of Christ-likeness."

"You know, I've gone to church all my life," said Peter thoughtfully. "In church, people say that they want to be like Jesus, but I never got the impression that they were including wisdom in that."

"No, when people say they want to be like Jesus, I don't think wisdom is very prominent in their thinking," Andrew said. "But wisdom and Christ-likeness go together. Certainly, James urged the early Christians to pursue wisdom. In order to help them, he describes what true wisdom is like. He outlines some of the characteristics of spiritual wisdom. And he was writing from experience."

Andrew had certainly given us a great deal to think about, and I looked forward to the class we would attend in the morning. We thanked him for devoting his time to us. Andrew thanked us and said, "I hope this gives you a little background to the study we will do in class tomorrow morning."

It had been a long day and both Peter and I were tired. We made our way to our cabin and retired for the night. I noticed that Lloyd and Elizabeth also looked tired. Elizabeth seemed troubled and uncomfortable. She was obviously having some sort of inward struggle that went back to the experience at the Lake of Mammon.

Topics for Discussion

1. Share your imaginations and thoughts as to what it would be like to live for years in the same house as Jesus as His little brother.

2. Do you agree with Andrew's statement that when people say they want to be like Jesus, wisdom isn't very prominent in their thinking?

Sixteen

James the Wise

WE GATHERED FOR THE FIRST CLASS AFTER BREAKFAST. THIS TIME, WE MET IN ONE of the classrooms. We sat at tables with all the students facing forward towards the teacher's desk. There were about fifteen of us. Peter, Lloyd, Elizabeth, and I sat together.

Andrew came in, and after greeting us he plunged right into his subject.

That seems to be his way, I thought. *He doesn't spend much time with social niceties.*

"The purpose of these classes is to expand your understanding of what wisdom is, especially the biblical understanding of wisdom. Some of you have indicated that you've had a very real experience with God but aren't sure what to do with it. You want to know how to apply Christian truth to the everyday events of life. To do that, you need to have a good understanding of what the Bible means when it talks about wisdom. During your time here, we'll study the subject in three ways. First, what is wisdom and what are the key elements that combine to make true wisdom? Second, we'll discuss the dark side of wisdom, for there are some types of wisdom available to us that need to be avoided. And third, what does true wisdom look like? How does it express itself? How do you see true wisdom in action? There will be, in addition, some homework for you to do, so you should plan to be here at least two days."

Definition of Wisdom

With that brief introduction, Andrew waited to see if there were any questions from us. When no one spoke, he continued.

"First let's consider what wisdom really is. Wikipedia gives us an extensive definition of wisdom. It says, 'Wisdom is a deep understanding and realization of people, things, events or situations, resulting in the ability to apply perceptions, judgments and actions in keeping with this understanding.'[2] There are two main elements in this definition. First, a wise person has a clear understanding and proper perception of reality. Second, they are able to apply this understanding so reality is properly dealt with.

"The same two aspects of wisdom emerge in the definition given in the Shorter Oxford Dictionary: 'The combination of experience and knowledge with the ability to apply them judiciously.'[3] So, true wisdom is two-sided. It is the ability to grasp and understand the reality of a situation and then, on the basis of this understanding, decide what is the best course of action. Wisdom comes with good comprehension and practical solutions. Both elements must be present for true wisdom to exist. The writer of Proverbs states it very simply by defining wisdom as *'knowing and doing right'* (Proverbs 3:21, TLB).

"To understand a situation and do nothing about it is neglectful. To do something about a situation when you don't properly understand it is rashness. Wisdom has a duel function; it understands correctly and responds appropriately. That's why Jesus said that a wise person is one who *'hears these words of mine and puts them into practice'* (Matthew 7:24).

"James endorses this duel function of wisdom as insight and action. From that base, he develops the Christian application for living."

---

2   "Wisdom," *Wikipedia,* 15 August 2013 (http://en.wikipedia.org/wiki/Wisdom).
3   *Shorter Oxford Dictionary, Fifth Edition* (Oxford, UK: Oxford University Press, 2002), 3653.

Applying Wisdom to the Christian life

"James wrote to new and young Christians, many of whom were only recently converted from lives lived in a pagan culture. They now accepted and believed in the basic truths of the Christian message but were inexperienced about how to apply the Christian faith to everyday life. They may not have lacked in enthusiasm and earnestness, but they weren't always wise in understanding how this new experience should be applied. To deal with this, James urged upon them the quality of Christian wisdom—the ability to grasp the truth and then apply it to the development of their Christian experience."

As Andrew spoke, I realized that I was in a very similar situation to those early Christians. I had only recently become interested in spiritual matters and made my commitment to follow Christ. I had lived life as if God didn't exist, and I had no experience in applying my new faith to real life.

"In addition, some of these young believers were experiencing resistance and persecution because of their Christian faith, and they weren't sure how to handle open persecution. James writes to them, telling them that if they can learn how to deal with their hard circumstances wisely, even these persecutions and difficulties will help them grow in their faith and increase the quality of their fellowship with the Lord. James was aware that the outcomes of personal opposition and difficult situations don't automatically benefit a person's faith. Indeed, far from helping, some people are hurt and discouraged by these hard events and find it difficult to keep their faith alive in the midst of trouble and doubt. If, on the other hand, they learn to handle these situations wisely and correctly, these trials can contribute to their development into mature, wise, and fruitful Christians.

"James explains that it's the insights and understandings of wisdom that help them adopt the right attitudes and responses so they'll know how to overcome trials. He writes,

> *Consider it pure joy, my brothers, whenever you face trials of many kinds, because you know that the testing of your faith develops perseverance. Perseverance must finish its work so that you may be mature and complete, not lacking anything. If any of you lacks wisdom, he should ask God, who gives generously to all without finding fault, and it will be given to him.* (James 1:2–5)

"As we read these verses, we begin to understand just what James meant by wisdom and how it works in our lives."

126

Wisdom Understands Truth

"First, wisdom has a clear grasp of truth. It has an accurate understanding of a concept or situation. It was fundamental to the New Testament writers that their audiences understand and believe the truth of the Christian message. This message gave clear insight into the grand realities of our existence. It focused on the great values of life. It encompassed eternity, as well as time. It recognized that we have a soul as well as a body. It pointed the way for the human heart to find its home in God. And the realities of these central truths find their greatest expression in the life, death, resurrection, and teachings of Jesus Christ. To a Christian, the center of truth is in Jesus Christ. For a person to have a wise understanding of life and reality, he must have a solid understanding of Jesus Christ, the source of true wisdom.

"The more you reflect the spirit of Jesus in your attitudes, values, and decisions, the wiser you'll be. Many of the statements made by Jesus confirm that He's the center of wisdom. Only Jesus can say, *'I am the way and the truth and the life'* (John 14:6). He alone is *'the light of the world'* (John 8:12). Only He can testify, *'I have come that they may have life, and have it to the full'* (John 10:10). In the New Testament, Christian truth is embodied in Jesus Christ. The foundation upon which wisdom will be built in our lives is knowing and believing in Him.

"To James, the center of wisdom is a proper understanding of the truth about Jesus Christ. A person must have a proper grasp of who Jesus Christ is and what He's like. Knowing and understanding Jesus Christ is the essential truth that must be understood for a person's wise development in the Christian life. When this truth is firmly established in our minds, we will begin to operate on principles that allow us to better grasp and understand what real truth is."

Wisdom Highlights What's Most Important

"The wisdom James is talking about gives us good insight into what's really important. It understands what the true priorities of life must be. It sees clearly which things ought to come first. If we lack this clear insight, we'll make decisions based on what seems to be good for us in the moment. But the urgency of present needs and desires can often lead us astray. Wisdom gives us the insight of having a clear understanding of the most important purposes and objectives of life. So many mistakes are made because we don't keep our priorities in view, but allow ourselves to be distracted by the conveniences, appeal, and desires of smaller and less important things. The voice of wisdom would say that it's important to keep first things first.

"Wisdom prioritizes the main values, but it also brings into focus the values that last. As we deal with the everyday details of life, wisdom helps us to keep the big picture in focus. It isn't wise to endanger long-range objectives in order to satisfy some passing pleasure or convenience. True wisdom impresses on our minds the importance of lasting values, motivating us to keep our hearts set on them in spite of temptations to get sidetracked.

"Jesus made it clear that it is wise to invest heavily in lasting values, not temporal values. He said,

> Do not store up for yourselves treasures on earth, where moth and rust destroy, and where thieves break in and steal. But store up for yourselves treasures in heaven, where moth and rust do not destroy, and where thieves do not break in and steal. For where your treasure is, there your heart will be also. (Matthew 6:19–21)

"Keeping the big picture in mind calls for disciplined maturity and wisdom. The insights of wisdom show us how to organize and control our lives so we give adequate time, energy, and attention to the things that really count. Wisdom is so captivated by the important, long-range issues of life that it helps us stay on course and not get confused. In the light of Christian wisdom, we understand that it isn't wise to emphasize the body to the neglect of the soul. It isn't wise to neglect God in the urgent pursuit of material gain. It isn't wise to live as if the only thing that counts is what happens in this world, giving no thought to our welfare in eternity. The Christian message continually emphasizes the importance of the soul, eternity, and our relationship with God, demanding that we give adequate attention to these values."

I asked a question here. "Is that why we were instructed to keep our eyes on Far Mountain when we started the journey?"

"That's right," replied Andrew. "Far Mountain represents the desired destination of our hearts, the ultimate and lasting values of existence. That's where you want to end up, so you use it for your guidance. If you get your eye off the mountain and start taking directions from the immediate circumstances around you, you'll soon lose your way.

"A great deal of trouble comes when we cease to view the big picture and see only the needs, desires, and demands of the present. The insight of wisdom keeps our eyes on what's important, showing us how to organize our lives and make present decisions."

One member of the class raised his hand at this. "I'm not quite sure I'm grasping this. Can you give us an illustration?"

With a little smile on his face, Andrew responded. "Many set the goal of dieting in order to keep their weight down and promote good health. This is a great long-term goal. Often, however, that goal is frustrated and never attained because the person gives in to the temptation of overeating and indulging their present appetites. This isn't wise.

"Another obvious example would be tobacco. Everyone knows that smoking is bad for you and can bring about many diseases. The goal to stop smoking is a great objective, yet the urgent need to satisfy the present craving for a cigarette is often too great. The overall goal is lost in yielding to the desire for comfort and pleasure. In these cases, wisdom becomes subservient to immediate desire."

Andrew paused. "This same principle holds true in the spiritual realm. Many have a desire to be right with God and enjoy a rich fellowship with Him. They want their hearts to be at peace and to sense His love. Yet in the actual performance of their lives, these values are neglected and forgotten under the pressure of everyday affairs. A wise grasp of the truth would help you bring the affairs of your soul to the forefront. Jesus explained that we shouldn't jeopardize our eternal good for the sake of some temporal benefit. He said,

> *If your right eye causes you to sin, gouge it out and throw it away.*
> *It is better for you to lose one part of your body than for your whole*
> *body to be thrown into hell.* (Matthew 5:29)

"You get the idea," said Andrew. "Wisdom gives you a clear grasp of what's really important, and this creates the stimulus and desire that motivates you to seek, work, and trust until you reach your goal. Wisdom helps you get your eyes fixed on the most worthy purposes of life and helps you organize your life so you give them priority. The greater the clarity with which you see these values, the more determined and committed you'll be towards realizing them."

The Greatest Values

I felt excited by all of this. "But what are the right things?" I asked. "What are the correct priorities and long-range values?"

Andrew smiled. "You aren't the first person to ask that. Jesus was asked a similar question and he answered it like this: *"Love the Lord your God with all your heart and with all your soul and with all your mind." This is the first and greatest commandment'* (Matthew 22:37–38). Let's make no mistake about it. The greatest value to the human heart is a loving relationship with God. The wise person understands this clearly and seeks to experience it. The psalmist expresses the central passion of the wise heart this way: *'As the deer pants for streams of water, so my soul pants for you, O God. My soul thirsts for God, for the living God'* (Psalm 42:1–2)

"A wise person grasps the truth that the quality of interaction between him and God is the most important thing in life. That's why Jesus could say, *'My food… is to do the will of him who sent me and to finish his work'* (John 4:34). And to those who think this must be a very burdensome way of life, the psalmist claims, *'I delight to do thy will, O my God: yea, thy law is within my heart'* (Psalm 40:8, KJV). Do not be deceived: the universal testimony of the great men and women of God is that nothing brings greater joy and satisfaction to the spirit than a harmonious relationship with God. A wise person is God-centered. This also confirms what you've been told that the beginning of wisdom is to fear the Lord.

"So to Jesus, the greatest value is to love God, but he went on to say that *'the second is like it: "Love your neighbor as yourself"'* (Matthew 22:39). Few things bring more delight and satisfaction to the human heart than harmonious and loving relationships with others. It is wise to place great emphasis on seeking benefit and blessing for others. The selfish way of life isn't satisfying; it leads to emptiness and frustration.

"We could go on and add a third value. Since you love God and others, a central factor in life is to pour yourself out in service to God and others. This, Jesus said, is a primary value. So there you have it. You can see Jesus' value system. Let's set our hearts on these things and become wise."

I nodded in understanding. "I agree with you, but sometimes, when I'm tempted, I wish it were not so."

"That is often the case," agreed Andrew. "The power of Jesus' message is that it lays out the eternal priorities of life very clearly. Making sure that you recognize and commit yourself to them was a constant issue for Jesus. He complained about those who *'strain out a gnat but swallow a camel'* (Matthew 23:24). That is, there are people who neglect the important issues of life while giving unjustified attention to things that ultimately don't matter much. A wise Christian is one who recognizes what's important and gives it priority. That's why Jesus said, *'But seek first his kingdom and his righteousness, and all these things will be given to you as well'* (Matthew 6:33). He is saying that we should get our priorities straight and devote ourselves to them."

Andrew paused here to make sure our questions were satisfied. Then, looking at our table, he added, "Remember your experience at the Lake of Mammon? Those people allowed their minds and hearts to become absorbed by wrong values. Well, it's not that the values were necessarily wrong, just that for them the secondary values had become dominant. They allowed themselves to be sidetracked and so will never arrive at the Sea of Tranquility.

"When wisdom helps us understand the important issues of life, and teaches us how to respond to them, it becomes a powerful ally in helping us handle whatever life brings."

I raised my hand to get Andrews' attention. "But it seems to me that since I committed to Jesus Christ, my need for wisdom has greatly increased."

"How so?" asked Andrew.

"Since I became a Christian, a lot of new things have been introduced into my life, things I didn't have to worry about before. For example, I'm now concerned about doing God's will. That was never an issue before; I just did what I wanted to do. Now I have to treat other people with love and respect, whereas before I didn't care. I just did what was right in my own eyes. I didn't have to worry about God, or my soul, or eternity. I could go my own way. I could look after my own interests. Now I have to consider God's interests, God's kingdom, and God's will. It makes it all much more complicated."

I noticed some others nodding their heads as I spoke, so I assumed I was expressing thoughts that they, too, had in their minds.

"You are, of course, correct," replied Andrew. "Becoming a committed Christian means introducing a whole new set of values and priorities. They have to be understood and accommodated. They call for changes and adjustments. New habits need to be developed in order to give them freedom to grow and mature. Some old habits will need to be dismissed. Space will have to be cleared to make room for new values. The presence of God in your life will demand attention. But the new values, if you obey and follow them, will move you into a way of life that's much more fruitful, effective, and meaningful. The introduction of these new values will be the most profitable thing you've ever done. There is no doubt that the introduction of all these new values calls for a reassessment of your life-style, and that, in turn, calls for wisdom.

"In fact, Colin, this is the center of our experience with Jesus Christ. Knowing Him and following Him make us passionate about new things. We deeply want to do His will. We have a hunger for righteousness. We become aware of our immortal souls and eternal spiritual nature. We want to labor for Him and His kingdom. The heart of one who is following Jesus changes. That's why we say that Jesus is the way, the truth, and the life, for He awakens these things in our hearts. Without this awakening, they lie dormant."

Lloyd spoke up at this point. "The decision to follow Jesus Christ is like the difference between deciding to let a patch of ground grow wild and turning it into a garden. It may be easier to let it grow wild, for then you don't have to worry about anything. But the results of this are the proliferation of weeds and thorns. Letting the parcel of ground grow wild won't yield good fruit or vegetables. However, cultivating the patch into a garden calls for skill, effort, and knowledge, and it yields a harvest which provides nourishment, beauty, and enjoyment. One method may be easier, but it's also unfruitful. The other is more difficult, but it produces useful and satisfying results."

"Well said," exclaimed Andrew. "A lot depends on what you want to make of yourself. If you want to develop a fruitful, useful, and effective life, you must introduce and care for the values and priorities that will make that happen. And nobody knows what these factors are better than Jesus Christ. Following Jesus usually means moving your life in a whole new direction. To do that, you need wisdom, with its insights and practicality.

"This is a good place for me to move on and talk about the second element in true wisdom. Wisdom isn't just having right understanding and correct insights; it also means that we have the ability to implement these truths."

Wisdom Is Practical

"True wisdom is practical. It's able to apply the understanding of the mind to the practical decisions and actions of everyday life. It helps us respond to life correctly. It helps balance our values so that all aspects of life are taken care of. It shows us how to provide space for the important and dismiss the unimportant.

"Practical wisdom also helps us deal with the road blocks that inevitably arise as we pursue our objectives. Many things come to us in life that we don't plan or expect but which discourage or distract us. Wisdom gives us the skill to negotiate successfully all the bruises and knocks that come our way. Life isn't always kind to us. Life brings successes and disappointments, blessings and hardships, victories and failures, rewards and frustrations. Wisdom helps us understand how to deal with these so we learn and profit from the experiences.

"Wisdom isn't something that flourishes in an ivory tower or prospers in splendid isolation. It doesn't belong only to those people who withdraw from living and spend their time reading and meditating. Wisdom is practical and helps us know how best to negotiate with life as it comes to us.

"While the way of wisdom is the right way for all people, it is particularly pertinent for Christians seeking to live for God in this world." Here, Andrew looked at me, making sure that I understood he was responding to my earlier statement. "Because we want to please and honor God, we're faced with unique situations that never troubled us before. For example, we earnestly want to do God's will, but we don't always know how to understand what His will is. That takes practical wisdom. We respect God and want to hear what He says to us, but we don't always know how to listen to what God is saying. That takes practical wisdom, for without it we can easily misunderstand what we think we hear. We want to pray effectively, but we don't always know how to do this. We want to love God but are hindered by all kinds of selfish and unloving attitudes in our own heart. We want to know how to deal with other people in our lives, some of whom are very difficult. We want to be able to help and encourage our loved ones. All of this requires wisdom.

"This practical wisdom is necessary even though we're sincere and dedicated. We can see the necessity of this even as we watch other Christians deal with life. We observe that often sincere and earnest Christians do very foolish things. Being devoted doesn't equate to always making the right decisions. There is no inherent wisdom resident in sincerity or earnestness. We can be very earnest for the wrong causes. Sincerity needs to be guided. We need to ask for wisdom. It will help us translate our earnestness into practical and effective living."

Wisdom Helps Us Interpret Our Faith

"Wisdom is a vital ingredient if we're going to properly express the spirit and attitudes of Jesus Christ. The need for wisdom doesn't arise so much in the initial days after accepting of Jesus Christ as our Savior, but becomes essential as we try to live out the implications of this new faith. We are redeemed through Jesus

Christ, and under the power of that redemption a whole new way of life opens up for us. R.G. Tasker says of the Epistle of James,

> *This Epistle would seem to be of special value to the individual Christian during what we might describe as the second stage in his pilgrim's progress. After he has been led to respond to the gospel of grace, and come to have the joyful assurance that he is a redeemed child of God, if he is to advance along the way of holiness, and if the ethical implication of his new faith are to be translated into practical realities then he needs the stimulus and the challenge of the Epistle of James.[4]*

"So the two basic elements in the quality of true wisdom are insight and application. Wisdom shows us both what is really important and also how to adapt our lifestyle and decision-making so that what's important gets priority. Always the guiding force in developing this is the spirit of Jesus Christ. For the Christian, wisdom centers in Jesus Christ. How do I please Him? How do I honor Him? How do I love and obey Him?

Wisdom Is the Compass

"That's why James urges us to ask for wisdom. Too much devastation is caused when we neglect it. Too much is lost and spoiled. We must urgently turn to God, the source of all wisdom, and ask Him to give us wisdom as we handle the issues of life. The wonderful promise is that if we ask, He'll share His wisdom with us. It's there for the asking, and we need to ask. Are we asking?"

Andrew closed his notebook. "Let's take a break now. When we come back, we'll turn our attention to the dark side of wisdom."

---

4   R.G. Tasker, *Beacon Bible Commentary* (Kansas City, MO: Beacon Hill Press, 1967), 189.

Topics for Discussion

1. From the definitions of wisdom given in this chapter, we concluded that wisdom has a duel function—it understands correctly and responds appropriately. Discuss the implications of this. Compare these definitions with the statement of Jesus that a wise person is one who hears His words and puts them into practice.

2. What are the three primary values listed in this chapter?

SEVENTEEN

The Dark Side

THE COFFEE BREAK WAS SHORT, AS ANDREW SEEMED ANXIOUS TO GET ON WITH class. He soon called us back, and again, without much fuss, he opened his notebook. He began by asking us to open our Bibles to James 3:13–18. One of the other students found the passage, then stood and read:

> *Who is wise and understanding among you? Let him show it by his good life, by deeds done in the humility that comes from wisdom. But if you harbor bitter envy and selfish ambition in your hearts, do not boast about it or deny the truth. Such 'wisdom' does not come down from heaven but is earthly, unspiritual, of the devil. For where you have envy and selfish ambition, there you find disorder and every evil practice. But the wisdom that comes from heaven is first of all pure; then peace-loving, considerate, submissive, full of mercy and good fruit, impartial and sincere.*

Peacemakers who sow in peace raise a harvest of righteousness. (James 3:13–18)

Andrew thanked the reader and then began. "James is particularly anxious that we understand that wisdom can take different forms, and some of the forms aren't good. A gardener can plant two seeds in the same garden, but depending on the nature of the seeds they will grow to be very different plants. One plant can grow to be beautiful and fruitful, while the other can be harmful and toxic. Similarly, wisdom can grow in the heart of man, but it can be good or harmful. In this passage, James describes the flowering of good wisdom, but he also explains that there is another form of wisdom that can grow, and it is bad. We must be careful not to confuse the two. There is, James says, a wisdom that is from heaven and a wisdom that is from below. Right now, we'll talk about the dark side of wisdom—the wisdom from below."

The Wisdom from Below

"Some time ago, I received from a friend a series of impressive photographs of the great city of Hong Kong. My friend had lived there for many years and was well-acquainted with the city. It is a thriving, bustling, enterprising place. Hong Kong is a modern success story. Its buildings, commerce, attractions, and pleasures are renowned around the world. Yet in the midst of all this material success and prosperity, there is an underlying emptiness. Each picture in the series portrays great technological success and material affluence. You get the idea that if you lived in the midst of this wealth and prosperity, you'd have everything you need for a happy, contented, meaningful life. Yet underneath each picture are sayings, written in Chinese and translated into English, which express the paradox that even while living in the midst of such abundance, there is emptiness and frustration:

> …*we have bigger houses and smaller families; more conveniences, yet less time; we have more degrees but less sense; more knowledge but less judgment; more experts, yet more problems… more medicine, yet less wellness…*
> *We have multiplied our possessions, but reduced our values… We've learned how to make a living, but not a life; we've added years to life, not life to years. We've been all the way to the moon and back, but have trouble crossing the street to meet the new neighbor. We've*

conquered outer space but not inner space... we've split the atom, but not our prejudice... we learned to rush, but not to wait; we have... higher incomes, but lower morals... We've become long on quantity, but short on quality.

These are the times of... more leisure and less fun... more kinds of food and less nutrition. These are days of two incomes, but more divorces; these are times of fancier houses, but broken homes... Indeed, these are the times![5]

"You may want to argue with some of these statements, but nevertheless they give us the picture of a society that's so engrossed in material advancement that it has neglected and forgotten other values. This isn't wise. This is the wisdom of the world, the wisdom from below. It's materialistic and fleshly and misses out whole dimensions of life and existence that are essential to a well-balanced and wholesome life. It depicts a way of life that in the end leaves us empty, frustrated, and poverty-stricken in spirit. This kind of wisdom downgrades the soul, neglects the spirit, and narrows the mind."

"On our canoe trip down the River of Wisdom," Elisabeth said, "we passed through a lake called Mammon. We were impressed by the opulent lifestyle of those who lived there, but they seemed strangely empty and dissatisfied while surrounded by wealth and comforts. They were polite and well-polished, but perhaps they were following the wrong type of wisdom?"

"Oh yes," said Andrew. "You certainly don't need to go to Hong Kong to find people being guided by this wisdom from below. It's very prevalent amongst us.

"You can tell by the language James used that he's unsympathetic to wisdom from below and warns us about giving too much credence to its value system. This wisdom may smell very appetizing and look appealing, but if not disciplined and controlled it can poison and destroy us. It has the effect of weakening our spiritual awareness while strengthening the false notion that all that matters in this world are the physical and material aspects of our existence. Filling ourselves with this wisdom and trusting its fruits to satisfy us leads to malnutrition and emptiness of soul. It has a lot of bulk but very little nutritional value. The final outcome of this wisdom is internal sickness and ill health, draining us of the energy and vitality we long for.

---

5   Bob Moorehead, "Words Aptly Spoken" (Kirkland, WA: Overlake Christian Press, 1995), 198.

"James gives this wisdom three unsavory characteristics. He says it is earthly, unspiritual, and of the devil. Let's look at these three characteristics and examine them. I want us to compare the wisdom from below with the wisdom from above, so that we can see the sharp distinction between them. They are plainly in opposition to each other.

Andrew looked to our table. "Elizabeth mentioned that those of you who have travelled down the River of Wisdom have in fact seen a good illustration of this kind of wisdom when you passed through the Lake of Mammon. It would help if you tried to describe for us some of the characteristics of the people who lived on that lake."

I looked at Peter, and we silently agreed that he should respond. "We talked about it after we left the lake, and we felt the people there ran their lives mainly in pursuit of three values. They were focused on money, pleasure, and power. Money seemed to be a dominant value. They believed the more of it you had, the more important and happier you would be."

"Money, pleasure, and power," repeated Andrew. "Yes, that's a good description. It reflects the same value system James is talking about here, only he calls it earthly, unspiritual, and devilish."

Andrew turned and wrote on the blackboard behind him: *The wisdom from below is earthly.*

"Earthly wisdom has a value system whose priorities, goals, and ambitions are focused on the affairs of the world. Wisdom from below trains us to believe that anything of real value is found in the affairs of this life. It suggests that everything we need to achieve for happiness and satisfaction comes from the temporal, physical plane of existence. According to this wisdom, wealth is a primary value. If you amass wealth, life will be wonderful. Earthly wisdom indicates that the more you accumulate, the more likely you are to find happiness and contentment.

"A major objective of this wisdom from below is that you seek more wealth, for only money will open the doors of pleasure, status, respect, honor, security, and contentment. This is very different from wisdom that comes from above, which would say that there's more to life than material possessions, which can never satisfy the heart.

"The second characteristic of wisdom from below is that it is sensual. Out of the three things you observed in the Lake of Mammon—money, pleasure, and power—probably the last two, pleasure and power, are included in what James means by sensual."

Andrew turned again to the board and wrote: *The wisdom from below is sensual.*

"The wisdom from below is earthly and then sensual. Sensual means that it belongs to the natural man. It is manufactured and dreamed up by humanity, without any meaningful reference to God or the spiritual world. It focuses primarily on the comforts, satisfactions, and success of our lives in this world. It has little interest in the guidance or will of God and is neglectful of the affairs of the soul. It believes that real wisdom is found in man and that we are quite capable of determining our own path to happiness without God.

"Thus, as you observed at the Lake of Mammon, the people had a great interest in the pleasures of this life. They surrounded themselves with luxury, entertainment, diversion, and comfort. They gloried in their material success. They came to the conclusion that they didn't need to journey any further down the river; they had enough wisdom where they were. They were very sensually focused."

Elizabeth fidgeted. She had been troubled in spirit since leaving the Lake of Mammon. She hadn't spoken to us about her discomfort, but now she spoke up to reveal her concerns.

"But surely this isn't all wrong," she said. "I like nice things, too. I want comforts and some luxuries. I would like to live in a nice house and even have a boat to sail in. Is this wrong? Am I sinful to want these things?"

On hearing the sharp edge in Elizabeth's voice, I knew she was expressing some deep feelings. In some ways, I could agree with her and understand where she was coming from. I listened carefully to Andrew's reply.

Andrew also seemed to sense how important this question was to her. He gave it a few minutes' thought, and then slowly and quietly answered.

"Yes, Elizabeth, we have physical bodies that must live in this world. We're part of the material world God has created; we're not all soul and spirit. Since we're part of the animal kingdom and share many of the instincts and needs of the animal world, it's clear that we must give attention to meeting these needs. It's important that we eat and drink, and we don't just do it to survive; we also enjoy it. We must find shelter and clothing. These are important to us if life is to be carried on. We need to have times of rest, relaxation, and pleasure if our lives are to have a healthy balance. Certainly these things do have some value

"The issue is one of balance. The problem is not whether these things are important and enjoyable or not. Of course they're important to us, and we do enjoy them. The problem is that their significance can grow out of proportion, and become unbalanced to the point that we organize our lives as if they're all that matter. Added to this is the spirit of competition—the desire to get on better than our fellows, to be above them, to have power over them, to be the top person. The need to have power and influence is often equated with how much money and wealth a person has. According to the wisdom from below, money and wealth bring power and influence.

"Jesus continually warned us about this. He realized that we're constantly tempted to become so focused on providing for this life that we neglect the other aspects of human existence—God, the immortal soul, and eternity. He says,

> *Therefore I tell you, do not worry about your life, what you will eat or drink; or about your body, what you will wear. Is not life more important than food, and the body more important than clothes… So do not worry, saying, 'What shall we eat?' or 'What shall we drink?' or 'What shall we wear?' For the pagans run after all these things, and your heavenly Father knows that you need them. But seek first his kingdom and his righteousness, and all these things will be given to you as well.* (Matthew 6:25, 31–33)

"So Elizabeth, you asked if it's wrong to want the good things of life. No, it's not wrong. All of us want our bodies to be well taken care of. All of us enjoy being comfortable. These are part of the good things God has made available to us. The issue is keeping them in balance and in proportion.

"We have to organize life so that the whole person—body, soul, and spirit—is taken care of. The feeding of the spirit must be adequately attended to as well as the physical affairs of the body. The trouble with wisdom from below is that it advises us to live as if what matters most are the affairs of this life. It seeks to guide us into devoting our attention to bettering our status. It wants us to be so dominated by the matters of this world that we forget about the other values and aspects of life. This unbalanced way of living is unwise and leads us to emptiness, division, and frustration. The danger of this is very real."

Elizabeth nodded her agreement. "I agree with that. I just had the impression after the Lake of Mammon that it was wrong to desire these things. Since I desired them, I thought I must be sinful in some way. But now I see that Jesus didn't say that these things are wrong; they are part of life, just not all of life. They must be kept in their place. Put the spiritual life of the Kingdom of God first and then these things will also be added to you."

Elizabeth seemed to be much more comfortable having arrived at this understanding.

Andrew turned and wrote on the board the third characteristic of the wisdom from below: *The wisdom from below is devilish.*

"The third characteristic listed by James is that wisdom from below is devilish. We tend to rebel against the term 'devilish.' We would be offended if our way of life was called devilish. While we readily admit that we may not be perfect, we certainly don't think of ourselves as devilish.

"What James means is that wisdom from below comes from Satan. It gives expression to the way of life he likes. This wisdom fulfills the devil's purposes, not God's. Those who follow this wisdom help to expand the kingdom of the devil. The wisdom of the world reflects the devil's priorities, values, and motives.

"This wisdom makes us think of ourselves more than others, and that pleases the devil. It makes us esteem worldly values. It engrosses us in worldly pursuits to the point that we neglect the welfare of our soul. It causes us to nurture antagonism, jealousies, and hostilities in our hearts. It promotes a way of life and value system that belongs to the devil, not God.

"Animals exhibit this kind of wisdom. When their interests are invaded, they growl and snap. When they're in danger, they fight. When they're hungry, they tear at others, and even kill. This wisdom tells us to look after ourselves, making it acceptable to harm others if they in any way threaten our interests. This wisdom makes it acceptable to allow our personal needs and ambitions dominate us. If we have to put others down, or trample them on our way up, then that's just part of being smart, moving ahead, and getting what you want.

"This wisdom makes us jealous when we see others get ahead. It makes us bitter when our desires are frustrated. It makes us hostile when we're opposed. It makes us envy when we see others with possessions, positions, or stature. James says that when you're guided by this kind of wisdom, you're likely to *'harbor bitter envy and selfish ambitions in your hearts'* (James 3:14). He goes on to say, *'For where you have envy and selfish ambition, there you find disorder and every evil practice'* (James 3:16). When you examine the fruits of this wisdom, you realize that so much of the disorder, tension, and hostility we encounter in life happens because we or the people we deal with are driven and motivated by this wisdom from below."

God's Wisdom Is Greater than Man's

"The Apostle Paul also seemed to have very little patience with the wisdom of the world. He says,

> *For it is written: 'I will destroy the wisdom of the wise; the intelligence of the intelligent I will frustrate.' Where is the wise man? Where is the scholar? Where is the philosopher of this age? Has not God made foolish the wisdom of the world?* (1 Corinthians 1:19–20)

"In Paul's mind, there is a wisdom from God and then wisdom of the world, and the wisdom of the world is a false, destructive, and divisive force that robs men of real life, separating them from God and from spiritual values."

At this point, Andrew let his eyes take in the whole class. His deep voice reflected sincerity and concern. "You are on a journey into wisdom. You want to follow Far Mountain and arrive at the Sea of Tranquility. Clearly, you must disclaim the wisdom of the world as any base for satisfying the needs of your heart. You're pursuing the wisdom of God. You're pursuing true wisdom, and that will take you in a very different direction to that of the wisdom from below."

With that, Andrew finished his session.

"In the next session," he said, "we'll turn to a much more pleasant and inspiring subject—the wisdom of God, or the wisdom from above. I'm anxious, however, that you be sure about the clear distinction between the two wisdoms. This afternoon, I have some homework for you to do. I want you to again read this passage from James and think about the nature of wisdom from below. Then I want you all to write a paper about the life of King Saul. As you read about King Saul, realize that this is the story of a man who had great promise and every opportunity, but he began to make decisions and guide his life on the basis of wisdom from below. Near the end of his life, Saul said, *'Surely I have acted like a fool and have erred greatly'* (1 Samuel 26:21). I want you to trace the decision-making and value system of a man who guides his life by the wisdom from below. You'll find his story in 1 Samuel 7–31. This will keep you busy for the rest of the day. Tomorrow, one of you will read your paper to the class, and then we'll move on to talk about wisdom from above."

As the class began to disband, I turned to Elizabeth. "Are you satisfied with the answer Andrew gave to your question?"

"Yes," she said. "I was disturbed after our discussion on the meaning of the Lake of Mammon. I thought we were saying that we shouldn't value material things at all, and if that was the case, I was out of step."

"I think we tended to overemphasize the rejection of these things," I mused. "It's not that they're sinful in themselves. In many ways, they are good and necessary and so should be valued and appreciated. We just need to make sure they don't dominate us and squeeze out our spiritual values."

"I feel relieved," Elisabeth said. "I realize, though, that I'll have to be careful about it. I must seek to be wise enough to know how to keep material values in their place and make sure I discipline my life in such a way as to allow spiritual values room to grow and develop."

Lloyd put his arm around Elizabeth's shoulder. "This is wonderful. I feel we're making progress and understanding things we never understood before. Our search for wisdom is moving us in the right direction.

"You know, it's difficult to keep the value of material things and spiritual things in a wise balance. The truly wise attitude towards material possessions is found in what Jesus calls stewardship. A steward is someone who, in trust, is given responsibility for managing his master's wealth and holdings. The steward doesn't own the wealth, but he's made responsible for it. A good steward is one who efficiently uses the wealth of his master to increase its value. A poor steward becomes lazy, foolish, or careless with his master's holdings, neglecting them or using them for his own pleasure and benefit. Sometimes a steward becomes greedy and assumes the wealth belongs to him. He begins to act and think like he owns it, thus violating his stewardship.

"So for me, the wisest attitude is to view material possessions as a good steward would. They don't belong to me and God will hold me responsible for how I use them. I came into this world with nothing and I will leave it with nothing. I have this stuff only for a period of time before giving it back. I'm his servant and He is the Lord, even of the possessions that have come to me. I should certainly use them and enjoy them, but I must hold them lightly and be ready to change how I control them."

I thanked Lloyd for his insights. I was learning to appreciate more and more that Lloyd was a thoughtful and stable person. I was glad he and Elisabeth had accompanied us on this important journey.

Topics for Discussion

1. What are the three unsavory characteristics of wisdom from below?

2. Compare the characteristics of wisdom from below with those of the people living by the Lake of Mammon—money, pleasure, and power.

3. In light of Elizabeth's struggle with material values, discuss the statement, "The issue isn't whether we like these things or want them. The issue is keeping them in balance and proportion."

4. Keeping in mind the explanation given for the word "devilish," is the life we're presently living more pleasing to the devil or God?

Eighteen

The Story of Saul

As soon as I was alone in my room that afternoon, I looked up the chapters in the Bible Andrew had referred to and read the story of Saul, the first king of Israel. It wasn't a happy story, and I could see why had Andrew asked us to study it and use it as an illustration of what happens when someone follows wisdom from below.

I spent the afternoon and evening studying these chapters and wrote out my version of the story, as Andrew had requested. I was quite satisfied with my work, but was greatly surprised when the group met the next morning and Andrew, right at the start, asked me to read my story to the rest of the class. With a bit of uncertainty and nervousness, I began to read:

"King Saul is a good example of a person who follows the wrong wisdom and ends up in deep conflict and unhappiness. Saul started out well. He had every intention of being a good and successful king, but he made some unwise choices and began to follow unwise paths. Nearing the end of his life, he looked back and made the following self-evaluation: *'Surely I have acted like a fool and have erred greatly'* (1 Samuel 26:21). Saul rejected the wisdom of God and embraced the wisdom from below, ending his life in sorrow and failure.

"Saul wasn't born to be king. He was the son of a prosperous farmer. He grew up to be a handsome and impressive young man. He was strong and tall. It was said that he stood head and shoulders above the other men in Israel. He seemed like a potential leader, if the opportunity ever came his way. The opportunity came. The people of Israel had never had a king. They had been guided by prophets and judges, but the lack of a recognized central authority led each local tribe do that which was right in their own eyes. The need for a central authority became evident to them, so they asked Samuel, the leading prophet of the day, to appoint a king over them.

"Samuel wasn't happy about this, but he yielded to the pressure and was guided by God to consider Saul, a tall, strong, attractive young man. Saul, much to his surprise, was appointed king.

"Neither the nation nor Saul himself had any experience with what a king should do, but after a few military successes against their national enemies, Saul's position and authority was accepted. He was king, though he remained unsure of himself and insecure in his position. Saul began to err in his judgments. He disregarded God's instructions, issued through the prophet Samuel. It's never wise to disobey God, but Saul began to do this in little ways.

"The issue of what type of wisdom Saul listened to emerged when he was called upon to lead his people in battle against the Amalekites, historical enemies of Israel. Saul's instructions were made clear by the prophet Samuel, who told him,

> *This is what the Lord Almighty says: 'I will punish the Amalekites for what they did to Israel when they waylaid them as they came up from Egypt. Now go, attack the Amalekites and totally destroy everything that belongs to them. Do not spare them; put to death men and women, children and infants, cattle and sheep, camels and donkeys.'* (1 Samuel 15:2–3)

"Saul and the Israelites were successful in battle against the Amalekites, but afterward Saul partially disobeyed the instructions by keeping for himself some of the best of the Amalekites' sheep and cattle. He also spared the life of the Amalekite king. He did this in defiance of God's clear instruction that all of them were to be destroyed.

"The first indication that Saul wasn't following wisdom from above came when Samuel arrived at the scene where the battle had taken place. He was told that Saul was no longer there but had *"gone to Carmel. There he has set up a monument in his own honor and has turned and gone on down to Gilgal"* (1 Samuel 15.12). In setting up a monument in his own honor, Saul was clearly paying attention to his own glory and stature—an important value of wisdom from below. It was, after all, important that the new king look good. He needed all the prestige and public honor he could get in order to establish his position. So, in his own interests and to enhance his own stature, he set up a monument to celebrate the victory. The monument was intended as a symbol to the nation that the new king had done well. This was all very correct according to the wisdom of the world, but he had disobeyed God and was intent on honoring himself rather than give God honor. Self before God is a basic ingredient of worldly wisdom.

"When Samuel finally caught up with Saul at Gilgal, Saul came out to meet him with the pretentious words, *'The Lord bless you! I have carried out the Lord's instructions'* (1 Samuel 15:13). This wasn't true; he had not carried out the Lord's instructions. Appearances were important to Saul. He had to give the impression that he had been successful and fully obeyed God. It's important in worldly wisdom to give the right impression, to appear happy and successful. This wisdom insists that you avoid looking weak and uncertain. You mustn't appear to be a failure.

"Samuel's reply to Saul's pretentious statement was both vivid and devastating. God's instructions had been clear—all of the sheep and cattle of the enemy were to be destroyed. Saul falsely declared that he had done this. Samuel's responded, *'What then is this bleating of the sheep in my ears? What is this lowing of cattle that I hear?'* (1 Samuel 15:14). Samuel, thinking in terms of wisdom from above, realized that Saul hadn't obeyed God's instructions. Saul said, *"The soldiers brought them from the Amalekites; they spared the best of the sheep and cattle to sacrifice to the Lord your God, but we totally destroyed the rest'* (1 Samuel 15:15).

"You can see the point of Saul's argument. He maintained that it wasn't his fault, but the soldiers were responsible for keeping the sheep and cattle. Worldly wisdom would whisper, 'Good thinking, Saul! That's the way to do it. Blame someone else. Don't admit personal responsibility. Sure, you didn't quite do what you were supposed to, but the instructions were a bit extreme anyway. You did the best you could, and you couldn't help what others did.' Who could argue with that?

"Saul was becoming skillful at worldly wisdom. In his eyes, it was alright to seek his own selfish interests. It was alright to be a little disobedient. He had every right to keep some of the spoils of battle for himself. He could make his disobedience look good and righteous by making a few token sacrifices to God. He did it all for a good cause.

"It's amazing how well worldly wisdom can dress itself up in the clothes of righteousness. That justifies it. That makes it alright. Make a few token gestures towards God, or charities, and that seems to justify one's obsession with worldly affairs. This is what Jesus warned us about when he said, *'Watch out for false prophets. They come to you in sheep's clothing, but inwardly they are ferocious wolves'* (Matthew 7:15).

Samuel was operating on a different wavelength altogether. He cut through all these false pretentions and selfish justifications, saying, *'Stop... Let me tell you what the Lord said to me last night'* (1 Samuel 15:16). Samuel spoke with wisdom from above. It was clear, plain, and simple. No pretentions or justifications. Samuel went on to remind Saul of what he used to be but no longer was:

> *Although you were once small in your own eyes, did you not become the head of the tribes of Israel? The Lord anointed you king over Israel.* (1 Samuel 15:17)

"Essentially, Samuel was saying, 'You've changed your outlook, and the new look isn't good. You're not what you used to be. You're captivated by your own importance. You're trying to make yourself great and popular. In order to be popular and gain wealth and prestige, you are willing to disobey God and neglect His commandments. This isn't wise, Saul. Your power is going to your head. When you were small in your own eyes, God elevated you to be king. Now that you're trying to be great in your own eyes, and popular with the people, you find yourself on a road that will diminish you in the eyes of all.'

"Samuel then went on to remind Saul of the instruction he had received from God about the war with the Amalekites. Samuel said,

> *And he sent you on a mission, saying, 'Go and completely destroy those wicked people, the Amalekites; make war on them until you have wiped them out.' Why did you not obey the Lord? Why did you pounce on the plunder and do evil in the eyes of the Lord?* (1 Samuel 15:18–19)

"Blinded by the persuasions of his worldly wisdom, Saul could hardly see what he had done. He felt the need to defend himself rather than admit the error of his ways. Perhaps if he had admitted his wrongness at this point, and got back to listening to wisdom from above, the story of the rest of his life would have been different. But Saul didn't listen to God; he listened to the wisdom of his own desires. He repeated his argument to Samuel:

> *'But I did obey the Lord,' Saul said. 'I went on the mission the Lord assigned me. I completely destroyed the Amalekites and brought back Agag their king. The soldiers took sheep and cattle from the plunder, the best of what was devoted to God, in order to sacrifice them to the Lord your God at Gilgal."* (1 Samuel 15:20–21)

"It's difficult to convince those who are traveling down the road of worldly wisdom that they're on the wrong road. They don't see it. They really think their way is right, and anyone with any sense about how the world works would agree with them.

"This is the same old, tired argument. Saul probably told himself, 'Sure, we didn't quite do it the way God told us to, but the way we did it was alright. We didn't kill them all. We did keep some of the sheep and cattle, but at heart we really are good people. We're going to sacrifice the best of them to God. This makes more sense.' In his mind, he was arguing with God's wisdom: 'God, you can't really expect us to kill all these valuable sheep and cattle, can you? It would be wasteful. The soldiers need a reward. That's how you wage war. That's how it's done. It's common sense.'

"Worldly wisdom is very convincing to those who listen to it.

"Again, Samuel's reply cuts thorough all the self-justification and gets to the heart of the matter:

> *Does the Lord delight in burnt offerings and sacrifices as much as in obeying the voice of the Lord? To obey is better than sacrifice, and to heed is better than the fat of rams. For rebellion is like the sin of divination, and arrogance like the evil of idolatry. Because you have rejected the word of the Lord, he has rejected you as king.*
> (1 Samuel 22–23)

"The wisdom of God comes out clearly in this outstanding statement. Listening and heeding are more valuable than giving sacrifices and making excuses after disobedience.

"But the wisdom of the world isn't about to concede the point. Saul, realizing he could lose his kingdom, was alarmed. Nothing fills a worldly person with more fear than the possibility of losing position, power, wealth, and honor. Saul saw this possibility and was greatly afraid. He liked being king. He liked being wealthy. He liked people showing him deference and respect. He liked the power and honor the position brought to him. He didn't want to go back to being a common farmer.

"Therefore, Saul faked repentance. Worldly wisdom, in its extremity, may indeed make a show of repentance. When it's faced with the loss of its values, it's quite willing to pay attention to God. But the motivation is fear—fear of losing the values and benefits it has fought so hard to attain. It's sham repentance and God sees through it, just as Samuel saw through Saul.

"Saul didn't really intend to change his ways. If he could just get by this difficulty and appease Samuel, he could settle down again to build his kingdom, amassing wealth while increasing his stature and popularity. So Saul said to Samuel,

> *'I have sinned. I violated the Lord's command and your instructions. I was afraid of the people and so I gave in to them. Now I beg you, forgive my sin and come back with me, so that I may worship the Lord.' But Samuel said to him, 'I will not go back with you. You have rejected the word of the Lord, and the Lord has rejected you as king over Israel!'* (1 Samuel 15:24–26)

"Samuel turns to leave. In desperation, Saul grabs hold of Samuel's robe and pulls, tearing it. Samuel's response to this is to turn to Saul and say, *'The Lord has torn the kingdom of Israel from you today and has given it to one of your neighbors— to one better than you'* (1 Samuel 15:28).

"A multitude of conflicting emotions must have crowded in on Saul's spirit at this pronouncement. But his response to Samuel is a good indication of how deeply the wisdom of the world had taken hold of his spirit. At this moment of crisis, Saul's dominant concern was the loss of worldly benefits. There may have been an element of sorrow in Saul's heart for his disobedience and carelessness in heeding God's instructions. Had those feelings been predominant, he might still have been rescued, but Saul's response makes it clear that what really mattered to him was his loss of face and prestige, the endangering of his position, and the end of stature and wealth. He said, *'I have sinned. But please honor me before the elders of my people and before Israel; come back with me, so that I may worship the Lord your God'* (1 Samuel 15:30).

"He was afraid of being embarrassed and shamed in the eyes of the people. Even though he had lost standing with God, he didn't want this to be evident to the people. Samuel's presence was essential if his honor was to be maintained. To Saul, the loss of standing before God was regrettable, but his standing before the people was essential. This reflects the value system of worldly wisdom. The trouble with worldly wisdom is that it leads us away from God and His wisdom. It promotes a way of life that moves us to devalue the things of God.

"Samuel agreed to Saul's request and went back with him and honored God with him. Saul continued to be king for some time, but his path went steadily downhill from that point on. He became a man wracked with jealousy as others seemed to ascend. After David the shepherd killed Goliath and the people of Israel celebrated the victory, they sang a song that went like this: *'Saul has slain his thousands, and David his tens of thousands'* (1 Samuel 18:7). The Bible describes Saul's reaction to this:

> Saul was very angry; this refrain galled him. 'They have cred-ited David with tens of thousands,' he thought, 'but me with only thousands. What more can he get but the kingdom?' And from that time on Saul kept a jealous eye on David. (1 Samuel 18:8–9)

"His downward path of worldly wisdom became more pronounced. He was subject to foul and violent moods. He was increasingly jealous. He had times of deep depression. In one episode of black depression, he tried to kill David. More and more of his energy and thoughts were consumed not by the affairs of state, but in finding David and killing him, so that he would no longer be a threat. His faith in God deteriorated. Even as his wealth and position in the kingdom increased, Saul's enjoyment in the benefits of being king was lost. He developed suspicions and hostilities towards his own family and faithful friends. He even tried to kill his own son in a fit of jealous fury. The meaning of life faded. The atmosphere of humble trust in his spirit dried up, replaced with hatred and fear. Such is the path of worldly wisdom. It leads us away from God and away from the values in life that satisfy and fill the human heart with joy and peace.

"Worldly wisdom does not produce happy and contented people. James, writing many years after Saul had died, expressed the same sentiment. He said,

> *But if you harbor bitter envy and selfish ambition in your hearts, do not boast about it or deny the truth. Such 'wisdom' does not come down from heaven but is earthly, unspiritual, of the devil. For where you have envy and selfish ambition, there you find disorder and every evil practice.* (James 3:14–16)

"For Saul, the end of the road was tragic. The nation was again at war with the Philistines. Saul, on the eve of battle, was worried about the outcome, but he got no response from God, even though he pleaded for help and guidance. Because God was silent, Saul sought the guidance of a witch and diviner, a woman who lived in a place called Endor. With her power of divination, she brought up what appeared to be the ghost of Samuel, who was long dead by this time. Saul said to the ghost,

> *I am in great distress… The Philistines are fighting against me, and God has turned away from me. He no longer answers me, either by prophets or by dreams. So I have called on you to tell me what to do.* (1 Samuel 28:15)

"Samuel confirmed that the battle the next day would be a catastrophe, that Saul and his sons would be killed, and that the army of Israel would be badly defeated. It was a sad, lonely, and painful end for a man who had trusted in the path of worldly wisdom."

I finished my presentation and sat down. There was silence in the room. *Either they're thinking about what I said or they're sound asleep,* I thought.

Andrew relieved my concerns by thanking me and asking the class if they had any comments.

"That was great," my good friend Peter said. "It makes me all the more anxious not to follow the principles and values of the wisdom from below. I want to learn better what the wisdom from above is, and live by it."

There were a number of "Amens" and grunts of approval from the rest of the class, which convinced me they had understood and agreed with what I had said.

153

"You've said it well, Colin," Andrew said. "We're all agreed that we don't want to follow the wisdom of the world, but rather the wisdom of God. Let's give our attention now to what the wisdom of God looks like."

Topics for Discussion

1. Was Saul's transgression with the Amalekites really so bad? Why did God react to it so strongly? At what points could Saul have changed his attitude? What were Saul's predominant interests throughout this episode?

Nineteen

Wisdom from Above, Part One

AFTER A SHORT BREAK, WE WERE READY FOR OUR NEXT LESSON ON WISDOM.

"We turn our attention now to the bright side of wisdom," said Andrew. "James leaves us in no doubt that the two types of wisdom are very different. One has its source in God, the other in diminished human nature. One is inspired by love and holiness, the other flows from inbred self-interest. One attempts to construct life so that the whole man, including his soul and spirit, are taken care of; the other neglects the spiritual aspects of life and focuses almost exclusively on the affairs of this world.

"James paints a vivid picture of what wisdom from above is like. He sketches for us its seven characteristics. These characteristics aren't incidental features, but rather flow from the depths of a person's personality. They are an expression of a heart in deep communion, absorbing the atmosphere of His Spirit. This wisdom forms in our lives when we accept and embrace the priorities of God.

Characteristics of Wisdom Come from God

"You've already heard the basic principle that the fear of the Lord is the beginning of wisdom. From this interaction, the rich, clear stream of the Spirit of God begins to flow in our hearts, and the strength of this flow influences the way we make decisions, relate with others, and view life. Wisdom from above begins to instill in us a deeper understanding of life, of other people, and even of ourselves. It helps us live to the fullest in all dimensions.

"As we examine these seven characteristics of wisdom from above, I want you to realize that they are very rewarding. They bring to us a richer, fuller, and more satisfying way of life. Desirable fruits will appear in our lives and in our personalities. These rewards may include, but far exceed, the rewards of following the wisdom from below. The book of Proverbs expresses this well:

> *Blessed is the man who finds wisdom, the man who gains understanding, for she is more profitable than silver and yields better returns than gold. She is more precious than rubies; nothing you desire can compare with her. Long life is in her right hand; in her left hand are riches and honor. Her ways are pleasant ways, and all her paths are peace. She is a tree of life to those who embrace her; those who lay hold of her will be blessed.* (Proverbs 3:13–18)

"Wisdom from above is more than an intellectual exercise of right thinking. While right thinking is important, this wisdom emerges mostly from right attitudes which filter through our minds, siphoning out falseness and nourishing rightness. This wisdom is a matter of the heart.

"If you want to know what true wisdom looks like, then here is the answer:

> *But the wisdom that comes from heaven is first of all pure; then peace-loving, considerate, submissive, full of mercy and good fruit, impartial and sincere. Peacemakers who sow in peace raise a harvest of righteousness."* (James 3:17–18)

1. Wisdom from Above Is Pure

"The first characteristic is that wisdom from above is pure. To help us understand what is meant by "pure," William Barkley says,

156

The Greek is hagnos *and its root meaning is* pure enough to approach the gods. *At first this could have meant primarily a ceremonial cleanness. You have gone through the correct rituals, made the right sacrifices to approach the gods. It soon, however, meant more than that. Purity meant cleanness of thinking; having holy thoughts, being cleansed from selfish and worldly motivations. The wisdom that is from above is pure, which means that in content and motivation it reflects the spirit and atmosphere of God. Those with this wisdom are moved by motives and purposes that are cleansed of selfish and ulterior motives so that they can be exposed to God's scrutiny and be comfortable.[6]*

"Jesus stated in the Sermon on the Mount, *'Blessed are the pure in heart, for they will see God'* (Matthew 5:8). The pure in heart can comfortably operate in God's presence and expose themselves to the eyes of God without discomfort. It is natural for the wisdom from above to move us towards purity of thought, motive, and value. When your heart is dominated by this wisdom, you make decisions, set your values, and define your purposes on a different basis than you would if you were motivated by the wisdom from below, with its focus on money, pleasure, and power. It is wise to seek a pure heart. It is unwise to accommodate selfish impurities.

"Jesus constantly urges us to embrace a way of life that's pure, that's free of selfishness and ulterior motives. Your decisions and values will become purified if you set your sights upon the honor of God and seek to do His will. Your direction and purposes will change if you seek first His Kingdom and His righteousness. Your motivations and attitudes will change if you love God *'with all of your heart and with all your soul and with all your mind... [and] love your neighbor as yourself'* (Matthew 22:37, 39).

"At its heart, true wisdom is pure. When your heart is governed by the true Spirit of wisdom, you'll be at peace with yourself. You'll build loving and compassionate relationships with others. When you make decisions in light of what God wants, and what's good for others, you'll expand your life into new dimensions of sensitivity and love.

---

6   William Barclay, *The Daily Study Bible: Letters of James and Peter* (Burlington, ON: Welch Publishing Company, 1976), 95.

"On the other hand, when you make selfish decisions in light of what's good for *you*, your view of what's important in life will deteriorate. Decisions made on this basis are narrow, small, and miss the greater values of life. Selfishness destroys wisdom."

As I listened to Andrew, I thought, *This is strong meat, indeed. I'm not at all sure I've reached this state of grace.*

For my encouragement more than anything else, I said to Andrew, "Purity in heart is something I should strive for, but I'm afraid I haven't quite attained it yet."

"But do not be discouraged," Andrew said. "Remember that God is more powerful than sin. There's no need for sin to reign in your heart. In fact, Paul states triumphantly,

> *The law was added so that the trespass might increase. But where sin increased, grace increased all the more, so that, just as sin reigned in death, so also grace might reign through righteousness to bring eternal life through Jesus Christ our Lord.* (Romans 5:20–21).

"Paul means that where sin is strong, God is stronger. Colin, there's no sin in your heart that's so powerful God cannot deal with it. In fact, we are encouraged to believe that *'if we confess our sins, he is faithful and just and will forgive us our sins and purify us from all unrighteousness'* (1 John 1:9)."

"So what do I do if I find that my attitudes are unclean?" I asked. "What if my motivation is greedy or hostile and I'm making decisions for selfish reasons? It's not enough to say I shouldn't do that. There must be a practical solution."

"Most certainly there is," Andrew said. "The verse from John promises that if you perceive sin in your heart, then confess it, for there is power in Jesus Christ to cleanse you. You don't need to operate on the basis of an impure heart. It's never wise to accommodate sin in our lives."

I would need some time to absorb this, so I said no more. But Andrew continued.

"It's significant to notice that 'pure' comes first in the list of characteristics of wisdom. It's an inner quality. The other characteristics will lay their emphasis on the outward expressions of wisdom and how it guides our lives. But purity is an expression of what we are, the condition of our own hearts, and the state of our own spirits. The other qualities are an outgrowth of purity. Purity is the fresh spring from which all the other characteristics flow. Wisdom begins here. If the heart is pure, then the motivations, values, and purposes upon which we base the decisions of our life will also be pure. If we try to live what appears to be a clean life in outward appearance, while inwardly we're self-seeking and worldly, we will fail. Wisdom begins with an inner purity."

Looking at me, he said, "So don't settle for an impure heart. Claim victory in your heart in the name of Jesus Christ. True wisdom always lies in the direction of purity, and never in the direction of sin and selfishness."

2. Wisdom from Above Is Peace-Loving

"The second characteristic of wisdom is that it is peaceable, or peace-loving. Because your heart is clean, you'll be able to be a genuinely peace-loving person. You'll strive to have harmonious relationships between yourself and others, including a good relationship with God.

"Some of the richest and most satisfying experiences we can have are harmonious, loving relationships with others. Wisdom from above gives us good insight that enables us to get on well with God and other people. Wisdom instructs us in developing attitudes of respect, dignity, and considerateness when it comes to our relationships.

"Being peaceable means desiring first of all to have a loving respect for other people. Wisdom shows us ways in which we seek to benefit others by being constructive and encouraging. It will help us grow an attitude of honor and acceptance for all people. Wisdom helps us to be kind about all the shortcomings we see in others and to be tolerant of the aggravations we suffer from them. When our attitude towards others is loving and peaceful, our decisions, judgments, and responses to them will be honorable. Jesus said, *'Blessed are the peacemakers, for they will be called the sons of God'* (Matthew 5:9).

"There is great benefit and blessing in creating an atmosphere of peace between people. You will greatly enhance the quality of your life, and also the quality you bring to the lives of others, if you learn the wisdom of being peaceable. Harmony, love, and happy fellowship issue from peace-loving people. Irritations and stress issue from those who are selfish and self-seeking in their relationships with others. Wisdom from above will show us how to be more skillful at living at peace with each other."

"But," someone asked, "what if others don't want peaceful relationships? What if they're hostile and want to create trouble?"

"The Bible understands this," replied Andrew. "The apostle Paul urges us to *'make every effort to do what leads to peace and to mutual edification'* (Romans 14:19). The writer to the Hebrews says much the same thing: *'Make every effort to live in peace with all men and to be holy'* (Hebrews 12:14). The responsibility of the peace-maker is to make every effort to bring peace, but it's understood that it takes two people to live at peace. Sometimes the effort will be in vain, but only if the other person makes a poor choice. Wisdom will give us insight to understand what it takes to be more effective in maintaining peaceful relationships."

Peace with Our Enemies

"In fact, developing this skill for peaceful relationships extends even to our enemies, or those who seem determined to cause us harm and stress. Jesus said, *'But I tell you: Love your enemies and pray for those who persecute you, that you may be sons of your Father in heaven'* (Matthew 5:44–45). When you're wise and other people aren't nice to you, seek to absorb their insults. Be patient with their idiosyncrasies. Respond quietly to their irritations. Do not easily take offence. Treat them with honor and respect, and always work towards building a good and harmonious relationship. Wisdom looks for ways to avoid bitter conflicts, and when conflict comes, it seeks solutions. Wisdom from above makes great effort and shows considerable skill at living peaceably with all. It doesn't easily take offence. It doesn't harbor resentment. It isn't boorish or ill-mannered in its treatment of others. It is prepared to overlook faults and failures in others in order to keep the peace.

"When you meet someone and they go out of their way to be unfriendly, or even hostile, you cannot help their attitude. They are responsible for that. But you can help your own attitude. Deal with them wisely and generously. Always look for ways to do good to them. Try to understand them. Always be prepared to forgive and overlook. This is wise."

"Those who are wise enough to seek peace usually find warmth, fellowship, and support in others. They are surrounded by people who help and encourage. When they themselves have a need, others rush in to help. They enjoy the company of others. They are free of the stresses and strains that seem so common in our society today. It is wise to be peaceable. Peaceful wisdom is also an inner state. Those who promote peace usually have peace within themselves. This is wise living. This is rich living. This is good living."

3. Wisdom from Above Is Gentle

"The next characteristic of wisdom is that it's gentle. This wisdom looks for ways to be kind in its judgments. It has an atmosphere of understanding mercy. It isn't quick to blame or jump to harsh criticisms.

"This is the kind of gentle wisdom Jesus showed. One day, He arrived at the temple in Jerusalem early and began to teach the people who gathered around Him. His teaching, however, was interrupted when a rough and noisy crowd of temple supporters arrived, led by some of the Pharisees. They were dragging with them a protesting and very unhappy, embarrassed woman. This hostile gang, as they had hoped, soon became the center of attention. They made the woman stand in front of Jesus. With the whole crowd watching and listening, they challenged Him, saying, *'Teacher, this woman was caught in the act of adultery. In the Law Moses commanded us to stone such women. Now what do you say?'* (John 8:4–5)

"To our ears today, this sounds extreme, but it was true. The law of Moses says, *'If a man commits adultery with another man's wife—with the wife of his neighbor—both the adulterer and the adulteress must be put to death'* (Leviticus 20:10). By the time of Jesus, this was no longer the practice, but nevertheless it was a statement of law put forward by Moses. Jesus' enemies had orchestrated this event so they could use it as a trap in which to catch Him. The Bible says, *'They were using this question as a trap, in order to have a basis for accusing him'* (John 8:6). If Jesus replied by saying, 'No. You must not do that. It is too harsh and extreme,' then He could be accused of contradicting the Law of Moses. If He said, 'Yes. You must keep the law. She should be stoned to death,' then the people would have resented His unforgiving attitude.

"In a remarkable show of gentle wisdom, Jesus didn't answer them, but stooped down and began to write with his finger in the dust of the ground. Time passed. Everyone waited. What would He say? The questioners persisted in urging Him for an answer. They thought they had cornered him. After a while,

> *[Jesus] straightened up and said to them, 'If any one of you is without sin, let him be the first to throw a stone at her.' Again he stooped down and wrote on the ground. At this, those who heard began to go away one at a time, the older ones first, until only Jesus was left, with the woman still standing there. Jesus straightened up and asked her, 'Woman, where are they? Has no one condemned you?'*

161

"'No one, sir,' she said.
"'Then neither do I condemn you,' Jesus declared. 'Go now and leave your life of sin.' (John 8:7–11)

"This is a beautiful example of gentle, merciful wisdom in action. Jesus didn't want the woman stoned. He wanted to relieve her of her public shame and embarrassment. He wasn't anxious to condemn but looked for a way for her to be relieved and forgiven. His spirit of wise mercy was revealed when He said to her, *'Then neither do I condemn you… Go now and leave your life of sin'* (John 8:11). No harshness there. No quick rush to judgment. No gloating over someone's fall. No criticism, saying, 'You're just getting what you deserve. If you'd been stronger, you would never have gotten into this situation.'

"Wise gentleness isn't anxious to condemn, but is skillful in finding a way to encourage forgiveness and a change of heart. Jesus was clear—the woman had sinned. She did something that she ought not to have done. Jesus in no way condoned or approved of her actions. He wasn't offering forgiveness without repentance. He wasn't shutting His eyes to the wrong that had been done.

"When a person is conscious of doing wrong and is hurting others, but insists on proceeding anyway, the call is not for gentle mercy. But if the person shows some sense of remorse and willingness to change. mercy kicks in and is a powerful tool for changing lives. Wise mercy doesn't dispense forgiveness without repentance. It doesn't cover up and make excuses for sin. It skillfully negotiates towards repentance and change.

"The objective of gentleness isn't just to make the person feel better, but to make them into a better person. Its motivation is to ease the stress of the situation and bring about reformation. In dealing with faults, failures, and weaknesses, wisdom believes it is better to take an attitude of gentleness and be kind and considerate than it is to be harsh, judgmental, and critical. The gentle attitude, wisely applied, is likely to have more impact on the person who's going astray than the harsh pronouncement of judgment."

Blessed Are the Merciful

"Jesus said in Matthew 5:7, *'Blessed are the merciful, for they will be shown mercy.'* Jesus endorses the attitude of mercy, saying that it's a blessed and rewarding way to live. A spirit of gentle mercy is easier to live with than a censorious spirit of judgment and condemnation. Kind mercy is rewarding to the person showing it as well as to the person receiving it. It brings peace and quietness to the heart of the one who is being merciful. A gentle understanding towards the failures and faults of others brings richness and reward to the spirit of the giver and an encouragement to the receiver. It brings quiet contentment to the soul."

"I think there's even an added blessing here," Lloyd said. "Jesus said that the merciful aren't only blessed, but that they shall also be shown mercy. I've found that we're much more willing to be gentle and kind to people who were gentle and kind with us when we failed. We're more likely to forgive those who are ready to forgive us. On the other hand, when we have been the recipient of someone's quick, unforgiving, gleeful judgment, we are tempted to be hard on them when their faults are revealed. When others have rushed to judgment on us and shown no mercy, it's more difficult for us to show mercy to them."

Andrew smiled at this and thanked Lloyd for his insight. "I think this is what Jesus was referring to when he said,

> *Do not judge, or you too will be judged. For in the same way you judge others, you will be judged, and with the measure you use, it will be measured to you.* (Matthew 7:1–2).

"It's true, Lloyd, that if you're gentle and generous with others, they'll be more inclined to be gentle and generous with you. Be gentle with the faults, failings, and sins of others. This is a much more fruitful way of life than tense, harsh condemnation."

4. Wisdom from Above Is Easy to Be Entreated

Andrew picked up his Bible again. "The next quality James lists is that it's easy to be entreated. This is difficult to translate and explain in English. William Barkley indicates that the Greek word *eupeithes* can be translated in two ways. First, it can mean "ever ready to obey." Second, it can mean "easy to persuade, not in the sense of being pliable, easily led and weak, but in the sense of not being stubborn and of being willing to listen to reason and to appeal."[7]

"It means that it's not wise to be stubborn, narrow-minded, and unyielding in our relationships with God and other people. It's not wise to close your mind and spirit, being unaccepting of new direction, truth, and ways of doing things.

---

7   Ibid., 96.

It is wise to be open to new truth and fresh light from God, and to be flexible and respectful in receiving the opinions and ideas of others.

"It's very important to be easily entreated in our relationship with God. Once a person begins to think they know all there is to know, they close themselves off to the flow of fresh light and life constantly coming from God. When a person says, 'I've learned how to pray, and the way I'm doing it is so right that I cannot see much need to change or improve,' then that person has cut himself off from a source of growing richness in the spiritual life. When a person assumes what they already know about God covers the essentials and that there's no need for significant change, that person will dry up and his spiritual life will grow dull and habitual. Wisdom has a humble spirit, so when it comes to our relationships with God, we humbly acknowledge that there are vast amounts of experience and understanding we have still to learn. It is wise to genuinely feel that we have a lot to learn and be open to learning it. When it comes to understanding God, we've hardly scratched the surface.

"This spirit of being easily entreated is the atmosphere of someone who's willing to listen to God, ready to obey, anxious to learn, prepared to confess when wrong, and humbly trust in the goodness of God. A wise person is one who seeks and searches for more of God. Jesus said a strange thing when He said,

> *I tell you the truth, unless you change and become like little children, you will never enter the kingdom of heaven. Therefore, whoever humbles himself like this child is the greatest in the kingdom of heaven.* (Matthew 18:3–4)

"It is wise to adopt the humble, meek attitude of the child, who understands he cannot yet do everything and needs constant help, support, and instruction. It is wise to say, 'I have a lot to learn.' This attitude opens the way for growth and maturity in the kingdom of God.

"The Apostle John expresses the same concept. He says,

> *But if we walk in the light, as he is in the light, we have fellowship with one another, and the blood of Jesus, his Son, purifies us from all sin.* (1 John 1:7)

"The assumption is that there's a lot of light still to dawn on us in our spiritual lives. We have a lot to learn. There are vast amounts of experience yet to be encountered. We must walk forward into the new light and experience new things in order to grow and develop in our walk with God. A refusal to walk into this new light means we'll cease to make progress in our spiritual growth.

"There's nothing more stifling than the idea that we already know most of what is essential, that there's not much more of importance to know. It's stale and arrogant to believe that what we have experienced of God is largely complete. Those who blandly assume they have covered all the necessary bases aren't likely to experience the thrill of scoring more runs. This is unwise. This is foolish."

Easy to Entreat in Our Relationships with Others

"When it comes to interacting with other people, it's wise not to be stubborn and dogmatic in our positions and opinions. It's wise to be open to see and respect the opinions and ideas of others. This wisdom tries to understand where others are coming from and shows understanding for why they have arrived at their opinion. You may not agree, but you should still understand and respect them. They know when they talk to you that they'll have a fair hearing. They appreciate the fact that you listen.

"In terms of maintaining friendly relationships with others, this is a winning attitude. It's a stance of non-aggression. It takes great skill and wisdom to know when to yield and when to take your stand. Many of the resentful divisions that take place between people could be avoided if a little more entreaty was demonstrated."

At this point, one of the young men in the class put his hand up, asking permission to speak. "I was looking up a statement made by the Apostle Paul, who wasn't always known for changing his mind on issues. But he demonstrated a great willingness to be entreated in this passage. He testifies,

> *Though I am free and belong to no man, I make myself a slave to everyone, to win as many as possible. To the Jews I became like a Jew, to win the Jews. To those under the law I became like one under the law (though I myself am not under the law), so as to win those under the law. To those not having the law I became like one not having the law (though I am not free from God's law but am under Christ's law), so as to win those not having the law. To the weak I became weak, to win the weak. I have become all things to all men so that by all possible means I might save some.* (1 Corinthians 9:19–22)

165

"That's a great reference," said Andrew. "Paul understood the wisdom of personally making adjustments and foregoing his own rights to keep the lines of respectful communication open to others and better persuade them. This flexibility is a wise way to deal with others, who will usually appreciate this and make concessions."

"However," said the young man, who had clearly thought a great deal about this, "the same Paul who was flexible and accommodating to the various cultural peculiarities of those to whom he ministered was very inflexible when he faced the challenge of those in the early church who wanted his gentile converts to become Jews and who insisted that these gentile converts adopt all Jewish laws and culture."

Andrew nodded. "Paul understood that a very basic and fundamental issue was at stake here, one that could change the whole nature and outlook of the Gospel he was preaching. He therefore took a strong stand against it. The matter of insisting on Jewishness for non-Jewish converts was a destiny-changing issue for the early church. It does, however, take great wisdom to know that while we can be open and generous in many issues, there are also some basic tenets upon which we cannot compromise. Paul was wise enough to understand this difference.

"We face similar choices today, and they still call for wisdom. When should we take a stand and when should we yield? Every parent faces this with their children. Every marriage encounters the same perplexities. It's good to be flexible and easily entreated on many issues, but there are some issues upon which we need to take our stand. It takes great wisdom to know the difference. This well-known prayer is appropriate here:

> *Lord, help me to change the things I can change, and accept the things I cannot change, and the wisdom to know the difference.*

"How different is the spirit of this prayer from the recorded prayer of the chairman of the board who prayed, 'Lord, help me always to be right, for Thou knowest I will never change my mind'?"

The class laughed at this, but Andrew nodded and said, "The spirit of wisdom brings into our lives and relationships an atmosphere of being respectfully and generously easy to be entreated."

Somebody spoke up at this time. "Andrew, this has been a good but heavy session. Could we entreat you to give us a break right now before we move on to the next quality?"

Andrew smiled. "I will gladly practice what I preach and give you a short break."

Topics for Discussion

1. The seven characteristics of wisdom from above are compared to the characteristics of the Kingdom of God as outlined by Jesus in the Beatitudes. Can you list the comparisons?

2. Discuss Andrew's response to Colin who felt that his heart was not yet pure.

3. What are some of the rewards of being peace-loving?

4. Can you explain the difference between being easily entreated and being weak and easily led?

Twenty

Wisdom from Above, Part Two

After a short break for lunch and refreshments, we came back and settled down for the rest of the class.

5. Wisdom from Above Is Full of Mercy and Good Fruits

Andrew started immediately. "The next characteristic James lists as an expression of wisdom is being full of mercy and good fruits. In other words, wisdom gives us insight into how to act towards others in a kind and redemptive way. Wisdom knows how to show mercy to those in need, but does it in such a way that it enriches and matures them. Wisdom wants its mercy to issue in good fruits, and not be wasted.

"The spirit of wisdom indicates that we want to help others by meeting immediate and urgent needs, but it also looks beyond the immediate and constructs plans to remedy the situation so that, if possible, it doesn't occur again. The old saying goes, 'Give a man a fish and you will feed him for a day. Teach a man to fish and he can feed himself for a lifetime.' The wisdom that's full of mercy and good fruits is interested not only in meeting needs, but in helping people so that their needs don't become chronic dependencies. The recipient becomes resourceful enough to take care of their needs themselves.

"The suggestion is that there can be unwise mercy. Out of pity for the suffering and need of others, unwise mercy will rush in and do whatever is necessary to meet that need. This is commendable, but if there's no change in the circumstances the need will arise again, and again and again. People who build their houses on a flood plain experience loss every spring when the river breaks its banks. It's good for the neighbors to move in and supply urgent food and shelter, but is this to be repeated the next year when the flood comes back, and the year after that, and the year after that? Wise mercy that's full of good fruits moves in and says, 'We'll help you relocate your home to higher and safer ground.' Wise mercy understands that it's not merciful to create unhealthy dependence in people so that they fail to take responsibility for themselves."

Someone put up her hand. "I understand. My father was a good man, but he was an alcoholic. My mother, who had to deal with it, finally accepted this principle of redemptive wisdom. She came to understand that showing mercy and pity without accompanying redemptive wisdom does more harm than good. At first, my mother would say to herself, and to us, 'We'll cover for him, and avoid embarrassment. We'll help him this time. We'll suffer his abuse because he doesn't really know what he's doing.' We kept this up for a long time until finally we came to see that all we were doing was confirming him in his alcoholism, making it easy for him to continue in it. When we finally refused to shelter him from the painful consequences of his addiction, and when he saw what his drinking was doing to us, he was finally able to admit his problem and seek help. What made the difference was this attitude of wise, redemptive mercy. We didn't only ask what we could do to help him in the present crisis; we asked what we could do to help him cure his alcoholism."

"That's a good illustration of wise mercy and good fruits at work," said Andrew.

Another lady made a contribution to the discussion by saying, "Those of us who are parents know that if we give our children everything they want, it develops a dependency that makes them incapable of working and striving for the things they want in life. While love may urge us to give them everything they want, wise mercy would ask, 'How can I train my children to grow up to be independent, fruitful, and productive persons?' Wisdom strives to be redemptive, not just helpful."

"Wise mercy is full of good fruits," Andrew said. "It's anxious to do things that are helpful. It's ready to step in and help others, but the help should be wise so that the benefits can be maintained and the person can become self-reliant and mature. It doesn't indiscriminately distribute wealth and mercy.

"A wise, merciful person enjoys making plans for the improvement of others. This mercy is clever at devising ways in which these plans can help people improve. It helps people in times of distress. It organizes ways to provide redemptive help. It turns weakness into strength. It turns need into sufficiency. It turns confusion into direction.

"This attitude of wise fruitfulness is taught by Jesus. He illustrated it to His disciples by telling them,

> *I am the true vine, and my Father is the gardener. He cuts off every branch in me that bears no fruit, while every branch that does bear fruit he prunes so that it will be even more fruitful.* (John 15:1–2)

"The purpose of the branches is to bear fruit. But in order to bear fruit, the branches have to go through a sometimes difficult process. The branches that bear fruit are pruned and cut so that they may bear more fruit. The objective of wise, redemptive mercy is to help others achieve a more fruitful and fulfilling life. This isn't always easy. It often demands effort, sacrifice, and discipline on the part of those being helped.

"It takes the thought, care, and insight of merciful wisdom to develop lasting fruit. Wisdom works for long-term values, not short term satisfaction. Wisdom plans more for eventual fruitfulness than present comfort."

6. Wisdom from Above Is Undivided

"The next characteristic of wisdom is that it is undivided. The Greek word used here for undivided isn't used anywhere else in the New Testament: *adiakritos*. It means 'not divided.' The RSV translates it as 'without uncertainty.' The NEB translates it 'straightforward,' while Moffat uses the word 'unambiguous.' It indicates that the spirit of true wisdom is trustworthy. It's solid, honest, and sincere. You can put your faith in a wise person, for he isn't fickle, changeable, or unreliable.

"Wisdom believes that when a course is correct, you persevere with it. Wisdom sets its values and then consistently pursues them. Wisdom decides on its priorities and builds on them. When wisdom gives its word, you can believe it. It's not wise to be forever changing your mind. It's not wise to be governed by your emotions, so that your decision changes with the mood of the day. There's nothing more frustrating, disappointing, and confusing than those people who keep reneging on their commitments. They let you down. Plans become mixed up, arrangements become confused. You cannot trust them. If things turn out badly, they'll leave you. This is a foolish way to live. You certainly wouldn't want them to be your business partner. The people we rely upon and trust are those who stay the course and persevere even when things are difficult. We think these people are wise.

"Jesus often reiterated this principle of wisdom. He consistently urged us to choose the right values and then commit ourselves to following them. He said that in the midst of trial and persecution, *'he who stands firm to the end will be saved'* (Matthew 10:22). The writer to the Hebrews lifts up Jesus Himself as an example of this stout-hearted, consistent reliability. He said,

> *Let us fix our eyes on Jesus, the author and perfecter of our faith, who for the joy set before him endured the cross, scorning its shame, and sat down at the right hand of the throne of God. Consider him who endured such opposition from sinful men, so that you will not grow weary and lose heart.* (Hebrews 12:2–3)

"In many ways," I said, "this is like the instructions we received when we set out on our journey down the River of Wisdom. We were told to keep our eye on Far Mountain, to use it to keep our direction correct, to not get sidetracked or give up. There were easier ways. There were simpler paths, but they wouldn't lead us where we wanted to go. We have persevered and kept our commitment to follow the river to Far Mountain."

"This principle of wisdom is reflected in Jesus' parable of the sower," Andrew said. "He speaks of seed that falls into shallow ground. It starts out well, but when the heat of the sun develops, Jesus said, *'They believe for a while, but in the time of testing they fall away'* (Luke 8:13). The Christian path, like Far Mountain, isn't always easy, but it would be unwise to let these difficulties cause us to change our minds about following Christ. Wisdom doesn't always choose paths that are broad and easy, but the end result is always rich and rewarding."

171

"So wisdom," said Peter, "helps us understand what our main purposes should be, and then it gives us strength to continue pursuing them even when things are hard?"

"Precisely," said Andrew. "It's not wise to live and make decisions only on what seems to be convenient for the short-term. It's wise to set viable long-term goals and then faithfully pursue them. James encourages us to ask God for wisdom, and then he goes on to say,

> *But when he asks, he must believe and not doubt, because he who doubts is like a wave of the sea, blown and tossed by the wind. That man should not think he will receive anything from the Lord; he is a double-minded man, unstable in all he does.* (James 1:6–8)

Wisdom Makes Strong Decisions

Peter, who was still listening carefully, said, "So, true wisdom doesn't come to easy decisions but strong decisions. We understand that we'll all have to make choices in life. The point of wisdom is that it guides us to make the best decisions and then helps us pursue them with perseverance."

"You all seem to understand the meaning of wisdom as being undivided. Jesus warned about these easy, convenient choices in life when he said,

> *Enter through the narrow gate. For wide is the gate and broad is the road that leads to destruction, and many enter through it. But small is the gate and narrow the road that leads to life, and only a few find it.* (Matthew 7:13–14)

Someone else added to the discussion. "Isn't that the power of temptation? Temptation usually offers us something immediate, convenient, and pleasurable."

"Temptation usually offers short-term satisfaction and easily attainable profits," Andrew said. "But wisdom has its eyes on something else and won't be sidetracked or tempted into actions and decisions that cause it to wander off-track. It's steady and determined. It won't be deterred from committing itself to the correct priorities in life."

7. Wisdom from Above Is Without Hypocrisy

"The last quality James describes is that wisdom is without hypocrisy. Wisdom doesn't deal in deception. It doesn't tell lies, even when there are clear benefits to not telling the truth. Wisdom doesn't strive to create a false image and give a false impression. Striving for a good public image of righteousness, while endorsing private corruption, isn't the lifestyle of the wise.

"The unhypocritical lifestyle helps wise people to remain at peace and be relaxed. They don't pretend to be something they're not. They don't live with the anxiety that their real selves will be exposed. They don't live under the stress of trying to convince people of something that isn't true. They don't live in fear that they'll make a mistake and the truth will come out.

"In this world, you're more relaxed when your yes means yes and your no means no. It's not easy to maintain a double life. When you have skeletons in the cupboard, you're always afraid that the door might be opened and the skeletons discovered. Truthful sincerity is a peaceful and relaxed way to live. True wisdom is honest, open, and above board. It doesn't play games to give false impressions or gain something under false pretenses."

The Rich Harvest of Wisdom

Andrew again picked up his Bible. "James concludes this section with a very beautiful verse: *'Peacemakers who sow in peace raise a harvest of righteousness'* (James 3:18). There grows from the seeds of true wisdom a beautiful harvest."

Looking up at us, Andrew concluded. "We're all seeking a full, rich, and rewarding life. The wise person understands that this will come through sowing peace and harmony and developing unity with God. This abundant harvest of peace and harmony will come when we're wise enough to understand the importance of the principles He outlines and have enough insight to know how to put them into practice. Satisfied lives don't come from jarring conflicts and hostile disagreements. Harmony and joy don't flow in an atmosphere of strife and bitterness. Righteousness doesn't flourish in a culture of deceit and untruth.

"I hope this has given you a good idea as to what real wisdom is like. Wisdom is more than a function of the mind; it's a state of the heart. It's more than correct thinking; it's correct objectives and purposes. Wisdom isn't something you call on in an emergency when you don't know what to do; it's a state of being. Wisdom is more than training your mind; it's disciplining your personality to accept and live by the right values. Wisdom is more than a sudden flash of insight or intuition; it's a lifestyle of commitment to priorities and causes that have lasting value. And the greatest values and priorities are those which are endorsed and favored by God.

"True wisdom harmonizes our hearts with the heart of God. That's why we're told that the beginning of wisdom is the fear of the Lord. True wisdom begins in having the right attitude towards God, and the things He says and the way of life He promotes. Jesus put it all very simply when he said, *'But seek first his kingdom and his righteousness, and all these things will be given to you as well'* (Matthew 6:33)."

There wasn't much movement in the class. It seemed we were all deeply affected by what Andrew had said, and in some ways we were unwilling to break the spell of the atmosphere he had created.

Finally, I whispered to my three companions, "Let's meet for a while in our room and talk about where we go from here." They all agreed, and we quietly left the room to gather in our cabin.

When we were comfortable, I said, "I was very impressed with what Andrew said and I want to grasp the kind of wisdom he was talking about. I'm ready now to move on, but I realize that if we're going to go, the journey will be different from what I thought. I now see this as primarily a journey of the soul. This isn't just an intellectual enterprise, but a spiritual one. I'm ready for that. In fact, I'm anxious for it."

I looked from one of my companions to another, realizing how attached to them I had become. "I am ready to move on, and I hope you are too. I just know we could do so much better if we journeyed as a team." Then, rather reluctantly I added, "But if I have to go alone, I'm prepared to do that."

I waited for some response from each of them. Lloyd spoke up first. "Elizabeth and I have to talk to make sure we're together on it, but I can say right now, for me, I'm ready. The direction of the journey is different than I would have anticipated, but I don't disagree with it. In fact, I'm satisfied it's the way to go."

Elizabeth spoke up next. She seemed to have recovered her bright spirits. "Count me in. I think wisdom comes from God. If becoming wiser gets me closer to Him, I'm in favor of it. My heart seems to be telling me, 'This is the way; walk in it.'"

Peter, always one to consider his decisions carefully, said, "I'm with you. I'm not sure where it will all end, but I do sense that we need to go on. The Sea of Tranquility certainly sounds like the kind of place I want to be experience."

I was encouraged with these positive responses. "I hope you're all keeping in mind that we've been told that this third phase of the journey goes through the mountains, and the river can be dangerous."

I was delighted when they all indicated that wouldn't discourage or deter them. They wanted to proceed regardless of the dangers.

My heart warmed to these friends of mine. While I would have been ready to continue the journey on my own, I understood just how much I had come to rely on them, and how deeply I would have missed them if I'd had to leave them behind.

"Why don't we pray together and ask for God's help and guidance as we go?" Elizabeth suggested. "Let's pray that we'll learn what needs to be learned and that we'll all safely end up by Far Mountain in the Sea of Tranquility."

She stretched out her hand and we all joined hands in fellowship.

"After we've prayed," I said, "we'll go to Andrew and tell him that we want to move on tomorrow morning and ask him for any advice he can give us."

The act of praying together seemed to unite our hearts in a deeper and stronger bond. We left each other with a sense of loyalty and profound fellowship. I knew that the rest of this journey was going to be rich and rewarding.

Topics for Discussion

1. Explain the difference between wise mercy and unwise mercy.

2. Why does wisdom from above produce a relaxed life?

3. List the fruit that comes from wisdom from above and the results of following wisdom from below. Compare the two.

Finding Wisdom

TWENTY-ONE

Company Along the Way

WITH A SENSE OF EXCITEMENT, WE GATHERED WITH ANDREW AROUND THE breakfast table the next morning.

"You're ready now to move into the third phase of your journey," he told us. "As you journey down the next section of the river, you'll experience some difficulties, but if you respond to these situations correctly they'll teach you important truths about how to develop wisdom. I would advise you to take time after each of these experiences to discuss them together so you learn from them."

We indicated our agreement with this advice.

"Before we go any further," said Andrew, "I want to ask you a question. Some of those who took the class with you are also interested in going down the river. Would you mind if they joined you?"

I looked at my companions. We had become comfortable with each other. Adding to the group would demand that we make adjustments.

Peter asked the question on all of our minds. "How many of them are there?"

"Two couples," responded Andrew. "Four altogether."

I spoke up for the group, "We'd be happy to have them, but we want to leave right after breakfast. Will they be ready?"

"Yes," said Andrew. "In fact, they're ready to go now. The reason I asked is that if you're to go as one group, I would like them to be part of this discussion."

Andrew withdrew and came back with two young couples. We welcomed them and Andrew introduced them as Gregory and Joyce, and Andrez and Margaretta. Gregory and Joyce were a well-dressed, fine-looking couple. They seemed to be used to a rather luxurious and easy lifestyle. I wasn't at all sure how well they would adapt to the rough and tumble of a canoe trip. On the other hand, Andrez and Margaretta seemed a sturdy pair, used to some hardship in life.

These people are going to make for some interesting times ahead, I thought.

"Now, you want to learn how to develop wisdom." Andrew looked at the four new additions and said to them, but indicating us, "These people have been on this journey for a while now. One of the early lessons they were taught is where the search for wisdom really begins." He turned to us. "Where does wisdom begin?"

I had been practicing this answer all the way down the river. "The beginning of wisdom is the fear of the Lord," I said.

"Right," said Andrew. "The soil in which wisdom grows in your heart is the soil of a reverent and respectful attitude towards God. If you don't cultivate this soil, godly wisdom won't grow successfully in your heart. You've already been taught this, so I won't say any more about it, except that it's important that you continue to develop this reverent attitude towards God.

"I want to tell you the second simple lesson that will help you gain wisdom. There is a verse of scripture I want you to notice and consider. In fact, we referred to it yesterday in class." He opened his Bible and read:

> *"If any of you lacks wisdom, he should ask God, who gives generously to all without finding fault, and it will be given to him. But when he asks, he must believe and not doubt, because he who doubts is like a wave of the sea, blown and tossed by the wind. That man should not think he will receive anything from the Lord; he is a double-minded man, unstable in all he does..* (James 1:5–8)

180

"This is a remarkably simple and open promise. If we lack wisdom, we should ask God for it. It places the growth of wisdom within the reach of all of us. No one need lack for wisdom. All the wisdom and insights of God are laid open for us to participate in. This is indeed an encouraging and wonderful invitation. Who would think that growth in wisdom is so simple and available? So, why are so few asking?"

Andrew didn't seem to expect us to answer.

"The nature of this promise also has a built-in encouragement for us. It's given to us so we understand that wisdom is something God wants to give us. He isn't reluctant, or parsimonious, or discriminatory. He's generous and wants to share with all of us His infinite understanding and eternal insights so we can use them to become authentic persons who deal with life victoriously and fruitfully.

"God's plan and purpose for us is that we grow into full and complete persons, mature and godly in our personalities. God has no desire to see us get mired down in the mud of poor relationships and hostile enmities. He doesn't want us to make wrong and short-sighted decisions that bring hurt and harm to people. He doesn't want us to be ground down to despair by the worries and anxieties of life. God wants to share His wisdom with us. He wants us to become confident so we know who we are, what our purpose is, and how we can go about attaining it."

"But that sounds so simple," I said. "How can it be that easy?"

"We usually think wisdom is incredibly complex, that it can only be entertained by those who have great minds and devote themselves to deep and profound thinking. We think it's not for simple everyday people. But that isn't true. The fact is that wisdom is a practical thing, a virtue that's available for us all to help us deal with life in a more effective way.

"God has a great reservoir of wisdom. He's generous and willing to open the gates of this reservoir, so it can pour into our lives, helping us produce large fertile fields of rich and healthy fruit. But we must ask for it."

"What does James mean when he says God will give us wisdom generously without finding fault?" Lloyd asked. "What has fault got to do with it?"

"Not only is God generous in wanting to give us wisdom," Andrew replied, "but He's also kind and nonjudgmental. He'll give wisdom without finding fault. It often happens that before we even get around to humbly asking, we'll often find ourselves in desperate situations. Through poor choices and shallow understanding, we blindly walk into swamps that mire us down, from which we cannot get out. Only when we come to the end of ourselves do we usually call on God to help us.

"If you were to put yourself in God's position, you might imagine He would be justified in saying, 'You got yourself into this, so you figure a way out of it.' God isn't even tempted to scold us and condemn us. We are assured that God will give wisdom generously without finding fault. Even when our problems are of our own making, He'll provide us with wisdom to deal with them and move us towards solutions."

"That's amazing," responded Lloyd. "So even if you have no one else to blame for your predicament, God will still grant wisdom? Even if you paid no attention to God's directions before?"

Andrew smiled. "It *is* amazing, Lloyd. Just remember that I'm not the one making the promise. God is."

"You mean we can ask for wisdom, even though we've been very foolish and blind?" I asked. "I've never in my life bothered to ask God for wisdom, until recently. I went my own way without reference to Him at all."

"It's never too late to ask for wisdom, whatever your situation and however you got here," Andrew said. "You can start now. God will reveal ways in which you can handle yourself better. The solutions might not be easy. The way out may require sacrifice and discipline, but allow God's wisdom to break through the darkness, and light and hope will begin to shine."

"But why do we have to ask at all?" I asked. "If God is so anxious to give us wisdom, why doesn't He just give it automatically?"

"The very act of asking instills into us the correct attitude towards God. When we humbly ask, we adopt a reverent spirit. The main reason we don't bother to ask God for wisdom is that we think we're wise enough. However, when we kneel before God, we realize that we don't have all the answers."

"I would think, too," added Peter, "that asking indicates that we think there's going to be an answer. We wouldn't bother to ask if we thought God wasn't going to answer. It also indicates that we think God is the real source of wisdom, not ourselves. God knows how to take care of things. When we ask, we recognize His authority and power."

"I want you to really remember this promise from God, that He will give us wisdom when we ask, without finding fault. Make this a regular part of your prayer lives. It's good to pray for wisdom, whether you're in trouble or not. If you wait until you're in trouble, it may be too late. Better to start now, so that day by day you make decisions that please Him, following His directions and accepting His values. Wisdom will grow out of a righteous and godly walk with Him. It will lead you into a life that's rich and full of His spirit and joy. The writer of Proverbs says it well:

> *Have two goals: wisdom—that is, knowing and doing right—and common sense. Don't let them slip away, for they will fill you with living energy, and are a feather in your cap. They keep you safe from defeat and disaster and from stumbling off the trail.* (Proverbs 3: 21–23, TLB)

"Now," said Andrew, "I think you're ready to go. Let's meet down at the dock. There's one more thing I want to tell you before you leave."

At the dock, we were met by Gregory and Joyce, and Andrez and Margaretta. Their canoes were already loaded up with equipment.

We gathered around Andrew.

"Remember what you've been taught," Andrew said. "First, the beginning of wisdom is the fear of the Lord. Second, if you lack wisdom, ask God. Build these thoughts into your daily fellowship with God. They must become the habits of your life, rather than occasional incidents. A third instruction comes from the book of Proverbs:

> *Get wisdom, get understanding; do not forget my words or swerve from them. Do not forsake wisdom, and she will protect you; love her, and she will watch over you. Wisdom is supreme; therefore get wisdom. Though it cost all you have, get understanding. Esteem her, and she will exalt you; embrace her, and she will honor you.* (Proverbs 4:5–8)

"The instruction is to seek for wisdom. See it as something worth pursuing. In this next part of the journey, you'll understand that wisdom is a valuable prize, but it won't be won easily or simply. The depth of your desire will be tested, and some of you may decide that wisdom isn't worth the effort. Only those who are deeply committed to developing wisdom will carry on

Andrew lifted his arm and pointed down the river. "You can see Far Mountain from here. It's nearer than when you started, but remember to keep it in your sights and be guided by it. Get your direction from the mountain or you'll easily be diverted. Now, be off with you. I wish you all the best."

With that, we got into the canoes and took off down the river.

Topics for Discussion

1. According to Andrew, not only is God generous in wanting to give us wisdom, but He's also kind and nonjudgmental in the giving. Discuss.

2. If God is so anxious to give us wisdom, why do we have to ask?

Twenty-Two

The Waterfall

AT FIRST, THE GOING WAS EASY AND WE MADE GOOD PROGRESS. PETER AND I took the lead in the first canoe, with Lloyd and Elizabeth following us. The two new couples brought up the rear of the convoy. There was not much opportunity for conversation, so we quietly enjoyed the surrounding scenery. We could see, however, that we were approaching some hills, and behind them was a rugged set of mountains. We understood that the river would cut a pathway through the mountains before reaching the Sea of Tranquility. We knew to expect rough water.

We reached the hills in the early afternoon. The river flowed smoothly but more quickly through a shallow valley between the hills. This ease was not to last. The valley got deeper, causing us to be carried downstream at increasing speed. The walls of the valley closed in, and I became concerned. We had to give full attention to the guidance of the canoes.

The Waterfall

It was Peter who first saw the danger and shouted back to us that he thought there was a waterfall ahead. I could see that the river ahead seemed to disappear, and behind the point of disappearance an ominous spray plumed into the air. Our fears were confirmed when we began to hear the roar of the waters. Fortunately, there was a convenient landing spot on the nearby bank, and Peter and I guided the canoes to it. This gave us the opportunity to pull the canoes safely onto the shore and examine just what we were facing.

We clambered up some rocks overlooking the river. It was a rather daunting sight. The waterfall wasn't high, but the river narrowed and surged over the edge with a fierce rush, hitting rocks at the bottom. It was a noisy display, awesome to watch but rather distressing for a group of canoeists.

"Well, I don't think our canoes can survive that," I said. "We're going to have to portage around this."

Andrez definitely didn't agree. "I believe we can canoe over it and continue our journey without delay."

I looked at the waterfall again and slowly shook my head. "It's too dangerous. A portage is a lot of trouble and work, but I think we have to do it."

"Absolutely not," Andrez declared. He was determined. "I know we can do it. After all, isn't God supposed to be with us? He will help us."

I looked to Peter, and he nodded his agreement with me.

"What you do is up to you," I said, "but Peter and I won't risk everything in a foolish attempt to navigate those wild waters."

Lloyd, not wanting to cause a rupture in the party, made a suggestion. "Look, it's getting rather late in the day. This is a good place for us to set up camp for the night. Why don't we stay here? That will give us time to think on this. After a night's sleep, we can make a decision in the morning."

This seemed a sensible suggestion and we all agreed to it, but I could see Andrez had a determined, stubborn expression on his face.

He won't change his mind, no matter what, I thought.

We set up our tents and prepared for a night's stay. When we were finished the camp chores, I noticed Andrez and Margaretta having a discussion down by their canoe. They both nodded and came to an agreement.

"There'll be no harm trying to negotiate the falls in our canoe," Andrez said. "We'll leave our equipment out and go alone. Even if we capsize, the worse thing that can happen is we'll get a soaking."

I could see that nothing I said would change his mind. "I don't think you should, but if you're going to do it anyway, let us go down river a bit with some ropes. That way, if you capsize we'll be there to pull you and the canoe out of the water."

"That's not necessary," said Andrez, "but if it makes you feel better, you can do it."

Peter and I walked down the river until we passed the rapids. Here, the frothing river emptied itself into a relatively calm pool and we decided to wait there for them.

When we were set, we signaled up to Lloyd, who was watching from the top of the waterfall. He, in turn, signaled to Andrez and Margaretta. They launched their canoe and paddled out into the center of the river. They were immediately caught up in the swift current. The power of the current didn't allow them much control over the canoe. When they reached the edge of the falls, the canoe had turned sideways. When they shot over the edge, the canoe turned on its side and capsized, spilling Andrez and Margaretta into the water.

They were wearing life jackets, so they bobbed to the surface in the relative calm of the pool. We threw the rope out. Andrez laid hold of the canoe and we were able to pull both them and the canoe to safety. I thought the experience made it clear that going over the waterfall wasn't a good idea, so I was rather shocked when a wet and dripping Andrez said to Margaretta, "We almost made it. Next time, if we can just keep the canoe straight, we'll make it."

"You mean you're going to try that again?" I said in amazement. I looked at Margaretta, who was wet and cold. I could tell she wasn't at all enthusiastic about a second attempt, but she went along with Andrez.

Peter and I waited while they carried their canoe back up to the top of the falls. They pushed it back into the water and managed to hit the falls straight this time, but the results were the same. They capsized and had to be pulled from the water again.

"There," I said to the cold and wet pair. "That makes it clear that portaging is the better way."

"Not at all," said Andrez. "I know we can do it. We'll give it another try."

I shook my head in disbelief. "You can't be serious. This is dangerous, you know. One of you could really get hurt."

"Nonsense," said Andrez. "You just watch."

Margaretta shook her head. "I'm not sure we should try it again, Andrez."

But Andrez was adamant. "Of course we will. Next time, we'll make it."

But they didn't. The canoe capsized and they had to be pulled from the water again. This time, they were too cold to try again. Much relieved, we made our way back to the camp and the warmth of the fire.

After Andrez and Margaretta had changed their clothes, they stood and warmed themselves next to the flames. Supper that night was a rather strained meal. Nobody said a word about the attempt to canoe over the falls, but it was obvious to all of us that it had been wild and reckless. We would portage around the falls tomorrow morning.

A Foolish Decision

We were therefore stunned when, in the morning, as we were packing up camp and making ready for the portage, we saw Andrez and Margaretta loading up their canoe.

There was an obvious disagreement between them. They were talking together, and Margaretta was shaking her head. She wasn't helping as he did all the work.

"What are you doing?" I asked. "Surely you're not going over the falls with a loaded canoe!"

"I believe we can make it," replied Andrez. "We capsized because the canoe was too light. It needs to be weighed down with all our equipment and luggage."

"But if it does capsize," I reasoned, "all your stuff will be lost in the river."

"I don't believe that will happen," said Andrez. "God is with us and we will take the risk."

"Andrez, it's too dangerous," Margaretta said.

"If you don't want to come with me, you can walk down," Andrez told her. "But I am going and I believe we can do it this time."

Margaretta seemed to think she had no choice and reluctantly acquiesced.

"Well, at least wait until we go below with the rope," I said.

Andrez shook his head. "That won't be necessary. In fact, we'll wait for you down river a bit while you walk around the falls."

I wasn't satisfied with this, so while Andrez and Margaretta finished loading up, I took Peter and some rope and we went down to the pool to await the outcome.

The outcome wasn't happy. Once again, the canoe tipped over, only this time all their gear and equipment spilled into the raging water. We managed again to pull Andrez and Margaretta out of the water, along with their canoe, but all their equipment was lost.

As we walked back to camp, an angry and unhappy Andrez said, "I can't understand that. Why didn't God help us? We wanted to go down the River of Wisdom so we could know Him better, but He's certainly not helping us."

"What are you going to do now?" I asked.

Andrez looked at me and with some hostility said, "What else can we do? We have no food, we have no equipment, and we have no fresh clothes. We'll have to go back. We cannot continue with the journey."

We were a sad and disappointed group as we made our way back to the camp. We did our best to fit Andrez and Margaretta with dry clothes and give them a little food from our own packs, but they were deeply disillusioned and disappointed. We sadly waved goodbye to them as they started back to the village where Andrew lived. I had the distinct impression that in spite of the hardship of this experience, Andrez hadn't learned a thing. If he were to ever come on this journey again, he would still get capsized on that waterfall. He would never get past it.

I looked at the others and then reminded them of the instructions we had received from Andrew. "He told us that we would have some vivid experiences in this portion of the journey and that after each experience we should sit down and discuss it so we would be sure to understand the lesson. I know we're anxious to get on with the journey, but why don't we take time to evaluate what has just happened?"

Everyone agreed, so we built up the fire again and sat around it.

Lessons Learned

"What can we learn from the experience with Andrez, Margaretta, and the waterfall?" I said, starting out.

"I think that the ones who needed to learn the lesson were Andrez and Margaretta," Peter said. "They kept doing the same thing, even when it was evident that it was wrong. They should have learned from the experience of going over the waterfall the first time. Instead they kept doing it, until it ruined their whole journey."

Wisdom and Experience

"So, to learn from experience," I said, "we shouldn't keep making the same mistakes."

189

"If the alcoholic keeps drinking and the gambler keeps gambling and the lazy person keeps being lazy," Peter said, "in spite of their experiences, they won't learn a thing from experience."

"The first thing we should learn from this is that just going through experiences doesn't necessarily make us wise," I said. "It's learning something from the experiences that helps us develop wisdom. Learning from experience means changing our behavior."

"Yes," said Lloyd. "This is why we generally assume older people should be wise, while younger people tend to be rash and thoughtless. Older people have a lifetime of experiences that should have taught them some things. Young people, we think, have still to learn from life's experiences. Yet the fact is that many older people aren't wise. They've gone through many experiences, but they still haven't found the things that give them satisfaction or fulfillment. They don't handle other people well. They don't control their finances properly. They don't look after their health. They harbor bitterness and resentment. They don't know how to show love and grace, and on and on. Two people can have the same experience, while one is wise and learns from it and the other reacts to the experience with doubt, excuses, and resentment, thus learning nothing."

"That's well said," agreed Gregory. "I remember once interviewing someone for a job. Their resume said they had twenty years of experience, which looked good. But I found out he had changed employers ten times and had done the same job for every employer. I said to myself, 'No, you don't have twenty years of experience; you have two years of experience repeated ten times.'" We all laughed at this, but Gregory went on. "He hadn't grown in the job. He hadn't developed or expanded. He just kept doing what he was used to doing and repeating it. He would spend his life doing that, never maturing and expanding to new and better things."

"So, how do we learn from experiences so the lessons are incorporated into our lives?" I asked.

Experience Enriches Knowledge

"Well, first," said Elizabeth, "it's sometimes not enough just to be told something. You have to experience it for yourself and the experience confirms what you've been told. A child is told not to touch a hot plate or it will burn him. That information doesn't mean much until one day when he reaches up and touches the hot plate when the mother isn't looking. The burn is painful and he has learned something, not only because he was told about it, but also because he experienced it for himself. He now knows from experience not to put his hand on the hot plate. A lesson from experience can be more impressive than just being told."

"So, are you saying wisdom is more than just knowing things?" I asked. "Can we possess a lot of knowledge, but not be wise?"

"Yes," replied Elizabeth. "Knowledge is certainly a good thing. We need all the knowledge we can get, but wisdom is more than knowledge. Wisdom knows how to apply knowledge properly. When we go through experiences, good or bad, wisdom is practical and shows us how to deal with the situation in the best way."

"Well," I said regretfully, "Andrez and Margaretta were advised not to go over the falls, and when they did it, they were urged not to do it again. They not only didn't listen to what they were told, they did not listen to the experience, either."

"If the child keeps putting his hand on the hot plate and getting burned, we would think he was a pretty foolish child," Lloyd said. "When it comes to Andrez and Margaretta, none of us were sure at first whether it would be better to portage around the falls or risk it in our canoes. After we watched the first capsizing, we learned that it was better to portage. We all seemed to learn this except for Andrez and Margaretta. We all told them that their canoe would capsize if they tried to go over again. They were given knowledge from two sources—they heard it from us, and they found out from experience. Wisdom is the quality that knows how to put knowledge into action. I think that is what Jesus meant when He said a wise man hears His words and puts them into practice."

Need for Flexibility

"Another vital part of learning from experience is to be flexible and open to learning," Peter said. "If you're stubborn, you won't learn anything. It's wise to be humble and ready to admit mistakes."

Lloyd nodded. "I remember a verse from the book of Proverbs which says, '*To learn, you must want to be taught. To refuse reproof is stupid*' (Proverbs 12:1, TLB)."

"So we understand that if we're going to learn from experience, we need to recognize our mistakes and stop repeating them," I said, in summary. "We understand that experience often confirms what we've been told. We also understand that going through experiences doesn't automatically make us wise. We must be willing to learn from them and change our behavior accordingly. What attitude must we have if we're going to learn from experience?"

"Humility," Peter answered. "We need to humbly accept that we're doing something wrong and then improve our performance."

"Okay, this is good," I said. "We learn from experiences when we're open and flexible and ready to modify our behavior. The startling thing about Andrez and Margaretta was that in spite of all that happened, they didn't seem to think they needed to change their approach."

Accept Responsibility

"I think another part of being open and learning from experience," added Peter, "is to accept responsibility for our own decisions. We all have experiences that come to us in life and we cannot anticipate them. Nor are we responsible for them; we just have to respond to them correctly. But there are other experiences that we bring on ourselves by our own decisions. We choose to do it. If our decisions are wrong, we must accept responsibility. It's easy to try and push responsibility for our mistakes onto other people or circumstances. If that's our attitude, we aren't going to learn from our experiences. We all make mistakes, but they can be valuable if we learn from them and never repeat them."

"That's right," said Lloyd. "If we blame others every time something doesn't turn out right, we'll conclude that it's others who have to change while seeing no need for change in ourselves. When we see no need for change, we aren't likely to change."

"I tend to think Andrez was quietly blaming Margareta for the failure in the canoe," Gregory remarked. "He might have thought she wasn't paddling correctly, or she wasn't strong enough. That's probably why he didn't learn from experience, because he thought she was the one who had to learn."

I said, "All of these thoughts are good. We understand that going through experiences doesn't automatically teach us things. We learn from experience when we realize that experience is a teacher and we're willing to be taught. Is there anything else we can learn from this experience?

Decisions Have Outcomes

Joyce now added her thoughts. "We can also learn from experience when we understand that our decisions have outcomes and consequences. Many foolish decisions could have been avoided if the person only took more thought about the consequences. I know from experience that my quick temper makes me say

192

angry and foolish things, and that my anger creates anger in others. I know this from experience, but then I need to be responsible for doing something about it. It would be foolish for me to go through life being quick-tempered and explosive while expecting other people to consistently respond to me with quiet love. I'm responsible for realizing that my actions, words, and attitudes have outcomes and results both for me and for others. It's therefore foolish for me to keep on with the same poor action and attitudes when I know what the results will be. Since I know from experience that shouting and yelling creates hostility and resentment in others, why do I keep on shouting and yelling? I know that when my spirit is loving and forgiving, it tends to solicit that same response in others. Do I not have a responsibility to try to be kind and forgiving?"

"I don't really think Andrez and Margaretta thought their decisions would result in them losing their equipment and giving up the journey," I said. "Their decisions had outcomes they didn't anticipate. Unwise people don't think beyond the immediate issues they face. But decisions have consequences and the decision-maker must take responsibility for the outcomes of his decision."

What You Put In Is What You Get Out

"I used to work in a butcher's shop," said Peter. "One of my responsibilities was to make the ground beef. I quickly learned that what you put into the meat grinder determines the quality of ground meat that comes out the other end. If you put in a lot of fat and gristly meat, you get poor quality ground beef. If you put in top-cut steak, you get good quality ground beef. What comes out is determined by what goes in. I think it would be the same in wise living. The outcomes we experience are largely determined by the qualities we put into our decisions. If we're careless, greedy, hostile, and jealous, then the outcome will reflect it. If we're loving, kind, faithful, and true, then our decisions will reflect those attitudes. It's foolish to think we can put poor quality meat into the grinder and produce high quality ground beef at the other end."

Lloyd agreed. "I think that's what James meant when he said, *'My brothers, can a fig tree bear olives, or a grapevine bear figs? Neither can a salt spring produce fresh water'* (James 3:12). That means it's foolish for us to harbor unwise attitudes, follow unwise values, and commit to unwise purposes while expecting to make wise decisions and reap the fruits of a wisely lived life."

"This has been good," I said. "We've learned that if experience is going to teach us anything, we have to be teachable. Often experience confirms the truth of what we've been told verbally. If the lessons of experience are to be effective, we need to be flexible and willing to change our behavior. We have to be humble to admit our mistakes and try to figure out how we can do better next time. Then, we must accept responsibility for the outcomes we experience from our own decisions. In addition to this, as Peter has pointed out, when it comes to decisions, we must expect the outcomes to reflect what we put into the decisions. Should we add anything else to that list?"

Decisions and Emotions

"I wonder what part our emotions play in this," Elisabeth said. "I tend to listen to my emotions and be guided by them. On days when I'm feeling confident, I make different decisions than I do on days when I'm discouraged. Should we be guided by our emotions?"

"Tell us what you think," I said.

"My experience with emotions is that they change and are unreliable. I shouldn't make decisions or set directions on the basis of how I happen to be feeling on any particular day. If I feel discouraged, I may make decisions while under the cloud of those feelings that I'll regret later when I'm feeling better. If I'm to be responsible for my decisions and their outcomes, I need a much better guide to follow than feelings. It's far better to have a set of principles that stay the same regardless of how I feel, and set my course in life according to them."

"I think that's why we've been instructed to look to Far Mountain for our guidance," I said. "If we were to set our course by the immediate situations we experience on the river, we would be constantly sidetracked and lost."

Elisabeth nodded. "Yes, but I have to confess that I find it hard to do. I'm much too influenced by how I happen to feel at the moment. The intensity of today's feelings can cause me to lose sight of my long-term objectives. From experience, I'm learning that I shouldn't be guided by my present circumstances and feelings, but keep the steady principles of Jesus in my mind."

"We can so easily get carried away with our emotions," said Peter. "For example, Andrez was determined. Determination is good, but when does good determination become blind stubbornness? It's good to be meek, but when does meekness become weakness? It's good to be forgiving, but when does a forgiving spirit become soft indulgence?"

Nobody seemed to have an answer, so I said, "I guess that's where wisdom becomes so vital. Wisdom helps us keep our emotions balanced. Wisdom helps us understand when emotions need to be listened to and when they should be disciplined."

"In that case," said Elizabeth, "I certainly need wisdom. Lots of it."

We all seemed to agree with this. Everybody was satisfied with the discussion, so we decided it was time to move on. We regretted having to go on without Andrez and Margaretta.

Negotiating the portage proved to be a fairly simple operation, and we soon launched our canoes into the river below the falls.

Topics for Discussion

1. What characteristics in Andrez contributed to his having to give up on the journey?

2. What qualities would help us learn from our experiences?

TWENTY-THREE

The Calm Before the Storm

THE RIVER CUT ITS WAY DEEPER INTO THE MOUNTAINS. THE FLOW WAS NOW MUCH faster and rougher. It took a great deal of effort and attention to guide the canoes.

Soon the mountains towered above us. Their elevation was so high that we could see snow on the peaks. We got occasional sightings of Far Mountain, so we knew we were on the right track and making progress. It was, however, tiring and exhausting work. It was a great relief to me when we came upon a suitable campsite. We decided to pull in early that day and stay for the night.

We were all tired, but I noticed Gregory and Joyce especially seemed to be at the point of exhaustion. They clearly weren't used to this hard work. They barely got their tent up when they crawled into it and lay down. With sighs of relief, they fell asleep.

While they slept, the rest of us set up camp, built the fire, and prepared supper. When everything was ready, we woke Gregory and Joyce and sat around the fire to eat.

Joyce seemed to be in some distress. Her hands were blistered from pulling on the paddles. Her muscles were sore and she complained about a pain in her back. She didn't eat much and soon excused herself, retiring into the tent. I wondered how well she would survive the rest of the journey.

When supper was over, we cleared up the camp, then stocked the fire and sat around it for a while. It was still fairly early and not yet dark, so Elizabeth came up with the proposition that we take time to follow the advice we had been given and pray together.

"We were instructed," she said, "to claim the promise, *'If any of you lacks wisdom, he should ask God, who gives generously to all without finding fault, and it will be given to him'* (James 1:5). We're travelling down the river of Wisdom, so we must not neglect to do what we were urged to do and ask God for help and guidance as we seek greater wisdom in our lives."

To this, the whole group agreed, except for Joyce, who was still asleep. We joined hands around the fire and each took time to pray. I wasn't used to verbalizing my prayers in front of a group, and felt somewhat hesitant and unsure of myself. Others, like Peter and Lloyd, had obviously done this before and were quite fluent and comfortable. I soon understood that no one was interested in each other's level of skill. As we prayed, we sensed a spirit of bonding take place amongst us. It had been a hard day, but we all had the satisfaction of knowing we had made progress. We were together on the same journey. We were united in our desire to be wise in our communion with God and in our interactions with each other. It was a good experience to join with these companions and feel united in our prayers. I only regretted that Joyce didn't participate.

After prayers, I felt I wanted some time alone, so I hiked up to the top of a hill just behind the camp. I sat down in a little clearing. It was a beautiful spot. I could see up the valley where we had come from, and also I downriver. I wondered what lay ahead as the river plunged into the heart of the mountains. Apart from the faraway noise of the river, it was peaceful here. I absorbed the quiet and felt comforted in my heart. It was reassuring to able to see the peak of Far Mountain just beyond the other mountains. A wonderful sense of peace settled on my soul, and I enjoyed my communion with God and nature as the sun set behind the mountains.

Reviewing the Journey

In the fading light, I was pleased to see my friend Peter climb up the hill towards me. We sat in companionable silence for a while, taking in the beauty of the world around us.

Finally, Peter asked, "Are you glad, Colin, that you've come on this journey?"

"Absolutely," I responded. "I wouldn't have missed this for anything. This has been the most enriching journey of my life."

"Do you feel you're making progress and learning anything about wisdom and how to live for God in a fruitful way?"

"Oh yes. Keep in mind that I didn't have the experience and background in church you had. This is all new to me. I feel I've come a long way." I turned and looked at my good friend. "How about you? Has this journey been good for you?"

"Indeed it has. I've lived in religious circles all my life, but I needed to know and understand just how important wisdom is for the successful development of my Christian life. I never realized just how significant a role it plays in the fruitful development of one's walk with God."

I was pleased to hear this. It was good to know we were both experiencing benefit from this journey.

"Way back at the beginning, after our life-changing experience with God and we were having breakfast together, remember when we saw that young couple preaching in the street? While we admired their devotion, we both felt we didn't want to do it that way. It didn't seem to be very effective. You were the one who suggested we go see Hermes."

"Yes, and Hermes was the one who advised us to come on this journey. And he introduced us to Charles."

"And didn't Charles tell us a lot? I remember him talking about the very first step, that the fear of the Lord is the beginning of wisdom. That's when it began to dawn on me that wisdom is more than an intellectual exercise or the gaining of more knowledge. Wisdom is something that develops in the very depths of your personality. It grows out of your values and priorities, the things that move you and motivate you."

"Right," said Peter, "and only as you absorb the Spirit of God into your life and heart do these wise values and priorities begin to merge with your personality. Charles was the one who convinced me that wisdom was important in Jesus' life, and if it was important to Him, it must be important for me."

"You remember the wise farmer and the foolish farmer? That taught us that it's wise to think ahead and not just do whatever seems convenient or easy.

Wisdom helps you cultivate the best values and not spend your life chasing empty values."

"I especially enjoyed my time with Phyllis and George," said Peter. "They told us again about how important wisdom was in the teachings of Jesus. I really needed to hear that, because I'd neglected its value in my life. I never realized how damaging lack of wisdom can be, or how vital it is to the proper outcomes of our lives with God."

"And I remember the swamp," I said. "How easy it is to get sidetracked from pursuing the long-term values of the Kingdom of God. I learned not to trust the easy ways that present themselves to us."

"Don't forget Craig," said Peter. "How good he was in telling us about wisdom in the life and teachings of the early church. That was what really convinced me."

"And of course there was the College of Wisdom," I said. "Andrew enlightened me about what wisdom is really like."

"Yes, wisdom is a way of life. It's about establishing the right values. It's about deciding to put the first things first, about absorbing the spirit and atmosphere of Christ. These things don't just pop into our hearts overnight; they must be acknowledged and cultivated. Remember, Andrew likened the development of wisdom to soil in the heart. If the soil is good, then wisdom will grow to a rich and fruitful harvest, but if the soil is poor, the harvest will be poor—or lost."

"That meant a lot to me," I said. "I've been working at trying to develop good soil in my heart. I take seriously what the instructors have told me. Wisdom begins with the fear of the Lord. I've been trying, in my times of communion with Him, to let a spirit of reverence and awe grow in my heart, for that is where it begins. If I don't have the right attitude towards God, godly wisdom will never flourish in my life. I'm enjoying the sense of being humble in His presence, of being possessed by His greatness, of being overwhelmed by his power and majesty. I'm learning to develop thankfulness for His love and grace.

"A second thing I've been trying to develop is trust and obedience to His values and priorities. As we paddled along, I've been taking time to remind myself about the things God values most. Because if I'm to become wise, I need to truly love what He loves, want what He wants, and desire what He desires. His will must become my will. I remember what Andrew told us about wisdom that is from above—it's peaceful, loving, forgiving, and holy. I try to make these traits dominate in my heart and life. I cannot do it without the help of God's Spirit.

"I've also been praying the prayer Andrew told us about. I need wisdom so I ask God for it. I believe He will impart His wisdom to me, filling me with His spirit of wisdom, because I need it and He wants to give it. I pray constantly for wisdom."

Peter looked at me and smiled. "All that sounds great, Colin. I do the same things. The only thing I would add is that I need to keep on reminding myself that this is important. It still haunts me that I've lived so long and never taken the matter of wisdom seriously. It wasn't something I thought I needed to pursue and develop. I remember especially the Lake of Mammon, and how easily those people fell prey to false and empty values. They made the subordinate values their priority. I keep reminding myself about that, renewing my commitment to seeking first the Kingdom of God."

It was almost dark now, but I peered downriver. In the fading light, it seemed threatening and uninviting.

I put my hand on Peter's shoulder. "Well, friend, we've come a long way. Tomorrow we will move on, but I think it's going to be a tough day. Let's go down and get our rest."

So Peter and I made our way down to the camp. We crawled into our tent and soon fell asleep with the satisfaction of knowing that there was much more still to come.

Topics for Discussion

1. Discuss how Colin's time alone was important for him as he developed in wisdom. Is time alone important for you?

2. Peter remembered that Andrew had likened the development of wisdom to soil in the heart, and if the soil is good, then wisdom will grow to a rich and fruitful harvest, but if the soil is poor, the harvest is either poor or will be lost. Colin then explained what he was doing to develop the soil in his heart. Can you list what he was doing?

TWENTY-FOUR

The Long Portage

PACKING UP CAMP IN THE MORNING WAS A SLOW AFFAIR. WE WERE ALL TIRED from the day before and so took our time. Joyce especially seemed stiff and weary. Her back was better, but her muscles ached and her blistered hands were in pain. The activity of packing up, however, seemed to loosen her up a bit, She was ready when we finally pushed the three canoes off and started into the river for what we anticipated was going to be a difficult day.

We were now in the heart of the mountains. The river ran through a deep valley that became a gorge with high cliffs towering up each side. The water was swift, but not too rough. That is, until we were swept around a corner and saw, to our consternation, that the river plunged into a wild and dark gorge. There was, however, a good landing place along the bank just before the start of the gorge. We pulled up to the landing to decide on what to do and were surprised to see another canoe already there.

As we dragged our canoes up on to the land, a man came down to meet us. We all introduced ourselves and then asked him about the situation on the river.

The Impossible Gorge

"Well," he said, pointing to the gorge, "there's no way you're going to be able to take your canoes through there. It's nothing but raging rapids all the way through. You'll have to portage to get around this gorge."

We didn't like this news, but he continued. "I've done a little exploring. The best portage is that one you can see." He pointed up the shoulder of the mountain. "It's extremely difficult and long, but it's the only way."

The pathway certainly didn't look inviting. The way was steep, rugged, and winding. At the steepest part of the climb, the pathway twisted and turned through hairpin bends. After that, the path finally disappeared over the top of the shoulder. But it was a long way up. The thought of carrying our canoes over that pass was daunting, indeed. Not only that, but we wouldn't be able to take the canoes and baggage all in one trip. It was a discouraging prospect.

"Are you sure we can't go through the gorge in the canoes?" I asked.

The man pointed to a high rock that pushed out into the river. "If you climb that rock, it will give you a good view into the gorge. Look for yourselves. You'll see there's no way to make it."

Peter, Lloyd, and I climbed up the rock while Elizabeth, Gregory, and Joyce waited by the canoes. From the top of the rock, we had a good view and it was, indeed, a wild and savage place. The water raged over rocks and sprayed vapor into the air. The roar and power of the foaming water was loud enough to make talking difficult. Even up here, the spray dampened our clothes and hair.

We made our way back to the canoes and told the others that we agreed with our new friend. The only way was to go over the shoulder of the mountain.

Joyce stood looking at the pathway winding its way up the steep mountain. She was quiet for a few moments, then turned to Gregory. "There's no way I'm going to carry a canoe over that." She was so definite and final in her statement that it was greeted with uncertain silence from us all. We didn't know how to respond. It was our new friend who rescued us from an embarrassing situation.

An Easier Way

"Actually, I've done some exploring and I think there may be another option." Pointing away from the river, he explained, "There's a track that's much simpler to follow. It seems to go in the wrong direction, but you never know… it may come back around. I've decided to give it a try, and you're all welcome to join me."

I sensed danger right away. "Where is this track?" I asked.

He pointed to a nearby valley hidden behind some trees. "It starts behind those trees. It isn't far. It follows a different valley, but I think that valley may lead us around the bottom of the mountain. If it does, then while it may be a long way around, you won't have to climb over the mountain. You can go around it."

It certainly sounded a plausible proposition, and if it was true then it would save us from a horrendous climb, loaded down with our canoes and baggage. I looked at Peter and sensed that we both agreed about what to do.

"No!" I said. "That track leads away from the river, away from Far Mountain. I've come too far to risk following some easy track that may end up getting us lost. We're going to go over the top."

Peter nodded in agreement. At that moment, I felt great affection for this good and faithful friend.

I was also very pleased when Lloyd and Elizabeth agreed that, while difficult, the way over the shoulder of the mountain was the right way to go. They would join Peter and me.

Gregory seemed undecided. Joyce, however, was insistent. "I'm not going to go over that. Look at it! It's far too long and far too steep. I'm already sore and stiff. There must be an easier way, and I want to look for it."

I realized that Gregory was in a difficult position. To try encouraging him, I said, "Yes, the right way looks hard, but I have found from experience that easy ways aren't always the best ways. Following the way of least resistance may lead you astray."

Lloyd agreed with me. "Remember what the book of Proverbs says: *'There is a way that seems right to a man, but in the end it leads to death'* (Proverbs 14:12). Jesus also said,

> *Enter through the narrow gate. For wide is the gate and broad is the road that leads to destruction, and many enter through it. But small is the gate and narrow the road that leads to life, and only a few find it."* (Matthew 7:13–14)

I thought to myself, *Good old Lloyd. He seems to have a scripture for every occasion.*

Gregory was still hesitant, but Joyce wasn't. She said to her husband, "I'm not going over that mountain. I can't! I need you to come with me the other way."

With great reluctance and uncertainty, Gregory replied, "Okay, we'll try this other path and see where it goes. But if it leads us astray, we'll come back and go over the mountain."

So the decisions were made. I was sure Gregory and Joyce were making the wrong choice, but I also recognized there wasn't much I could do about it. We began immediate preparations for the portage.

The Long Portage

The portage proved to be even harder and longer than we thought. We decided to carry the canoes over the pass first. We hoisted them onto our shoulders, with one person in the front and the other at the back. To ease the incline, the path followed a zigzag of switchbacks. It was hard, grinding work. We often paused to rest and catch our breath. The weight and awkwardness of the canoe soon made my shoulders ache. But we persevered.

It was with great relief that we finally reached the top. We eased the canoes down to the ground and collapsed. We had to rest our aching muscles. When we had somewhat recovered our breath, we were able to look around, realizing with some surprise just how high was the elevation we had reached. The view was beautiful. We could see where we had come from, far back up the valley of the River of Wisdom. But in the other direction we were disappointed. We had thought that when we got to the top, we would immediately go down the other side. To our surprise, instead of the land falling away, there now stretched before us a large, flat alpine plain. The portage would be even longer than expected.

After we refreshed ourselves, we picked up the canoes and started across the high alpine meadow. Two things encouraged us on the journey. First, during one of our frequent rests, we decided to walk to the edge of the canyon and look down. We were a great height above the river. The canyon was cold, gloomy, and wild. Even at this height, we could still faintly hear the roar of the water as it smashed its way through the rocks. We would never have survived if we had tried to go through there in our canoes. We had done the right thing to portage over this part of the journey.

"The second encouragement came when we reached the end of the plain and began our descent. From this vantage point, we could see the river as it emerged from the gorge. The river was not yet free of the mountains. In fact, a massive height of stone and rock still towered above the river. But what excited us and filled us with anticipation and joy was that we could now see Far Mountain, very plainly. It was nearer and clearer than we had ever seen it before. Even more thrilling, in the distance we could see what looked like a strip of blue water.

"That must be the Sea of Tranquility," cried Elizabeth, shouting in her excitement. "I can see it! Isn't it wonderful?"

It was wonderful, indeed. The sight of it renewed our spirits and gave us fresh strength. With rejoicing hearts, we picked up our canoes and made our way down.

At the bottom of the mountain and at the edge of the river, there was a pleasant place that would make an excellent camping spot. We deposited our canoes there and undertook the return journey to pick up the rest of our equipment and luggage. The hike back was no easier, except that the uncertainty was gone and we knew our labors were coming to an end. We were possessed by a spirit of excitement and anticipation, knowing that soon we would arrive at the foot of Far Mountain and enter the Sea of Tranquility. One thing we did notice was that the canoes belonging to Gregory and Joyce and their friend were still there. Wherever they had ended up, they hadn't come back for them.

It took us the whole day to successfully manage the portage. It was four exhausted but satisfied people who finally set up camp at the edge of the River of Wisdom. We treated ourselves to a well-deserved meal.

Lessons from the Portage

As we sat around the campfire that evening resting our weary but contented bodies, I raised the subject of evaluation. "We were told that we would have experiences in this part of the journey that would teach us how to develop wisdom. We've had a very important experience today. What do you think the lessons are?"

"The lesson I see," said Peter, "is that the road to wisdom sometimes calls for a great deal of discipline, work, and perseverance."

I nodded. "We've learned on a number of occasions that the easy way isn't always the right way. There are times when it isn't wise to yield to our own feelings. It is wise to keep ourselves in check and keep on doing what we know we should do. What else have we learned?"

"Well, I'm beginning to see that wisdom, or the lack of it, is revealed in the decisions we make," Peter said. "This is especially the case when we're under pressure. We're always tempted to go in the direction that eases the pressure or avoids the difficulty. If we're weak and unwise, we'll often yield to these temptations and they'll lead us into confusion and emptiness."

"I rather think Joyce allowed her tiredness and soreness to make the decision for her," I said. "I fear it was the wrong decision."

"Wisdom makes it clear where our own personal responsibility and accountability lie," Lloyd said. "We're responsible for the decisions that we make. Other people may influence us, but ultimately we stand alone. Nobody can force us into anything. The crucial moment of personal responsibility is the point of decision, and the outcomes of these decisions determine the direction and quality of our lives."

Elizabeth changed the subject. "I deeply regret what happened to Gregory and Joyce. You remember how surprised we were when we got to the top of the mountain's shoulder and discovered that instead of coming down there was this great upper plain that had to be crossed? They hoped that their easier path would lead them around the bottom of the mountain and they would end up here. But they didn't realize that the mountain extended a long way out. It may never allow them to circle around. I don't think they'll ever get here, going the way they went."

Lloyd said, "That's what the Bible refers to when it says, *'There is a way that seems right to a man, but in the end it leads to death'* (Proverbs 14:12). The way of the world, the way of ease, the way of selfishness, and the way of yielding to temptation all seem best ways, but they don't take us where we want to go."

"We've been given some basic instructions about how to develop wisdom," I said. "Keep Far Mountain in view, develop in our hearts deep reverence for God, acknowledge our need for wisdom, keep asking God for it, and allow the principles and spirit of wisdom from above to saturate our characters. If we persevere at these things, true wisdom will grow in our hearts."

"And I think we need to be careful of our friends," added Peter. "If we had followed some of the advice we received from them, we wouldn't be here today. Unwise friends and loved ones may mean well, but they can lead us astray. Their advice isn't always good. Think of how many young people allow themselves to be attracted into the wrong company and end in disaster!"

We were all tired after the heavy day, and no one seemed to have any more to contribute to the discussion.

"We're not out of the mountains yet, but we're making progress," I said. "We don't know what tomorrow may bring, but probably it'll be another testing experience. I think we should all get our rest so we'll be ready."

Everyone agreed to this and we retired to our tents, tired but satisfied.

In spite of being so tired, I was too excited to sleep. After a while, I quietly slipped out of the tent and sat by the riverside in quiet meditation.

I found that I could move into a spirit of respectful and appreciative worship much easier now than when I had started out on the journey. Even this realization encouraged me!

The soil of reverently respecting God is deepening in my heart, I thought. *It's beginning to bear fruit. The whole experience of worship is becoming much more natural to me.*

I felt the spirit of worship and reverence flow through my being. I wanted to bathe in the presence of God and be filled with His love and grace. I loved His nearness and was filled with joy over the beauty of nature.

This spiritual consciousness hadn't been prominent in my life before. In fact, it hadn't been part of my life at all. I realized what I had been missing. This was life. This was reality. I was in touch with a whole new dimension of experience. This was satisfying to my soul and my heart. This was truly the way to satisfaction and fulfillment.

Topics for Discussion

1. As they toiled over the long portage, what two things encouraged the group?

2. The influence of wisdom is particularly strong at the point at which we make decisions. Are we responsible for the decisions we make? Are we responsible for the outcomes of those decisions? On what basis does wisdom guide us in our decisions?

Twenty-Five

The Dark Tunnel

Anticipating a full day, we were up early in the morning. After breakfast, as we packed the canoes, Lloyd remarked to me, "I noticed that the name printed on your canoe is *Love*."

"Yes," I replied. "And did you notice that the names on the paddles are *Trust* and *Obey*?"

"Love, Trust, and Obey," Lloyd said thoughtfully. "There must be some significance."

"These names were painted on by the man who equipped us for the journey. He said that they represented the three great qualities that would help us."

Neither Lloyd nor I knew at the time that our reliance on *Love*, *Trust*, and *Obey* would be tested to the full before the day was done.

Even though we were still in the mountains, the first part of the journey was smooth. We began to think that we might emerge from the mountains without any further difficulties.

We quickly found out how very wrong we were in that hope. The river swept around a corner and moved straight towards a great mountain. I assumed the river would curve away and find a way around it. As we closed in on the base of the mountain, however, I could see no indication that the river was going to change its course. With growing concern, the river carried us straight towards the mountain. With mounting anxiety and considerable disbelief, we guided our canoes over to the side of the river to assess what was happening.

The Dark Tunnel

We could see now that the river, indeed, flowed right into the bowels of this great mountain. It wasn't a gorge, but a tunnel through which the river followed an underground passageway.

"It's obviously not a short tunnel," said Peter. "It must go right through the mountain. It'll be dark in there and who knows what will happen to the river before it emerges on the other side?"

"Not only that," said Lloyd, adding to the gloom, "the mountain is too precipitous to climb and there's no way around it for us to portage. If we're going to continue on, we'll have to go through it."

Elizabeth spoke up. "But the river looks smooth enough here. It might just carry us through without incident."

"Sure, the river looks good right here," said Peter with a little panic in his voice, "but who's to say what it will be like inside? Once we're in, there is no turning back."

We sat in stunned, unbelieving silence for a while. No one had any suggestions, and no one wanted to push our canoes into that dark, foreboding hole in the wall. What was waiting for us in the tunnel? What twists and turns might the river take? What rocks, rapids, or falls might be hidden in that dark unknown? Not going in, however, would spell the end of our journey into wisdom. We had come so far and learned so much; it would be a great loss to give up now. We sat there, struggling with an impossible decision.

Love, Trust, and Obey

It was Elizabeth who saved the day. "You and Lloyd were talking about the names of your canoe and the paddles," she reminded us. "*Love, Trust,* and *Obey.* The man who gave them to you said that if you had faith in them, they would get you through anything that came your way. Well, it seems to me the time has come to put this to the test. We need to have faith in *Love, Trust,* and *Obey* to get through this. If we don't go in there and follow this river to its end, then we're not obeying. When we cannot see how best to guide our canoes, we need to rely on *Trust.* And most of all, *Love* will keep us upright and on the right course when we don't know what that course is."

This didn't relieve our doubts any, but it did give us extra courage.

I looked at the others. "Elizabeth is right. We either have to go on and trust our canoes and paddles or turn back and never reach our destination."

"I'm ready to go, if you are," proclaimed Peter.

Lloyd, looking at Elizabeth, didn't say anything, but solemnly nodded his head in agreement. Elizabeth concurred.

So the decisions were made. We would launch into the dark and unknown tunnel.

"When we get in there, we won't be able to see where we're going," I said. "But we should try to stay together. After all, we're in this together. Let's tie a rope to the back of our canoe and Elizabeth, in the front of your canoe, can hold onto it. If we get into trouble, Elizabeth can let go of the rope and hopefully one of our canoes will survive."

"Elizabeth, can you also hold a flashlight?" Lloyd asked. "That way, we'll have a light. It's going to be dreadfully dark in there."

We agreed that this was an excellent idea and made the necessary preparations.

Before we pushed off, Lloyd suggested that we pray first. We anxiously agreed. Lloyd prayed for our safety and committed us into the hands of God.

With that, we pushed off.

The mountain towered above us, a vast fortress of dark, unscalable rock. As we approached the entrance to the tunnel, the banks of the river climbed to two high cliffs on each side. The river here was very slow, as if it too hesitated to enter the dark unknown.

We entered the tunnel and quietness seemed to envelope us. We let the canoes float along with the river current. I peered into the darkness ahead but could see nothing. I looked back and could see the mouth of the watery cave. The ceiling was quite high, so we weren't in danger of banging our heads on the ceiling rocks.

In the Dark

With great trepidation, we watched the mouth of the cave recede and felt the darkness deepen. The river took a curve and suddenly the half-circle of light disappeared and we were swallowed entirely by darkness. Thankfully, Elizabeth turned on the flashlight. It didn't help very much, but it gave us comfort.

"It's so quiet in here," Peter ventured.

Our progress was slow and the river was quiet. I hoped it would stay that way. Elizabeth, as an experiment, turned off the flashlight. The darkness was absolute. I couldn't see a thing, not even my hands on the paddles. Thankfully, she turned the light on again. This was going to be a long part of the journey.

I sensed rather than saw our speed of descent begin to pick up. I heard ripples from the water as it flowed past rock. I was in a hurry to get out of here, yes, but I also knew encountering rapids in this blackness could be the death of us.

Peter said, "Listen."

We listened and could faintly hear noise ahead. I didn't like it, for it sounded like the noise of water rushing and gurgling. We were definitely moving faster and knew we were in for a rough ride in total darkness.

Elizabeth tried to point the light in the direction we were going, but the thin ray of light wasn't strong enough. The canoe began to heave up and down. I felt water splash on my hands and I realized we were in the midst of rapids. Elizabeth, having to hold on to the rope with both hands, dropped the flashlight. We were helpless.

The surge of the water seemed furious, and the noise in that confined space was ominous. Clearly the river was dashing over invisible rocks. With dread, I waited for us to hit a rock or be swept over, but we plunged on.

As quickly as it started, it was over. The noise receded and the heaving of the canoe began to settle.

"Are you two alright?" I shouted back to Lloyd and Elizabeth.

"So far so good," replied Lloyd. His voice was strong and confident and gave me a little courage.

"Remember," Elizabeth shouted. "*Love, Trust,* and *Obey.*"

We floated on for what seemed like an eternity but could have been better measured in minutes.

"I think I can see some light," Peter said. We all peered ahead, and it did seem as if the darkness wasn't quite as dense. Utter black turned to deep grey, and the grey grew lighter all of the time. We knew we were coming to the end of the underground river. We couldn't yet see the opening, but the light had to be coming from somewhere. I had never been so glad to see light!

We turned a corner and Peter again shouted out, "There, I can see it."

The opening was still some distance away, but it was clearly the end of the tunnel. We now paddled with unbridled excitement. Our exit from the tunnel was a moment of triumph, but we weren't at all ready for the sight that awaited us in the bright sunshine.

Victory

The river emptied itself into a great and beautiful body of clear blue water which lay before us, open and warm. To our left was the base of the great mountain which we had traveled through and which now towered above us. We couldn't see the top from where we were, but we knew it was massive.

With joy and delight, we realized we had arrived at the Sea of Tranquility. I let out a whoop. The others cheered at the top of their voices. We waved our paddles in the air as a sign of victory. We had arrived!

We rested for a while letting the canoes float randomly. We simply sat and drank in the scene around us, enjoying the sense of accomplishment and peace that quietly settled on our souls. The atmosphere was mellow. We absorbed it, letting it flow gently into our souls. What a beautiful place!

After a while, I remembered that Charles had told us that when we arrived we would see an island out in the sea and that we should make our way to it. I could see the island. Pointing to it, I suggested that we go to it and make camp.

The island wasn't far and we soon reached its shore, which was skirted with a fine beach of white sand. We pulled our canoes up on the beach and decided on a good place to pitch our tents back a bit from the water's edge. I looked back towards the mainland and was awed at the sight. I could see where the River of Wisdom emerged from the mountain and emptied itself into the Sea of Tranquility, but towering above it in massive grandeur was Far Mountain. Shaped like a pyramid, it reached up into the sky with a snow-capped peak that sparkled against the clear blue sky. It had been our guide all the way here, and now it seemed to stand guard over us. What amazed me was the realization that the fearsome dark tunnel had actually flowed through Far Mountain.

If I had known that, I thought, *I might not have been so afraid.*

After we had set up camp, we gathered on the beach to appreciate the grandeur all around us and luxuriate in the satisfying sense of accomplishment.

I smiled at the group. We felt satisfied and joyful, and although the journey through the dark river had only occurred that morning, it now seemed a long time ago. Already the vivid experience was receding in our minds. We needed to talk about it right away while it remained fresh.

Lessons from the Dark Tunnel

The others agreed that if they had known the mountain we were flowing through had been Far Mountain, they might have had more confidence.

"Part of developing wisdom is to learn from experiences," I said. "Coming through that underground river was certainly a powerful experience, but we need to consider what we should learn from it."

"I think the names given to your canoe and paddles were very important," suggested Elizabeth. "We had no idea where we were going or what would happen, so we committed ourselves to *Love*, *Trust*, and *Obey*, and we came through safely. It seems to me that in the experiences of life, we are often operating in the dark. We don't know what's ahead or which way to go. In times like that, you must have faith. When you're uncertain, act out of love and you won't go far wrong. When the future looks dark, trust in God and move ahead. When all seems lost, just obey what you understand is the will and guidance of God and you won't end up in the wrong place."

Elizabeth's excitement and sincerity affected us all.

"You're right," Peter said. "In times of conflict, it is wise to act out of love, not hatred, anger, or resentment. In times of uncertainty, you can always hear two voices—the voice of doubt and the voice of faith. It's wiser to act out of trust than it is to listen to your doubts. Doubts usually tell us, 'Don't risk it. Cut back. Be safe.' Listening to your doubts usually means you won't venture forward into new and creative ways of life. Doubts are confining and limiting. Trust always asks us to take some risks. And it's always wise to obey God."

I smiled a little to myself as I listened to Peter.

These friends of mine are really beginning to talk, I thought. *They're beginning to see and understand important truth and are confident enough to express them.*

Lloyd, in keeping with his philosophical bent, took a different but interesting approach. "In times of crisis and at turning points in life, in order to act out of love, trust, and obedience, you must have developed them strongly before the time of crisis came upon you. When you have learned to develop and strengthen these qualities in your heart, you establish them. They sing in your heart with beauty and harmony. But if you neglect them, they aren't able to motivate and guide you when times of uncertainty come."

"In my fellowship with God, His Holy Spirit has grown these qualities in my heart," I said. "I'm glad the dark tunnel was at the end of the journey and not the beginning. If we had started out by having to go through that tunnel, I wouldn't have done it. But over time, my fellowship with God grew and the soil of wisdom developed in my heart. When we eventually faced the dark tunnel, I had enough experience with God and His ways that I was able to undertake the test." I added, almost as an afterthought, "And if I had been alone, I don't think I would have done it even then. The companionship and strength I got from my friends gave me the courage to move ahead."

"Which brings us to the important point," said Lloyd. "We understand that you didn't provide yourselves with your canoe and paddles. They came from your friend Charles. In the same way, the development of love, trust, and obedience are provided for us by God. They develop in our hearts by the inner work of the Holy Spirit. We cannot, by our own efforts, produce the spirit of love, trust, and obedience. They are the gift of God. The Bible says that *'God has poured out his love into our hearts by the Holy Spirit, whom he has given us'* (Romans 5:5).

"That's correct," I said. "But remember what George told us about being a farmer. We must cultivate, tend, and help them to grow by constantly nourishing them. We do this by attending to the means of grace—through prayer, fellowship, Bible reading. These qualities don't grow in unyielding, hard, and untilled soil. I've been trying to cultivate a spirit in my heart that's conducive to the growth of wisdom. I remember that the fear of the Lord is the beginning of wisdom. I open my heart to the wonder of God's presence. He certainly produces love, trust, and obedience in our lives, but He won't do it without our cooperation and participation."

"On the other hand," Lloyd said, "no matter how hard we try to discipline ourselves, we cannot produce them ourselves without the presence and activity of God in our hearts."

I looked around the group. "Anything else we should take from that experience?

Peter spoke up. "We have consistently been told that wisdom isn't so much an intellectual development, although that's part of it; it is a movement of the heart. Wisdom flows out from the springs of our personalities. It's what makes us act and think the way we do. When we act out of righteousness, we act wisely. When we're guided by the spirit of holiness, we are guided correctly. The development of righteousness in our hearts and the development of wisdom happen together. They complement one another, like a hand in a glove."

"You've just defined the process of becoming wise so well," Lloyd agreed. "To live righteously is wise. To be wise is to live righteously. True wisdom points to a righteous way of life. A righteous way of life points us in the direction of true wisdom. How well you have said it!"

Feeling encouraged, Peter added, "I've experienced many very fine people who try to be righteous but do it without wisdom. When people try to be righteous while neglecting wisdom, they fall prey to all kinds of extremism and narrow thinking. In their sincerity, they're attracted to all kinds of foolish side issues. On the other hand, some try to be wise without being righteous and they pursue empty, destructive values. They don't realize that sin and unrighteousness have within them the seeds of their own destruction. What seems wise to them ends in emptiness and disillusionment. So yes, we should seek wise righteousness, or righteous wisdom."

"And the wise righteousness we seek is the righteousness Jesus taught and exhibited," I concluded.

This seemed to sum up our thoughts very well.

As we continued to take in the scenery, Elizabeth interrupted us with an excited cry: "Look, there's a boat coming out to our island."

Sure enough, we could see a small boat with only two passengers coming towards us. It was clear they had seen us.

Topics for Discussion

1. Discuss the importance of *Love, Trust,* and *Obey* as the group faced the dark tunnel.

2. How did the group decide that the spirit of *Love, Trust,* and *Obey* grew in their hearts?

3. Discuss the conclusion Lloyd came to, that to live righteously is wise, and to be wise is to live righteously.

The Sea of Tranquility and the Great Mountain

TWENTY-SIX

Old Friends

THE FOUR OF US WATCHED WITH GREAT INTEREST AS THE SMALL MOTORBOAT
chugged towards our beach. One of the two men sat at the back, guiding the
boat. The other stood up and waved to us. We waved back and moved down to
the edge of the water to meet them.

As they approached the shore, I was stunned. I grasped Peter by the arm.
"Do you recognize them?"

"Yes," said Peter with quiet intensity. "It's Hermes, and unless I'm mistaken,
the man guiding the boat is Charles."

With childlike joy and excitement, Peter and I hugged Hermes as he stepped
out of the boat. He laughed with obvious pleasure.

"You made it," Hermes said. "Welcome to the Sea of Tranquility."

Charles now got out of the boat and we engaged in another round of hugs
and handshakes. When the enthusiasm of our reunion had cooled a little, we
remembered Lloyd and Elizabeth and introduced them to Hermes and Charles.

With much talk and chatter, we made our way back to the fire and sat around it, telling Hermes and Charles all about the journey down the River of Wisdom. They listened with interest and understanding. We ended our tale by sharing with them the conclusion that we had so recently arrived at, that to live righteously is wise and to be wise is to live righteously. They were clearly delighted with this and felt we had learned the lessons of the river very well.

"So, now that we're here, what do we do next?" I asked.

"This is a beautiful place," replied Hermes, "and we want you to consider staying here permanently, making your life here. The central community is right at the bottom of the Great Mountain. If you decide to stay, that's where you'll live. Before you decide, however, there are a number of lessons we would like you to learn. They are practical lessons on how wisdom works in the everyday facets of life. Living around the sea are a number of very wise people we would like you to meet. They'll tell you some things about wisdom that will be very useful to you if you decide to make this your home."

Hermes pointed to Far Mountain. "To those who live here, that is no longer called Far Mountain. It's called the Great Mountain."

None of us had any response to this, so Hermes continued, "We'll leave you here on the island for a day or two. No one will disturb you. We suggest you give some time to absorbing the lessons you learned as you came down the river, and we especially want you to think about the Great Mountain. Think about its significance. Afterward, we'll come back and take you to the first of the wise people we want you to meet."

I was really grateful for this suggestion, as I was weary from the journey and needed time to refresh myself physically and absorb the experiences of the trip.

"But where do you live?" Peter asked. The same question had been on my mind,

"We would love to live here," replied Hermes, "but our task is to live where you came from and encourage others to find this place. It's an important job. I assure you that wherever we are, we carry with us the spirit and atmosphere you feel here."

We could all see the sense in this.

With reluctance, we waved goodbye to Hermes and Charles, comforted by their promise to return. We then proceeded to organize our camp for a longer stay. We enjoyed a good meal together. All of us felt tired but satisfied.

In the evening I walked alone to a stretch of beach out of sight of our camp. I sat down to enjoy some time of meditation. It was a beautiful spot. The sea lived up to its name; it was tranquil and the water was smooth, with scarcely a ripple. While everybody called it a sea, its water was fresh and clear. Unsalty. I concluded that it was actually a large lake.

The far side of the sea was surrounded by well-wooded hills, but straight across from where I sat arose the mighty fortress of the Great Mountain. In the quiet stillness of this warm evening, I continued to be awed by its size and majesty. It radiated power and strength. Although it was a mighty mountain, it was also very beautiful. Its power didn't repel; it attracted you. It seemed to invite more than challenge. I wondered if I would ever be able to climb to the top of its white peak.

In this awesome setting, once again my spirit rose within me. God seemed to be so close. In my heart, I sensed His presence. All of nature was quiet and still in His nearness. The beauty all around reflected His greatness and power. I felt a river of joy well up within my soul. I was in contact with the reality of the universe and the spirit of the ages. I rested in it. A deep reverence for the reality of God filled my being. I worshiped Him. I praised Him. If the fear of the Lord was the beginning of wisdom, then I knew I had achieved it. The fear of the Lord enveloped my soul, and I allowed my being to get lost in it, letting it roll over me in great waves of peace and joy. Experiences like this, when I was being filled with the awareness of the presence of God, were becoming more frequent and vivid. I loved it.

I'm not sure how long I sat engrossed in my meditation, but my solitude was interrupted by Lloyd, who came along the beach and sat down beside me. He sensed the mood and wonder of my spirit, quietly sharing the moment with me.

Finally, I said, "Hermes told us to think about the Great Mountain and its meaning for developing our wisdom. It's been our guide through the whole journey down the River of Wisdom. Now that we're here at the Sea of Tranquility, it seems to dominate everything. Nothing compares with it in stature, beauty, or power. What do you think it means?"

"I've been thinking," Lloyd said. "In the life of righteous wisdom, I think the Great Mountain represents the Lord Jesus Christ."

I looked at him in amazement. "I never thought of that."

"You were on the river longer than I was, but Far Mountain was always our guide. It guided us through difficult times. It kept us straight when it was easy to get sidetracked. Following it gave us direction when we could easily have been lost. Now that we're developing the spirit of wisdom, it's the mountain that dominates the scene. Its presence is felt everywhere. It is the great central feature of the sea. Everything revolves around it. In every way, it reflects the role Jesus Christ should play in our lives."

I looked at Lloyd with more appreciation. Once again, his insights helped me see and define what was happening to me. Once I saw it, it seemed so clear and obvious. But he was the one who saw it first.

"Of course," I said. "And no one was ever as wise as Jesus. No one ever lived as He lived or taught as He taught."

Lloyd took out a New Testament from his pocket. "There are some verses I want to show you. Look here. In 1 Corinthians, Paul speaks about the centrality of Jesus Christ in the lives of His followers. He says that Christ is the central message of the Christian church. He goes on to say that Jesus is *'to those whom God has called, both Jews and Greeks, Christ the power of God and the wisdom of God'* (1 Corinthians 1:24). That means that all the infinite wisdom and power of God was embodied in Jesus Christ, and He makes them available to us. In the same chapter, Paul says another amazing thing: *'It is because of him that you are in Christ Jesus, who has become for us wisdom from God—that is, our righteousness, holiness and redemption'* (1 Corinthians 1:30). God is willing to pass on to us through Jesus Christ all the wisdom necessary for us to live a wise and righteous life.

"I'm surprised at how much the Apostle Paul speaks of wisdom. He even tells us that the wisdom of the ages was hidden and is only revealed in these days through Jesus Christ. He says, *'No, we speak of God's secret wisdom, a wisdom that has been hidden and that God destined for our glory before time began'* (1 Corinthians 2:7). That wisdom has now been revealed through Jesus Christ. He says again to the Colossians,

> *My purpose is that they may be encouraged in heart and united in*
> *love, so that they may have the full riches of complete understanding,*
> *in order that they may know the mystery of God, namely, Christ,*
> *in whom are hidden all the treasures of wisdom and knowledge.*
> (Colossians 2:2–3)

"These truths about wisdom seem to focus on Jesus Christ. God's wisdom comes to us as we get to know Jesus Christ, trust His teaching, and obey His way of life."

"So, the secret of wisdom is wrapped up in knowing and following Jesus Christ," I said. "The more you know Him, and the better you absorb His spirit and reflect Him in the way you live, then the wiser you'll be."

"That's right."

I sat back in overwhelmed silence, looking at the Great Mountain with new eyes. *To live wisely here in the Sea of Tranquility, we must see the mountain as representing Jesus Christ. From Him comes all the wisdom of God. He is central to the life of righteous wisdom.*

This was something we were anxious to share with the others. Lloyd and I made our way back to the camp and joined Peter and Elizabeth as they sat around the campfire. We shared with them the revelation that had come to us.

"Of course!" Elizabeth exclaimed. "Jesus was the wisest person who ever lived. The more we can absorb His Spirit, thoughts, and attitudes, the wiser we'll be. To be like Jesus is to be wise, and the more you are like Him the wiser you are."

I was so glad Lloyd and Elizabeth were with us on this journey. They had insights and experience I didn't have.

Peter, always the careful one, still had some questions. "I wonder why God would hide all the treasures of wisdom and knowledge in Jesus Christ. Why are they hidden?"

"Perhaps," I answered, "they're not so much hidden as they are neglected, forgotten, and unfound. Those who don't following the wisdom of Jesus must have a very hard time understanding how His way of life could possibly be wise. They don't see it, experience it, or understand it. You remember the lessons we got about wisdom from above and wisdom from below? Those who follow the wisdom from below see His priorities, values, commitments, and spirit as foolish. So wisdom isn't hidden. We're just blind to it."

We continued to discuss this late into the night, concluding that, just as the Great Mountain dominated the scene here, it would be wise for us to absorb the Spirit of Jesus and try to express His Spirit in every way in your lives. This was a thrilling revelation to us. I looked forward with increasing anticipation to the return of Hermes and Charles and the fulfillment of the promise that we would enter more fully into this new, wise lifestyle by the Sea of Tranquility.

Topics for Discussion

1. Lloyd understood that the Great Mountain represents for us the Lord Jesus Christ. In what ways do you think the Great Mountain represents Jesus Christ in our lives?

2. In explaining why God's wisdom is embodied in Jesus Christ, Lloyd concludes that wisdom focuses on Jesus Christ. God's wisdom comes to us as we get to know Jesus Christ, trust His teachings, and obey His way of life. Do you agree with this conclusion? What are its implications? What does it mean in our lives?

TWENTY-SEVEN

Wisdom in Words

THE QUIET DAYS ON THE ISLAND WERE VERY REFRESHING. IT WAS NEVERTHELESS exciting to see Hermes and Charles arrive again. I had found myself looking forward to their coming and to the anticipated excursion they had planned for us.

"The people I want you to meet in the next few days are schooled in wisdom," Hermes said. "They'll help you in some of the very practical matters of being wise. I want you to hear them before you decide whether to stay or not.

"Today I want you to meet Pierre. Pierre isn't only a very wise man. He's also a great storyteller and I want him to tell you the story of Herod, who was the king of the Jews at the time of Jesus.

"The Bible makes a clear connection between the depth of wisdom in a person's heart and how they use their tongue. I'd like you to think of your words as a kind of thermometer of your heart. It's surprising how much the Bible has to say about our words. I think you'll find Pierre tough but helpful."

The journey to Pierre's home took us to the other side of the Sea of Tranquility. As we landed on the opposite shore, I glanced back at the Great Mountain and noted that even on this side of the sea it stood dominant and majestic in the morning light. On the Sea of Tranquility, you could never get away from the presence of the Great Mountain.

Pierre's home was on a high bank close to the water's edge, and it had a splendid view of the sea and the Great Mountain. It didn't take us long, after basic introductions, to get down to the business of the day.

"I'd like you to tell them the story of Herod," Hermes told Pierre. "Some of them may have heard it before, but I don't think Colin has heard it."

Pierre, who spoke with a French accent, seemed happy to do this and began immediately. Words certainly weren't being wasted here!

"King Herod was feeling good," Pierre began. "It was his birthday and he had organized a lavish party to celebrate the occasion. All the important people of the nation were there, showing proper deference to him. As the evening progressed and the wine began to take effect, Herod's feeling of expansive goodwill increased. The time came for the presentation of one of the highlights of the evening's entertainment, when Salome, the beautiful daughter of Herod's present wife, was to dance for the benefit of the guests. The dance was rather lewd and suggestive, but extremely well done. She received an enthusiastic applause from the rather jaded guests.

"As Herod basked in the pleasure of the applause, his feeling of generous well-being burst out and he loudly announced to all the guests that Salome had done so well that she could have, as a reward, anything she asked for, up to half his kingdom. This was an extremely foolish oath to announce publicly before all his guests, officials, and counselors. But in the emotion of the moment, and under the influence of wine, Herod had made a vow he would deeply regret."

Pierre nodded his head quietly to emphasize what he was saying. "Herod, like all men in authority and public office, should have known to speak carefully and watch his words. He couldn't afford to let his emotions get away from him. But the foolish words were spoken and the vow could not, with honor, be withdrawn.

"Salome, realizing the importance of this public pledge, asked for a little time to formulate her request. Herod agreed to this, perhaps already regretting his rashness. The girl went to her mother to ask advice. The mother, Herodias, knew exactly how to take advantage of the situation and instructed Salome on what she should request.

"Salome went back into the banquet hall. As she approached Herod, the raucous group of partiers became suddenly silent. Every eye followed her as she bowed before her stepfather. Then, in a clear voice for all to hear, she made her request: 'I would like the head of John the Baptist brought to me on a silver platter—now.' It was a shocking, gruesome request. Nobody, including Herod, had expected this."

I listened intently. The story was indeed new to me.

"John the Baptist was in prison under Herod's jurisdiction," Pierre continued. "John had publicly denounced Herod for marrying Herodias, who had been his brother's wife and thus, according to John, the union was unlawful. For this, Herod had John put in prison, but he had no inclination to make a martyr out of him. In many ways, John's preaching had impressed Herod; he'd followed John's ministry with some interest. He considered John to be a man of God, with a special message from God to the nation. Herodias, however, had no such scruples. She deeply resented John's questioning of her marriage and wanted rid of this embarrassing voice that exposed her private immorality. She had wanted Herod to destroy John for some time, but Herod had always resisted. Now, she saw the opportunity.

"The banquet hall fell deathly silent after Salome's request. Herod's eyes roamed the hall, looking for some way out of this—some compromise, some excuse, some delay. There were those present who were secretly pleased to see him caught in this embarrassing situation. But from all his guests, Herod received no advice, suggestion, or alternative. Very reluctantly, he gave the order for John to be beheaded, and for the head to be brought before them on a platter. His order was carried out."

Pierre paused here to let the significance of the story sink in.

"Herod's birthday party soon began to break up," Pierre continued. "The fun had gone out of the evening. Many people were appalled at what had happened. Some thought Herod should have just said to Salome, 'No! Ask for something else.' Others were even pleased, for their consciences had been pricked by the forthright preaching of the Baptist. But all were unanimous as they talked about it afterwards—Herod shouldn't have made such an unwise and foolish vow.

"Herod wasn't the first, nor will he be the last, to speak unwise words. Words are powerful and need to be used with care. Many have regretted unwise words, spoken in haste and without thought. Great damage has been done by thoughtless words spoken in the heat of the moment. All of us have been the target of hurtful and wounding words and opinions, sometimes justified, but often inaccurate and wrong. Words can be used for good and they can be used for evil—intended or unintended.

"There's a clear connection to be made between a person's inherent wisdom and his or her use of language. A wise person is restrained and careful about what he says. A wise person isn't given to rash statements. A good person uses words to encourage and to help. A thoughtful person uses words to teach and guide. A bitter person uses words to hurt and destroy. A deceitful person uses words to deceive and mislead. A loving person uses words to heal and build. For all of us, the words that come from our mouths are like bullets from a gun; once they're shot, they cannot taken back. A wise person, therefore, is known for his judicious use of words."

When Pierre had finished this story, Elizabeth and Lloyd glanced at each other and smiled. I knew there was some unspoken conversation going on between them.

Hermes interjected at this point. "Tell us, Pierre, what the Bible says about words and wisdom."

Pierre opened his Bible. "James makes clear the connection between wisdom and the use of words when he says, *'We all stumble in many ways. If anyone is never at fault in what he says, he is a perfect man, able to keep his whole body in check'* (James 3:2). Perfection is measured by a person's ability to speak wisely and well. Since none of us are perfect, we all stand in need of improvement in the use of our tongue.

"James goes on to say that the disciplined use of the tongue is an essential part of personal wisdom. He says,

> *When we put bits into the mouths of horses to make them obey us, we can turn the whole animal. Or take ships as an example. Although they are so large and are driven by strong winds, they are steered by a very small rudder wherever the pilot wants to go. Likewise the tongue is a small part of the body, but it makes great boasts. Consider what a great forest is set on fire by a small spark.*
> (James 3:3–5)

"It takes a strong and disciplined person to be able to control and guide the tongue." Pierre turned the pages of his Bible and continued. "Jesus confirms the principle that your tongue reflects who you really are at your heart. In talking about the importance of words, He said,

Make a tree good and its fruit will be good, or make a tree bad and its fruit will be bad, for a tree is recognized by its fruit. You brood of vipers, how can you who are evil say anything good? For out of the overflow of the heart the mouth speaks. The good man brings good things out of the good stored up in him, and the evil man brings evil things out of the evil stored up in him. But I tell you that men will have to give account on the day of judgment for every careless word they have spoken. For by your words you will be acquitted, and by your words you will be condemned. (Matthew 12:33–37)

"These are strong and carefully chosen words, but they indicate that what's really in our hearts will come out in the way we talk. As Hermes has said, wisdom in words is a thermometer measuring the condition of our inner being.

"The tongue has tremendous power and influence. It can be used for good or evil, but its impact on us and others should not be doubted. In vivid language, James says,

The tongue also is a fire, a world of evil among the parts of the body. It corrupts the whole person, sets the whole course of his life on fire, and is itself set on fire by hell. (James 3:6)

"This is powerful language, but James is at pains to impress upon us that the tongue, though small, is a powerful member of our body. If used foolishly and selfishly, it can spread great discord and set our own lives on a course that leads to personal destruction. The tongue has to be tamed and disciplined, guided by a wise heart. It cannot be undisciplined or allowed to run amok.

"James goes on to say that our tongues give each of us an effective tool for communication. We are responsible for how we use that tool. James says,

With the tongue we praise our Lord and Father, and with it we curse men, who have been made in God's likeness. Out of the same mouth come praise and cursing. My brothers, this should not be. Can both fresh water and salt water flow from the same spring? My brothers, can a fig tree bear olives, or a grapevine bear figs? Neither can a salt spring produce fresh water." (James 3:9–12)

Here, Pierre paused to give us time to absorb all he had said.

Peter, who was always careful before expressing his opinions, spoke up. "The tongue, of course, is in itself neither good nor evil. It is neutral. It's the person who controls the tongue that creates the good or evil. The tongue is an instrument."

"Right," said Pierre. "To each of us is given the power to communicate. This is an awesome power. Almost everything you say has some influence on the people around you. Speech is very seldom neutral."

Peter reached out and laid his hand on my arm. With a voice full of emotion, he said, "I've been amazed at the power some people have had on my life. Their speech encourages and help me. In times of despair and defeat, their words revive and renew me. Some have expressed words and opinions that inspired me with vision and gave me direction in life." Peter lifted his hand off my arm. "Others have hurt me. If I had listened to some, I would have quickly given up on a project. They were negative and depressing and they urged their doubts on me. They have knowingly spread gossip about me. Others have brought hurt to me but didn't do it deliberately. Nonetheless, their thoughtless, careless flippancy has added pain to my life."

The others in the company nodded at what Peter was saying. I gathered we'd all had similar experiences with the power of words. But Peter wasn't finished.

"I also realize that while the words of others have been influential in my life," he continued, "I expect my words to also have an influence on the lives of others. I need to ask myself, *What kind of effect do my words have? Do I encourage and build? Do I give good guidance and direction? Do I help and inspire? Do I bring praise and cheerfulness?* I need to know what that influence is. I pray that when people meet me and hear me, I'll spread cheer, encouragement, hope, and strength and not doubt, fear, discouragement, and weariness. Using the tool of the tongue well takes great wisdom. It requires a mind that is wise, mature, generous, and godly. This is something I need to seriously think about. I need to ask the Lord for His help."

Peter had obviously been speaking from his heart, and in saying this he revealed much about himself. The power of his testimony affected all of us and when he was finished, we spontaneously gave him a round of applause.

Hermes now turned our attention back to Pierre. "Pierre has given a great deal of thought to this matter. I would like him to guide us in some of the other wise things the Bible says about the tongue."

"Fortunately, the Bible gives us good direction for the wise use of the tongue," Pierre said. "Taming the tongue is difficult, but the ability to control it reflects maturity and wisdom. Here are some pointers from the Bible about the wise, proper, and fruitful use of the tongue."

Speak with Honesty

"First, speak the truth. Jesus said it plainly when He said, *'Simply let your "Yes" be "Yes," and your "No," "No"; anything beyond this comes from the evil one'* (Matthew 5:37) Be a person of your word. Establish trust and credibility, by saying what you mean and meaning what you say. Unless unforeseen circumstances make it impossible, when you say you'll be somewhere—be there. When you say you'll do something—do it. It's wise for you to become known as a person whose words can be trusted and believed.

"Trust between people isn't given; it's earned. People learn to have confidence in you or they learn to have no confidence in you. Once you start to lie, or not quite tell the truth, your relationships go downhill. It's foolish to deceive just because you think telling the truth would be inconvenient. It isn't wise to avoid the truth by shading the news to your own advantage. The book of Proverbs states it bluntly: *'The Lord detests lying lips, but he delights in men who are truthful'* (Proverbs 12:22).

"David, in writing the fifteenth Psalm, describes the characteristics of a person who is strong and reliable. One of the characteristics of such a person is his use of the tongue. He says this strong and steady person is one who *'speaks the truth from his heart and has no slander on his tongue... who keeps his oath even when it hurts'* (Psalm 15:2-4). Cheating, deceiving, and misleading are all devices for conveniently avoiding the truth, and they can create mistrust, disappointment, and grief."

Lloyd, who seemed to have experience in business, interjected here. "Consider how different our society would be if all business transactions were honest, if our leaders and politicians spoke only the truth, if our friends and family were honest with each other. Incredible harm and hurt is created by not telling the truth. In the world of commerce, horrendous costs are incurred because we cannot trust people. In order for us to have assurance that people will do what they say they'll do, we have to put in place systems that cost a great deal of money and time. It is wise to become a person whose words and commitments can be trusted. Then you will be honored and respected. We should strive to be like God in this respect. I think about what's said of God in the book of Proverbs:

Every word of God is flawless; he is a shield to those who take refuge in him. Do not add to his words, or he will rebuke you and prove you a liar." (Proverbs 30:5–6).

Speak Less

"The second piece of advice I would give you from the Bible is to speak less. Proverbs says, *'When words are many, sin is not absent, but he who holds his tongue is wise'* (Proverbs 10:19). There can be a lot of useless chatter about stuff that really doesn't matter. James is rather emphatic about this. He says, *'My dear brothers, take note of this: Everyone should be quick to listen, slow to speak and slow to become angry'* (James 1:19). It's wise for us to be quick to listen and slow to speak.

"There is much to talk about that's worthwhile and meaningful and brings help, understanding, and growth. There is also much to talk about that's empty, shallow, and does no one any good and may easily slip over into doing others harm. A wise person does not indulge in empty and meaningless chatter."

Again I saw Elizabeth and Lloyd looking at each other and smiling.

"In today's electronic age," Lloyd said, "we communicate in many ways beyond just speaking and writing. Useless chatter can be applied to emails, texting, phone calls, and social media. Apart from the wastage of time involved in passing back and forth trifling pieces of information, communications are often harmful and demeaning. In keeping with James' exhortation, it would be wise, even in electronic communications, to say less but make what you say more meaningful. Proverbs 15: 2 says, *'The tongue of the wise commends knowledge, but the mouth of the fool gushes folly.'*"

Think Before You Speak

"Think before you speak, or write or text," Pierre continued, making his next point. "The wise man of Proverbs says, *'Reckless words pierce like a sword, but the tongue of the wise brings healing'* (Proverbs 12:18). We've all experienced the regret of saying something in the heat of the moment and then wishing we could recall the words. Wise people learn to discipline their emotional impulses and refrain from saying the first thing that comes into their heads. There is wisdom in learning to think before you speak. Initial reactions are often immature and ill thought out. Take time to think about what you're going to say before you say it, for after you have said it you cannot bring it back."

Gossip Is Sin

"The next piece of guidance is obvious: gossip is sin. Proverbs says that spreading slander about others is foolish: *'He who conceals his hatred has lying lips, and whoever spreads slander is a fool'* (Proverbs 10:18). Even in the New Testament, gossip and slander are considered sin. In writing to the troubled church in Corinth, Paul lists gossip amongst the demeaning practices that were taking place in the church there:

> For I am afraid that when I come I may not find you as I want you to be, and you may not find me as you want me to be. I fear that there may be quarreling, jealousy, outbursts of anger, factions, slander, gossip, arrogance and disorder. (1 Corinthians 12:20).

"In addition, when Paul writes to the Galatians, he lists the spreading of discord and dissentions as one of the expressions of the sinful nature:

> The acts of the sinful nature are obvious: sexual immorality, impurity and debauchery; idolatry and witchcraft; hatred, discord, jealousy, fits of rage, selfish ambition, dissensions, factions and envy; drunkenness, orgies, and the like. I warn you, as I did before, that those who live like this will not inherit the kingdom of God."
> (Galatians 5:19–21)

"What exactly is gossip?" asked Elizabeth.

"Gossip is repeating stories or information about other people, whether true or not, that are designed to be injurious to their good name," Peter said. "There is a strange anxiety amongst some people to pass on bad news or spicy information. This can cause no end of trouble. Often the gossip isn't true or it's exaggerated for better effect. Wise people don't indulge themselves in this kind of destructive talk and behavior. It is contrary to the spirit of love and the Spirit of Christ. It doesn't create goodwill or generate confidence. There is a clear call for those who would be wise and mature in their Christian lives to refrain from gossip and not make it part of their conversations."

Speak the Truth in Love

"Speak the truth in love," Pierre continued. "This calls for a great deal of wisdom and maturity. When someone is in error, or is going astray, or is making decisions we consider foolish, we want to tell them the truth, that what they're about to do is ill-considered and harmful. But it takes a great deal of wisdom to be able to speak the truth to them in such a way that will not turn them off or create offense."

"Yes, I have experienced that," said Elizabeth with considerable feeling. "Some people like to use the truth as a lash to whip you for your failures and shortcomings."

"I'm afraid so," replied Pierre gently. "The truth can be spoken in a harsh and critical way, not in love. When this happens, it generates resentment, rebellion, and stubbornness, but it won't prevent the person from following the ill-conceived path they have in mind."

Elizabeth interrupted again. Obviously this was an area where she had been hurt in the past. "Yes, as you say, sometimes the truth can be spoken, but not in love. The person speaks out of their own need to get something off their chest or give us a piece of their mind or relieve their own conscience. This motivation behind speaking the truth doesn't help. It just allows that person to vent their frustrations. Sometimes they might even take secret pleasure from pointing out other people's weaknesses."

Pierre agreed. "If you've ever been the unfortunate person who has made a mistake, you probably know that the last thing you need is for someone to come along and let you know a thing or two about what you did wrong. They may enjoy scolding you and get satisfaction from it. What they're saying may be correct, but the truth doesn't make you want to reform, apologize, or make amends; instead you become defensive. Truth spoken from ulterior motives creates hostility, anger, and division."

"I wonder if the concept of 'truth' means more than just correct information," Lloyd mused. "If you speak a truth in a way that's destructive and demeaning, it may be correct, but is it truth? Truth, in the full sense of the word, also contains purpose, motivation, and the desire to use the information in a redemptive way."

As I listened to Lloyd, I was once again fascinated by his sharp and profound thinking processes.

"That's a very good insight," Pierre said. "It certainly points out the fact that speaking the truth in love calls for a great deal of wisdom and insight. It means you carefully and caringly want to help the other person improve. The motive is not to scold or demean or punish or pass judgment, but to be redemptive and create solutions."

I had something I wanted to share with the others at this point. "Back in my schoolboy days, we had a great variety of teachers," I said. "Some would get angry and shout and yell and give us the strap in order to punish us for our poor performance. As I remember, they weren't the really effective teachers. The most effective teacher I ever had, the one who inspired the best results out of me, never once gave me the strap, lost her temper, humiliated me before the whole class, but rather created in me a desire to please her. She gave me encouraging rewards for work well done and words of praise. She knew how to teach the truth in ways that made us want to learn and feel good about ourselves."

"Thank you," said Pierre. "That's a good illustration. It's not enough to speak the truth. Wisdom comes in when you speak the truth in love, so that the person is moved and motivated to better performance. James says,

> *My brothers, if one of you should wander from the truth and some-one should bring him back, remember this: Whoever turns a sinner from the error of his way will save him from death and cover over a multitude of sins.* (James 5:19—20)

"Proverbs tells us, *'The fruit of the righteous is a tree of life, and he who wins souls is wise'* (Proverbs 11:30). It takes wisdom and gentleness to present the truth in such a way that the other person will accept it and apply it to themselves in a useful and redemptive way. There are, indeed, times when rebuke and condemnation are called for in order to awaken a person to the realities of what they're doing; at other times, gentleness and respect are called for. It takes a wise person to know the difference."

Words Can Bring Peace to Conflict

"Another piece of guidance is that wise words can bring peace in the midst of conflict. It doesn't take much wisdom to stir up trouble. Anybody who wishes can create conflict and bad feelings. What does call for wisdom is bringing calm into stormy sessions, bringing peace to conflicting ideas, bringing understanding into arguments that are getting out of control. Proverbs 15:1 says it well: *'A gentle answer turns away wrath, but a harsh word stirs up anger.'* It takes a wise person to be in a situation where there is strong difference of opinion and yet be able to remain controlled and understanding. *'A wise man's heart guides his mouth'* (Proverbs 16:23)."

Know When to Speak and When to Be Quiet

"Next, we must know when to speak and when to be quiet," Pierre said.

Elizabeth let out a little groan, "Uh-oh!" she exclaimed. Lloyd laughed and put his arm around her shoulder. They obviously had an understanding on this subject that escaped the rest of us.

"There are times, when saying something only inflames the situation," Pierre said, "when anything you have to say, no matter how right you are, won't help. At other times, you could say the same thing to the same person and it would be considered good advice and timely guidance.

"Sometimes peoples' minds are consumed by other matters and they won't accept what you saying. It takes great wisdom to know when difficult subjects need to be broached and when it is better to leave them alone. Marriage partners learn that there are times when the atmosphere isn't conducive to serious talks. This kind of wisdom takes understanding and sensitivity. It is wise to discipline and control your speech in such situations."

"To do this effectively is very delicate," said Elizabeth. "Can you give us some pointers about when we can appropriately speak the truth in love?"

Pierre nodded. "First, be sure of your facts. Be sure your criticism is accurate. Second, check your motive. Why do you want to say this to the person? Why do you want to say it now? Third, always surround the criticism with praise. There are many good things you can say that will encourage the person. Fourth, say it gently. Perhaps I should add a fifth pointer, which is that if you can't honestly do all of the above, then don't say anything."

Elizabeth smiled at this, but nodded her head in agreement.

Pierre moved to summarize his remarks. "In the Bible, the tongue is seen as a very powerful and important instrument. It takes considerable wisdom to be able to use this instrument well. A wise person uses his tongue and speech to develop a voice of encouragement. He uses his tongue to express praise and thanksgiving. With his mouth, he seeks to do good and spread a positive atmosphere. In his interactions with others, he seeks to build up and create confidence, not tear down and destroy. So much good can be done, so much goodwill can be generated, so much positive atmosphere can be created and courage renewed by good and wise talk.

"Not one of us is perfect when it comes to the use of our tongues. We could all do better. But a wise man's words and conversation is guided by the wisdom of his heart and is therefore a source of blessing and a conveyor of goodwill. He won't knowingly let his tongue be used by evil. Nor will he use his tongue to express the ill tempers of his spirit, the poor attitudes of his mind, or the hurts that are in his soul. The stream that flows from him will be pure, fruitful, blessed, and positive, producing good fruit wherever it goes."

When Pierre was finished, Elizabeth spoke up. "I want to thank you for what you've said today about wisdom and the words we speak. I know that I tend to speak too much. When I'm excited, I talk and talk and talk. A lot of it is quite frivolous and empty. Sometimes I say things I wish later on I had never said. I realize that I need to exercise some discipline and thoughtfulness before I speak and not let my speech be governed by how I feel. I need wisdom and strength here. What you've said will help me."

"Elizabeth isn't the only one who needs help here," I said. "Let's all pray for each other that we be given wisdom in all the things we say. Were we not told that if we lack wisdom, we should ask God for it? I've been asking for it, but now it might be helpful for us to pray for each other."

We knelt together in Pierre's home and prayed that wisdom would be given to us in what we say. It was a solemn occasion.

As we sailed back to our island, I sat at the back of the boat and quietly surveyed my friends. I felt a strong bond with them. I loved and appreciated each one of them.

I'll have to make a point of telling them this more often. I then looked past the boat to the Great Mountain. *I love it here. It's so beautiful and restful. This is where I want to live, and I want my friends to stay as well so we can be together. This is where I belong, and this is where I want to stay, on the Great Mountain beside the Sea of Tranquility.*

Topics for Discussion

1. Pierre said that a wise person is restrained and careful about what he says. Consider just how wise you are on the basis of what you say and how you say it.

2. From the Bible, Pierre lists practical ways in which we can guide the use of our tongues. List and discuss these practical Bible instructions.

TWENTY-EIGHT

Wisdom of Listening

THE NEXT MORNING, HERMES AND CHARLES RETURNED TO OUR ISLAND. I WAS a little disappointed when Hermes said we wouldn't go anywhere that day. Charles wanted to talk to us about another quality in wisdom that we would find helpful if we were to become citizens of the Great Mountain.

I had hoped we would move on and see some new territory, but I was willing to abide by the guidance of Hermes and Charles, who were so much more experienced than I was.

When we had gathered round the fire, Hermes said, "One of the great characteristics of wise people is that they have developed the ability to listen, and to listen carefully. Charles is one of the best listeners I have ever met, so listen to him as he talks to you today. Our purpose is to help you become good and wise listeners.

Charles took up a stick and poked the fire a bit. When it was burning to his satisfaction, he began his talk. "Jesus had a phrase that He used often. He would say, 'He who has ears to hear, let him hear.' He used this phrase as a way of urging people to listen carefully to what He was saying. Jesus understood that you could hear, but not really listen. You could hear words, but not absorb their meaning. You could see a situation, but not really understand it. Listening requires more than just hearing. It requires that we have an understanding of what we're hearing and be able to apply it to ourselves. Truly wise people develop this ability. They often hear things no one else hears and see things no one else sees. Good listening usually requires concentration, as well as appropriate responses. Listening adds understanding and insight beyond just hearing words."

It's Wise to Listen

"Jesus clearly associated wisdom with the ability to listen. Do you remember the story Jesus told about the wise man and the foolish man? The wise man built his house upon the rock, so that when the winds and floods came it would able to withstand the fury of the storm. On the other hand, the foolish man built his house upon the sand, and when the wind and floods came the house collapsed. Jesus said that *everyone who hears these words of mine and puts them into practice is like a wise man who built his house on the rock* (Matthew 7:24.) The characteristic of the wise man was that he was the one who heard and obeyed, who listened and responded.

"Wisdom is hearing, understanding, and then responding appropriately to what you hear. If you're going to act wisely in a certain situation, you had better understand what the situation really is. It's foolish to act without being fully aware of the facts. Every counselor knows that you have to listen to the whole story before rendering judgment. The ability to listen, absorb, understand and apply is an essential function of wisdom.

"One day, Jesus wept in grief over the city of Jerusalem. In spite of all the people had seen and heard, they still didn't understand or accept what was being said to them or done for them. Because they didn't really hear what God was saying to them, Jesus made that haunting cry,

> *O Jerusalem, Jerusalem, you who kill the prophets and stone those sent to you, how often I have longed to gather your children together, as a hen gathers her chicks under her wings, but you were not willing.* (Matthew 23:37)

"Lack of true listening is a major factor in people's downfall. God often mourned that He had to send prophets to the nation of Israel to warn them and plead with them to listen. God gave them the written law to guide them personally and nationally in the right direction, but they didn't pay attention to these instructions and constantly disobeyed them.

"Likewise, Jesus mourned over some of the great towns of Israel, like Capernaum and Bethsaida, towns on which He had concentrated much of His ministry efforts. He indicated that if places renowned for their wickedness, like Sodom and Gomorrah, had seen and heard the same things that had been seen and heard in these towns, they would have repented long ago. To Jesus, listening was an essential part of wise living."

Listen to the Whole Message

"It's wise to learn to listen to what others are really saying. It's wise to cultivate the ability to listen carefully. To really listen, you need to give your full attention. Listen carefully not only to what is said, but how it is said. Try to pick up the emotional content of the message. Sometimes people try to hide their true feelings when they speak. A good listener hears not just the sound of the voice, but also the emotional vibrations. Often people don't mean what they say. They may try to shrug something off, but the emotional overtones make it clear that they care very deeply. A good listener can hear the unspoken message. He listens to the heart as well as the voice.

"A good listener listens to all that is said. He doesn't let his mind wander when another person is speaking. He doesn't jump in with opinions before he has heard the whole story. He doesn't spend his time thinking about how he will respond when the other person is done talking. When people are arguing, they seldom listen. They only think about how they can properly oppose what the other says.

"A good listener tries to completely understand the opinion or problem of the other person. If they don't understand, they will ask questions and probe until they have a good understanding. They don't offer advice or bring up arguments until they completely understand. Wisdom is able to listen below the surface. It hears beyond words. It understands the spirit and heart of the other person."

Elizabeth reached over and took Lloyd by the hand. "That's one of things I love about Lloyd. He listens. He seems to understand how I feel. He doesn't always have an answer, but just the fact that he listens with understanding helps me. In fact, I don't always *want* a solution; I just want the opportunity to talk it out with someone who doesn't judge."

"Yes," agreed Charles. "Just listening and understanding can be enough to bring relief. On the other hand, so many misunderstandings arise when we don't listen. So many feelings are hurt. So many arguments are inflamed. There is a gift to listening; many a person or situation have been redeemed because someone listened to them."

Listening and Modern Devices

"Today, in spite of our multiplicity of communication tools, we don't listen very well," Charles said. "One of the drawbacks of modern technology, like email or texting, is that it's difficult by these means to pick up the language of the heart. Often what is being said isn't the whole message."

I looked over at Elizabeth and Lloyd. *They are such a wonderful couple and have such a strong relationship. They obviously care enough about each other to listen and understand.*

"I think that listening indicates a spirit of caring and love," I said to the group, "and that's what people respond to. If you cannot take time or interest to really listen, it indicates that you don't really care, and that your interest is somewhere else."

Charles nodded. "A loving, caring listener can have a powerful influence. Good listening conveys care, respect, and acceptance."

Listening to God

Charles paused while he put more logs on the fire. He then continued, but changed the focus. "Even more important than learning to listen to other people is the wisdom of learning to listen to God. It might just be that God has important things to say to us, but we don't listen. God has tremendous wisdom, far above ours; it would be wise to listen to Him. He knows us better than we know ourselves. While to us the future is blind mystery, He knows what lies ahead. He could truly guide us. He could show the best way for us to go, but we need to listen."

I really need to listen to this, I thought. *I don't think I understand how to listen to God.*

Peter put my thoughts into words. "I've been in religious circles all my life and people always say that God talks to them. But as far as I know, nobody has ever heard an actual voice they could hear with their ears. When you say God is talking, what do you mean?"

"Listening is about more than listening to an audible voice," Charles said. "God communicates in many different ways, and we need to learn to listen. God is a spirit and communicates spirit to spirit, heart to heart, soul to soul. The fact is that God is constantly trying to communicate with us. If there's a lack of communication between us and God, it's not because He doesn't speak but because we aren't listening very well. Learning to listen to God takes wisdom. He is the source of all wisdom. He knows and understands better than anyone else, but we need to know how to pick up His communications."

"How do you know when He's talking to you?" insisted Peter.

Listening and Communicating

Charles thought for a moment. "When it comes to our interaction with God, the word 'communicate' is better than the word 'talking.' Communication means much more than talking. I can talk without communicating. I can communicate without talking. Talking is one method of communication, but there are many other methods. When people say God is talking to them, they don't mean they hear a voice that speaks to them out of the sky."

Pointing to Lloyd and Elizabeth, Charles said, "I'm sure Lloyd and Elizabeth communicate in many ways other than talking to each other."

"You're right about that," said Lloyd with enthusiasm. "We've been married for quite a few years now. Being that close to someone for that length of time means you get to know a thing or two. Often when I mention to her what's on my mind, she responds, 'Why, I was just thinking about that myself.' There's a kind of telepathy going on. When she goes to the bank to check on her finances, when she comes out I can tell, without a word being spoken, whether the news is good or bad. She knows when I'm discouraged. I know when she's displeased with me. We communicate a great deal without actually talking."

Charles laughed at this.

Communication Needs a Transmitter and a Receiver

"For real communication to take place, you need both a transmitter and a receiver. I can speak, but if nobody is listening or understanding, I'm not communicating. So it is in our interaction with God; we not only talk to Him and tell Him all the things we want, but we also listen to him and pick up His messages to us.

"It's convenient to think of His communications in two ways. First, there is a general communication that's for everyone. Second, there is a personal communication that's private and personal, just for you. The general communications of God are like the transmissions of a radio station. They send out their signals which are designed for everybody, for the whole community. Anyone who has a receiver can pick up the message. On the other hand, the personal messages are like telephone calls. Nobody gets them but you.

"Because listening to God is an important part of developing the spirit of wisdom, let's look at these two methods in which God communicates."

God Communicates through Nature

"God communicates to all of us through the natural world. There's a beauty and wonder about nature that can stir the human spirit and make us aware that behind all this marvelous creation there is a Presence and Creator. When we see and appreciate this, it nudges us into a spiritual frame of mind. The natural world can stir within us wonder and awe that moves our soul and stimulates our minds, making us aware that we're something more than flesh and blood, skin and bones. Nature encourages us to think beyond the physical and reach out to the meaning and wonder beyond the atoms and molecules. Through nature, we can communicate with God.

"The Psalmist picks up this sense when he writes,

> *The heavens declare the glory of God; the skies proclaim the work of his hands. Day after day they pour forth speech; night after night they display knowledge. There is no speech or language where their voice is not heard. Their voice goes out into all the earth, their words to the ends of the world.* (Psalm 19:1–4)

"The poet William Wordsworth senses the same communication in nature. He wrote, in 'Tintern Abbey,'

And I have felt a presence
That disturbs me with the joy
Of elevated thought; a sense sublime
Of something far more deeply interfused.[8]

"Not everyone, of course picks up the message. Not everyone is listening. Most of us now live in cities, where the tendency is to become so engrossed in our houses and roads, our cars and equipment, our conveniences and comforts, that we miss it. We don't hear anything in nature. It takes skill and concentration to hear the messages of nature. But the fact that some don't hear the message doesn't mean it's not being transmitted."

I interrupted with a quiet voice, "Since I started on this journey and understood that a spirit of reverent awe towards God is the beginning of wisdom, I've taken time to cultivate this sense of God's presence in nature. I have become increasingly aware of this presence and find more and more joy and wonder in appreciating God's natural creation. It has become a source of spiritual food for my soul. I love nature and can sense my appreciation for God grow as I absorb the beauty and wonder all around me."

"Thank you for that," said Charles. "This is a good testimony, confirming how God does communicate through nature if we tune in and learn to listen."

God Communicates through Conscience

"Another way in which God tries to communicate with us is through our conscience. I'm sure God has spoken to every one of us here through our consciences. God has placed a spiritual receiver in the heart of every person, and we receive these spiritual vibrations from Him, telling us what's right and wrong. When we do something that our conscience thinks is wrong, the voice we hear disturbs us and we are not at peace. When we do what is right, the voice gives us a sense of approval. Some of us have more enlightened and sensitive consciences than others, but God has spoken to everyone at some point through their consciences. A wise man develops a mature conscience. Not all consciences are mature, but a wise man gives time and attention to listening to his conscience and seeks to develop its sensitivity."

---

8   William Wordsworth, *Selection from Wordsworth* (London, UK: Ginn and Company, 1956), 132.

God Communicates through Writing

"In our society, a lot of communication is done through writing. We write letters and books. We issue newspapers and magazines. We have email and we carry around our cellphones. It's common practice to hear from each other through some form of writing. God, too, communicates through writing. Through inspiration and revelation, God communicated with man the written word we call the Bible. Under His inspiration, the Bible writers expressed His thoughts, told His story, described His value system, and revealed Him through the life and death of His Son Jesus Christ. God has wonderfully and powerfully spoken to us through the Bible. It is wise to give great attention to absorbing and understanding the message of the Bible. For those who learn to listen, the Bible is full of messages from God. A man or woman who soaks themselves in the stories and principles of the Bible is likely to hear from God and receive wise and true guidance for their lives. To effectively hear from God, a person needs uncluttered time to meditate and concentrate on the word of God"

"Is that why some people call the Bible the Word of God?" asked Lloyd.

"Exactly," Charles said. "The Bible is God's word to us. In fact, the psalmist proclaims, *'Your word is a lamp to my feet and a light for my path'* (Psalm 119:104). God will talk to you through the Bible. You should spend time every day reading and meditating on the Bible and its messages."

God Communicates through People

"God can communicate with us through other people. Others influence and affect us. When God has people He can rely upon to be faithful in promoting His message, then He has a great treasure. Often the church does this."

Charles looked at Peter and smiled. "As our friend Peter can tell us, the church isn't perfect. It's full of people with limitations and imperfections. Down through the centuries, the church has sometimes gotten the message garbled and mixed up, yet in spite of it all the church has helped God get the message out. God has spoken through the church. The Gospel has been proclaimed. His Son has been revealed, and many have been enlightened and guided by the church.

"There are wise and godly people in the world who have had a great influence in the lives of others and in the outcomes of history. They have explained the workings of God to us and exhibited the likeness of God in the way they have lived. God often speaks to us through the lives and witness of godly people. Some of us have been privileged to have godly fathers and mother, wives or husbands, friends or acquaintances who have deeply influenced us. God has spoken to us through them."

God Communicates through the Holy Spirit

"God communicates with us by means of the Holy Spirit. God's presence and activity in the world today are centered in the work and ministry of His Holy Spirit. God does a lot of communicating today through the Holy Spirit, but we have to be able to hear Him. Jesus promised that after He left the disciples to go back to His Father in heaven, He would send someone to take His place. This other person is the Holy Spirit, who has become the voice and expression of God's presence and activity in the world. Jesus said to His disciples,

> *But I tell you the truth: It is for your good that I am going away. Unless I go away, the Counselor will not come to you; but if I go, I will send him to you. When he comes, he will convict the world of guilt in regard to sin and righteousness and judgment: in regard to sin, because men do not believe in me; in regard to righteousness, because I am going to the Father, where you can see me no longer; and in regard to judgment, because the prince of this world now stands condemned.* (John 16:7–11)

"God is at work around the world today through the Holy Spirit. He does this by creating sensitivity in the hearts of men to spiritual truths, moving us towards God. Jesus said the Holy Spirit would convict us of sin so we would reject it. He motivates us towards righteousness, encouraging us to seek Him. He makes us aware of our spiritual lives. The Holy Spirit is the great motivator and encourager. He restrains men from sin and points them to God. He communicates with us all the time, and we hear Him primarily in the privacy and intimacy of our own hearts.

"It may well be that many aren't listening to Him, acknowledging Him, or understanding what He's doing. Many don't heed his promptings or pay attention to his rebukes, but I believe He has spoken to us all in our hearts and consciences. It is the height of foolishness to turn a deaf ear to this inner voice of God and not hear what He's trying to accomplish in our lives."

"You know," I said, "I had very little to do with religion all of my life, but nevertheless I can understand this. Now that you describe the work of the Holy

Spirit, I see that I've often felt His inner stirring. I had a hunger in my heart for something more. I felt that there were more dimensions to life than I was experiencing. There were times when I wondered about God and felt guilty about my way of life. All these inner feelings and promptings could have been the voice of God speaking to me through the Holy Spirit."

"I think we've all been aware of the voice of the Holy Spirit in our lives," Peter said, "although we may not have known what to call it. I, too, often felt a hunger for God. I have felt my spirit searching for a better spiritual experience. I somehow knew it was there but didn't know how to reach it."

"Yes, God has been trying to communicate with us all," Charles said. "You may not be tuned in. You may not always understand the message. You may not be acknowledging Him. You may not like what you hear, but the message is being transmitted. It is indeed wise to tune into the voice of God and hear what He has to say."

By this time, the fire had died down. Charles got more wood and piled it onto the fire. When he had done this to his satisfaction, he returned to the conversation.

Personal Communication

"God, in addition to these general methods of communication, can communicate with you in very personal and private ways. In a sense God has your spiritual telephone number. He has things to say that are directed to you. He has insights that will apply to you and to your purpose. These personal communications are for your eyes only. But to receive these messages, you need to pick up the telephone and listen.

"You can imagine that these personal calls from God are very important. If I'm sitting at home reading the newspaper, or listening to the general communications coming from the television, and the telephone rings, almost inevitably I will give precedence to the telephone call. This call is for me and I give it priority attention."

I felt that this would be very pertinent to where I was in my spiritual journey. "This is really helping," I said. "On this journey, I've been trying to listen to God in the general sense you mentioned, and I'm finding it vivid and real. But now I'm fascinated by the idea that God would speak to me personally. So how does God communicate with us in this personal way?"

God Communicates Spirit to Spirit

"We can develop an awareness that, if acknowledged, can grow into an inner conviction that God is trying to convey messages to us. There comes an assurance that there is something in particular God wants you to do. Through the sensitive ears of the soul, many have become aware of a voice from God. As they acknowledged and obeyed it, this voice opened up new areas of fellowship and service to them."

Peter said, "I've heard many pastors and missionaries say they have heard the call of God to move into a life of service. Many preachers and prophets have sensed that they've received a message from God that must be proclaimed."

"Yes. Some have had a clear inner conviction that God is calling them to special kinds of service and work," Charles said. "They are so assured and confident in this that they may change their whole life in order to fulfill what they feel God has called them to do. God doesn't do this with everybody. They have received a telephone call and have answered it.

"This inner voice of God, however, isn't reserved only for a few who are called to some kind of special service. God has things He wants to say to all of us, and what He has to say can vary, but it's always important. Sometimes God's voice within us brings a sense of assurance that what we are doing is correct and meets with His approval. It can come as a beautiful sense of peace and harmony as God whispers to us that all is well. At other times, the voice warns us by a sense of inner resistance that what we're planning is not in keeping with His will. God can let us know that He's not pleased with what we're doing and He would like us to change.

"At times, the Holy Spirit can come to us with a message of enlightenment. When this happens, we see a truth in a vivid way that we have never experienced before. Our spirit is inspired and excited about a spiritual enlightenment. We may become aware of God's presence and support in a way that we need right at that moment. If we learn to listen to this quiet inner voice of God, we become increasingly aware of the reality of the spiritual dimension in our lives.

"God communicates in many different ways to our spirit, and always the message we receive is meaningful and wonderful and practical. But in order for us to receive these messages, we need to develop the ability to listen and be wise enough to interpret the voice correctly. Listening to God requires sensitivity in the spirit. We need to develop ears that gently open us to receive and understand what is being said. While there's no audible voice, the impression of His Spirit can be quite clear and understandable for those who learn to listen and obey."

"Please, Charles, I need help here," I said. "All kinds of questions come to my mind. How do we develop this spiritual wisdom of listening to God? How do we know how to interpret correctly what God is saying? How do we learn to know the difference between the voice of God and the voice of our own desires and wishes? How do we know when it's evil talking to us and not God?"

Listening to God Requires Wisdom

Charles smiled at my urgency. "You're on a journey into wisdom. Well, this is where wisdom becomes so very important. Too many people, in the absence of wisdom, jump to false conclusions or foolishly listen to inner promptings that aren't from God. Some have never learned to be sensitive to the promptings of the Holy Spirit, living their lives with the ears of their spirit clogged. They never hear. They never listen. Here are some pointers that can help us develop this skill of listening to and communicating with God."

You Must Want to Learn

"First, you have to really want to learn from God. If you don't think God has anything important to tell you, if you don't care whether you hear from Him or not, you'll be tuned out. If you only want to listen to your own way, following your own desires and fulfilling your own wishes, you won't have the right attitude to receive inner promptings from God. Though the promptings may come, they'll be largely ignored. You must want it, hunger for it, seek it. Jesus said, *'Ask and it will be given to you; seek and you will find; knock and the door will be opened to you'* (Matthew 7:7)."

You Must Practice

"Second, you must patiently practice this. We aren't good at listening to God. If we've attempted to communicate with God at all, it's usually in trying to get God to listen to us. We aren't experienced at reversing the process and listening to God, so we need to learn to do this and recognize our immaturity in it. When we speak to an infant, we may say things that are perfectly sensible and important, but the infant has no idea what we're saying. The baby may hear the noise, but that's it. But as we continue to talk, and the infant hears us repeat the same things over and over, he or she begins to discern some words. The baby begins to respond, to discern his or her own name, to comprehend simple things like 'Dad' and "Mom.' After a while, the child can put together basic sentences and grasp what we're saying. As time goes on, the mysteries of language become second nature to the child, who becomes proficient in the use of language.

"In the spiritual realm, we are like infants. God talks, but we cannot understand. As we practice and work at it, though, we become proficient. We begin to accurately pick up some messages. As time goes on, our spirits become wise enough to understand what God is saying and what God wants. This takes time and practice. This is where wisdom and the development of wisdom are so important. Just because a child doesn't understand us the first time we say something, we don't dismiss the whole exercise of learning the language. We keep on working at it, repeating the same thing until the message is received and the response given.

"So it is wise for us to earnestly desire to hear from God and practice listening for Him. Take time to open your spirit to the promptings of His Spirit. At first, it will seem strange and unfamiliar, but keep practicing with a humble sensitivity and keen desire. The process will become easier and more familiar. Soon you'll begin to hear, discern, and understand. One of life's most exciting and wonderful experiences will open up to you. You will be able to talk to God, and God will talk to you. There is a spiritual wisdom here that will be of vast value to you and the development of your soul.

Let God Take the Initiative

"Third, let God take the initiative. Remember that you're listening, not talking. We keep wanting to urge our agenda on God, wanting Him to listen to our desires. We want to project onto Him our plans and want Him to assure us of the correctness of our decisions. Because we want to impress God with the importance of what we're saying, we monopolize the conversation. While we like to imagine that what we're hearing is the voice of God, in reality it's the echo of our own words coming back to us.

"As long as you're talking, you're not listening. Don't jump to conclusions. Present yourself to God with an open and empty mind, and let Him begin to fill it. Take your time. God usually doesn't hurry. Don't make false assumptions about what He's going to say. It's not easy. We're so used to pursuing our own wishes that we find it difficult to strip ourselves of this habit and start listening to God with open hearts. Sorting this out requires wisdom indeed."

Ask for Wisdom

"Fourth, ask for wisdom. You ask for wisdom because you recognize that you're only a child in this matter. You're a rank amateur and have much to learn. Ask for wisdom to understand when you make mistakes. Pray for wisdom to understand what the voice of God is really saying to you. Pray for wisdom to be able to differentiate between the voice of God and the voice of our own wishes. Godly wisdom is vitally important."

There Are Other Voices

"Fifth, understand that there are more voices speaking to you than just the voice of God. We need to develop the ability to differentiate between all the voices that speak to us. We often hear the voice of our own wishes and desires, and they can disguise themselves so that they sound like the voice of God to the unwary. There is the voice of the devil, who tempts us and subtly tries to lead us astray. There are voices that come to us from other people; they want us to please them, or appease them; they want us to act in certain ways. In the midst of all this clamor, wisdom and spiritual understanding are needed to discern the voice of God and His message. We need to pray for wisdom, guidance, and discernment."

Listening to God for Personal Maturity

"Lastly, understand that this process of learning to listen is for your own spiritual development. God wants you to grow in your soul. He wants you to mature in your spiritual life. He wants you to experience more and more the wonders and joys of the spiritual dimension. God wants us to develop strong and mature experiences with Him. He wants us to become wise in the ways of the spirit.

"When a child is small, his parents make all of the decisions for him. They decide what he will eat, what he will wear, when he will go to bed. The child is too immature and helpless to make these decisions for himself. But as the child grows older, the child begins to choose and do some things for himself. The growing child chooses his own friends, decides what his interests are, and goes places without being accompanied by his parents. When a person reaches adulthood, he is expected to be wise enough to make decisions for himself. He doesn't phone his parents every morning to ask what to wear or what to have for breakfast. We expect mature adults to make these decisions for themselves. We believe mature adults can choose their own friends, determine their own entertainments, and figure out their own career and direction in life. We give them the responsibility to make their own decisions about marriage, family, and religion. The parents need to instill in them the values, abilities, and discipline to make wise and meaningful decisions. Parents don't expect to make these decisions for their children all their lives; they want their children to grow up.

"So, too, God wants you to grow up. He wants you to mature so you don't look to Him to micromanage your life. He wants you to develop the ability to make wise decisions. He wants you to be wise enough to set your life on the right course. He wants you to be mature enough to stick to the right values even when tempted to go wrong. He looks to you to become mature enough to know how to handle difficult people and stay strong in adverse situations. God's objective is not to protect you and keep you from all difficulty; His objective is to make you a wise and mature adult Christian who knows how to handle life with strength, faith, and maturity. He's always there when guidance is needed. He's always there with strength and grace, but our decisions are our own. Don't anticipate that God will direct you in every decision. He's trying to help you grow to maturity so you'll know understand in your own heart the right direction. So, God does talk, but it takes wisdom and discernment to learn how to listen and interpret what is being said, and how to apply it to victorious living."

This had been a long but very enlightening conversation. We clearly had many things to think about.

I thanked Charles on behalf of our group and was glad that there was still time left in the day for me to get some time alone to meditate on the things we had been taught. Rushing the process would short-circuit it and do damage in the long run.

As Hermes and Charles were leaving, Hermes told us they would return the next day to take us for a trip across the Sea of Tranquility to meet a woman named Gladys. This sounded exciting, so we waved goodbye and looked forward to the morning.

Topics for Discussion

1. What do you think Jesus meant by the phrase, "He that has ears, let him hear"?

2. Discuss the concept of the power of the listening ear. How important is good listening? How does good listening affect others? How does good listening affect you?

3. What methods does God use in His general communications?

4. Can you describe experiences when you were sure God was speaking to you personally?

5. What advice is given to us that would improve our ability to listen to God?

Twenty-Nine

Wisdom of the Mind

THE NEXT MORNING, RIGHT ON TIME, HERMES AND CHARLES ARRIVED AND WE quickly got into the boat with them.

"Today we're going to see an elderly woman named Gladys," Hermes said. "While Gladys lives alone, she's really very busy. Because of her age, she isn't able to move around very much, but she has developed such wisdom that people constantly come to her for advice and guidance. I'll ask Gladys to talk to you about the wisdom of the mind. She has a lifetime of experience in developing it."

Gladys lived in a small but appealing cottage at the foot of the Mountain, but she seemed entirely content in her simple surroundings. We followed Gladys into a sitting room and settled into comfortable chairs by a warm fire. She smiled at us and welcomed us to her home. I realized right away that while Gladys was frail in body, her mind was fresh and alive. She was going to talk to us about a subject she knew and understood well.

"There's an almost universal agreement," she began, "that anyone seeking to develop wisdom will need to give disciplined attention to his or her mind and what goes on in there. We understand that wisdom and what happens in a person's mind are closely tied together. While a wise person knows how to think, not all thinking is necessarily wise. We understand that if our thoughts are wrong, our decisions and actions won't be wise. If our thoughts are false, our attitudes will be affected.

"The book of Proverbs says of a person, *'as he thinketh in his heart, so is he'* (Proverbs 23:7, KJV). What goes on in the mind comes out eventually in the decisions, attitudes, reactions, and values that a person lives by. If a person is selfish in their thinking, that's going to be reflected in a selfish outlook on life. A person who only thinks shallow and superficial thoughts isn't going to follow a deep and thoughtful direction in life. A person who often thinks of God and His ways is going to give serious attention to God in the patterns of his life. Your thoughts are like seeds, and they'll eventually grow into fruit. If you sow weeds, you aren't going to harvest grapes. What you feed your mind will eventually affect the health and vigor of your soul.

"Jesus indicated that many of the real battles for supremacy in the human heart are the battles of the mind. He said,

> *Make a tree good and its fruit will be good, or make a tree bad and its fruit will be bad, for a tree is recognized by its fruit... The good man brings good things out of the good stored up in him, and the evil man brings evil things out of the evil stored up in him.* (Matthew 12:33–35)

"To Jesus, the real moral and spiritual battles are often fought in a person's heart and mind. In His Sermon on the Mount, He said that adultery can happen in the mind, in the thinking and imagination of a person, long before it becomes a physical fact. He said,

> *You have heard that it was said, 'Do not commit adultery.' But I tell you that anyone who looks at a woman lustfully has already committed adultery with her in his heart.* (Matthew 5:27–28)

"The thoughts we welcome into our minds have a powerful effect on who we are and what we do. The imaginations we allow to dominate our thinking, whether good or bad, will eventually filter down and color our personality and our lifestyle.

"There is little purpose in talking about being wise and having a wise approach to life if we aren't going to address the matter of what we think and how we think. Wrong thoughts eventually issue in wrong decisions and bad action. Good thoughts eventually bring goodness into our decisions and actions."

Gladys paused to see if any of us had comments. We were uncharacteristically quiet; we all understood what she was saying and were in agreement with her. I was so amazed at the clarity and sharpness of her thinking for one so advanced in years.

"A good illustration of this is found right at the beginning of the Bible, with the catastrophic story of Eve. Eve was the first woman created and was introduced to the Garden of Eden. The garden was a beautiful place and life there was happy and fulfilling. Her relationship with Adam was peaceful and loving, as was her relationship with the natural world, and with God.

"In our minds, the Garden of Eden was the ideal world, the perfect place for humanity to live. Eve wasn't troubled by discord, hostility, greed, or cruelty. Today we can only imagine what life would have been like there. The garden provided all that was necessary for happy, contented, and satisfied living. Here in the garden, she worked, played, and rested, and found her heart was full of goodwill and love towards all."

It All Started in the Mind

"That is, until Eve allowed some wrong thoughts to enter her mind. She welcomed and entertained those thoughts, allowing them to grow and develop until she finally acted upon them, spoiling forever the idealistic existence that had been designed for her by God.

"It was into this idealistic situation that the devil came. His objective was to try and disrupt the plan and purpose of God for the world. The devil wasn't out to bring blessing and benefits; he was out to destroy. With a keen insight and understanding, he started the process by inserting some wrong seeds of thought into Eve's mind."

Seeds of Thought

"One day, as Eve was enjoying the warmth and security of the garden, the devil came to her and suggested a thought she hadn't considered before: *'He said to*

the woman, "Did God really say, 'You must not eat from any tree in the garden'?'"
(Genesis 3:1). That statement wasn't true. That isn't what God said. But the devil
doesn't adhere to the truth when it's to his advantage to lie.

"Eve's first reaction to this wrong thought was to correct it, by stating what
God really said:

> *We may eat fruit from the trees in the garden, but God did say, 'You*
> *must not eat fruit from the tree that is in the middle of the garden,*
> *and you must not touch it, or you will die.'* (Genesis 3:2–3)

"So far, everything was fine. Eve initially rejected the negative thought that
came to her mind and didn't accept the false statement about what God had said.
If the story had ended there, catastrophe would have been avoided.

"How easy it is at the early stages to reject negative and hostile thoughts. At
this stage, they can be dealt with simply. They can easily be rejected. Life can go
on as normal without any harm done. But the story didn't end there."

The Seed Takes Root

"The devil pushed the process to the next stage, but the battle was still in Eve's
mind. The devil knew he had to change the way Eve thought. To do this, he now
inserted a false notion by expanding his lies in a new direction and insinuating
bad motives to God. He contradicted what God had said by saying,

> *You will not surely die… For God knows that when you eat of it*
> *your eyes will be opened, and you will be like God, knowing good*
> *and evil.* (Genesis 3:4–5)

"The fact that the statement was false was of no significance to the devil;
he just wanted Eve to entertain the thought. He wanted her to think God
was withholding something from her and that it would be to her benefit to
discount what God had said. He implied that all kinds of benefits would come
to her if she disregarded God and ate the fruit of the forbidden tree. He also
promised that the dire results God had predicted if she ate the fruit wouldn't
happen.

"The issue was now becoming more critical. Instead of rejecting the suggestions of the devil outright, Eve entertained the thoughts."

Gladys shook her head sadly. "In the mind, it is fairly easy to reject and dismiss negative, hostile, and antagonistic thoughts when they first come. They have no strength. They have not taken root. They are easily destroyed. But when we begin to entertain them, wonder about them, nurse them, accept them, then they do take root and establish themselves. When we do this, their strength and influence grows. It is wise, in the battleground of the mind, to destroy enemy thoughts early before they gain strength and influence."

The Seed Matures

"Eve, however, wasn't wise in how she dealt with these suggestions from the devil. She thought to herself, *Could this be true? Is God really withholding something? Will I really become wise and enlightened if I eat the fruit? Will eating the fruit usher me into a new dimension of understanding and insight? Will I really be wiser and more like God? If I eat the fruit, will I really die?* And so she mulled over these thoughts, giving them credence. She showed respect for them by allowing them to settle in her mind. This nourishing and encouraging of negative thoughts is the start of the downward slide into chaos."

Gladys again paused, but all of us were captivated by the story and made no comment. "The next step in the process was that Eve decided to go and have a look at the tree. You can see that her thoughts were now beginning to be translated into action. *It won't do any harm just to go and look at it. I'm not doing anything wrong, I'm only looking.* It's true that she hadn't yet outwardly disobeyed God, but inwardly she was toying with the idea. She was considering it. While she wasn't saying yes, neither was she saying no. With every step she took towards the tree, the evil suggestions gained credibility and power. She could still have stopped the whole process by turning around and dismissing the evil suggestions from her mind. But Eve wasn't wise enough to do that."

The Seed Becomes Fruit

"Once Eve got to the tree, the process took on a new and more alluring dimension—she could now physically do what before she had only thought about:

> *When the woman saw that the fruit of the tree was good for food and pleasing to the eye, and also desirable for gaining wisdom, she took some and ate it.* (Genesis 3:6)

"When Eve looked at the tree, she saw that there were things about it that were desirable. It was a beautiful tree and the fruit looked good to eat. The issue was now spilling out of her thought life and into the physical world. She felt within her a growing desire for the fruit of the tree. Her appetites were awakened. The more she looked, the more she wanted it. She hungered for the fruit. She wanted to experience this thing for herself. She felt less and less like denying herself and more and more like indulging.

"She stood there, with so much at stake, and knew she had to make a vital decision. It was still possible for her to say no, to reject the thought, to not eat the fruit, to turn around and go back. But at the point of decision, Eve made her choice and it was the wrong one. She reached out. She picked the fruit. She ate it. The deed was done. The choice was made.

"Eve made a critical decision. She agreed to act upon her thoughts and give in to her desires. She did this in clear violation of God's wishes and command. Before she actually reached out her hand and picked the fruit, she had already consented to it in her mind. The battle had already been fought and lost in her thoughts.

"She was, of course, able to justify her wrong actions by excuses manufactured in her own mind. She gave credence to the suggestions of the devil that eating this fruit would make her wise. It would help her to be more like God. It would assist her in seeing what was right and wrong. She imagined, wrongly, that this would open up all kinds of doors for her and usher in new, beneficial experiences. With these thoughts in her mind, she justified herself for disobeying God."

Unwise Thinking Leads to Unwise Actions

At this point, Gladys leaned back in her chair and sighed. "Allowing a negative thought to fester eventually brings us to the point of decision. Do we accept this thought? Do we agree with it? Will we do something to implement it? Will we act on it? When we get to this stage, whether we actually turn our thoughts into action or not, the fact is that the battle of the mind has been lost.

"Another interesting factor in this story is that once she ate the fruit, she immediately turned to Adam and gave it to him to eat. She became a missionary for evil. She wanted company in her wrongdoing. She wanted to win others over so they would join her in her folly. This is the nature of evil; it wants to draw others in, to feel the security that others are doing the same thing and endorsing it. This multiplies the pain. This spreads the corruption. The desire of sin to evangelize is extremely strong. It spreads the corruption by getting others to think as it thinks, do as it does, and say as it says.

"What started as a simple but bad thought in Eve's mind grew and evolved until it became a full-blown passionate temptation, to which she yielded and brought incredible harm to herself and others. How foolish. It could all have been stopped so easily."

This story fascinated me, so I said to Gladys, "Tell me, is the opposite true? You traced the evolution of a bad thought, which grew and developed in Eve's mind until she acted upon it. But if you entertain good thoughts and nourish them and give them attention, will they, too, grow and develop into good actions and good decisions?"

"Oh yes," said Gladys. "The evolution of the mind can develop towards righteousness or unrighteousness, to wisdom or folly, to growth and maturity or shrinking and selfishness. The same process of thinking that encouraged Eve into sin can encourage us to righteousness. True wisdom understands this process and knows how to encourage and nourish the development of righteousness through the wise use of the mind. The important thing is what you feed into your mind. Let's trace the thought processes we must all go through and see how to deal with them wisely. The importance of dealing wisely with our thought life is vital to the health and vigor of our personalities and souls."

The First Step

First, the simple thought comes. It could be a thought to praise and worship God, a thought of thankfulness, a thought of goodwill and happiness… or it could be a thought towards lust, a thought towards anger and bitterness, a thought towards hurt or discouragement. Thoughts come to all of us. This cannot be helped. But a wise person will avoid situations where one's thoughts trend towards the negative, lustful, or hostile. You can deliberately feed into your mind good or bad thoughts. You do it by what you read, what you look at, what you talk about. You do it in the places you go and the company you keep.

"But are there not times when thoughts arrive in your mind unheralded and unforeseen?" Elizabeth asked with some hesitation. "Sometimes bad thoughts just seem to pop up without any conscious effort on my part."

Lloyd supported her. "Yes, thoughts come and we cannot prevent them. We are the gatekeepers of the mind, and we can encourage the right thoughts to enter and prevent wrong thoughts by dismissing them. There are times when the gatekeeper is asleep, though, or at least not alert. This seems to be part of being human. I remember someone saying that you cannot prevent birds from flying over your head, but you can stop them from building a nest in your hair."

Gladys laughed at this. "You're right. While we cannot prevent all negative thoughts from entering our minds, we can prevent them from settling in. The best way to do it is both to reject them and deliberately focus our thoughts on things that are good. We can cultivate a lifestyle where the larger portion of our thought life can be devoted to the good, the righteous, and the positive. When bad thoughts do enter our minds, and they will, they don't need to be accepted and entertained. We are not a slave to our minds. We are masters of them."

What Is Accepted and Rejected

"Second, we decide whether we're going to accept the thought or reject it," Gladys continued. "You are, as Lloyd said, the gatekeeper. A wise gatekeeper will only allow thoughts which are good and positive. An unwise gatekeeper will allow in all kinds of wayward thoughts. Wisdom is being able to determine which thoughts should be rejected and which should be welcomed. In the early stages, we can fairly easily decide if we're going to welcome or dismiss a thought. We are very much in control.

"For example, let's say a thought of thankfulness comes to your mind. It is wise to immediately latch on to this and develop it. There is much to be thankful for—God has been good, the world is so beautiful, people have been so kind. So, you accept this thought as something that's worthy of pursuit. This is good and wise. Suppose a thought of goodwill comes to you. You suddenly conceive that you could build a bridge of friendship to someone, or you see a way in which you could create some goodwill, or you believe there's a way for you to break down a barrier between you and another person. You think of the good things about them, remembering the good things they've done. You endorse this, accept it, and nourish it. This is wise."

Having thought carefully about this, I felt I had to make a confession to the group. "But isn't the very opposite true as well? A man with whom I worked once wronged me and didn't treat me the way I thought I should be treated. It wasn't a big issue, but I mulled over the offense in my mind. I relived the grievance. I inflamed the supposed insult over and over again. I was, as you say, welcoming and endorsing this bad way of thinking instead of dismissing it. I was being unwise. The more I fed the bad thoughts, the stronger they became. If I had been wise, I would have realized that this could lead to all kinds of bad feelings and negative attitudes. But I didn't reject the thoughts, or even combat them. I nourished them and let them settle in my mind. What happened to Eve happened to me. My thoughts influenced my actions. I avoided the man. I said some things to him that weren't nice. I didn't like him, and when making decisions at work, I found myself disagreeing with him, even when I knew that what he was saying was correct. Now that I'm alert to the power of thought, I'll be wiser and more careful."

"Thank you for sharing that, Colin," Gladys gently said. "It does, indeed, show us the power of thought once it gets flowing in our minds. The important thing is to guide good, pure water into the channels of our minds and keep out anything that would pollute or shame us."

Nourishing Our Thoughts

"Third, once the thought has entered, we either reject it or we move on and consciously encourage and cultivate the thought. We feed it or starve it. This is our choice. There's an interesting story told of an ancient Indian tribal chief. His grandson was deeply troubled by the bad way people in the tribe sometimes treated each other. He asked his grandfather, 'Why can people be so nasty and hateful?' The grandfather gave the question some thought, realizing that it was important for his grandson.

"Finally he said, 'There are two wolves that live in the heart of every person. One is a good wolf and the other is a bad wolf, and these two wolves are constantly fighting for control over the person's heart.'

"The boy thought about this for a while and then asked again, 'But grandfather, which one of the wolves wins the fight?'

"The grandfather replied, 'Whichever one you feed.'

"There is a lot of wisdom there. Into all of our minds comes good thoughts and bad thoughts. These thoughts can wilt through lack of nourishment, or flourish if they are fed. If you focus on bad thoughts, as Colin said, they will increase in strength until they're the dominant spirit and attitude in your mind. It's amazing how quickly thoughts of bitterness, hatred, hostility, selfishness, and pride can grow when they're given attention."

"We are warned in the Bible to watch and be careful about which thoughts we entertain in our minds," Lloyd said. "The book of Hebrews says, *'See to it that no one misses the grace of God and that no bitter root grows up to cause trouble and defile many'* (Hebrews 12:15).

Gladys nodded. "Yes, that's the perfect verse for this. We must give care to the thoughts we allow to live in our minds. The fact is that our personality and decision-making functions are greatly affected by our thoughts. The more time and focus you give to them, the healthier and the stronger they become. The message of wisdom is clear here. Consciously feed those thoughts that are positive and good and healthy, and dismiss the thoughts that are negative and selfish and hostile.

"The Bible is clear that the battle for the mind is crucial for the healthy and strong development of our personalities and walk with God. The Apostle Paul urges the Christians in Philippi by saying,

> *Finally, brothers, whatever is true, whatever is noble, whatever is right, whatever is pure, whatever is lovely, whatever is admirable—if anything is excellent or praiseworthy—think about such things.*
> (Philippians 4:8)

"We all have the power to control our thoughts. We have the choice to saturate our minds with the positive, the lovely, and the good, and dismiss that which is unworthy, tarnished, and demeaning. The river of the mind divides here. We have a choice as to which channel we will take. One channel is positive and leads to God and a healthy personality. The other is unhealthy and will carry us into rough and dangerous waters that could eventually ruin and destroy us.

"Because we have the ability to control our thoughts, Paul urges us to *'take captive every thought to make it obedient to Christ'* (2 Corinthians 10:5). We can control how we think and what we allow to dominate our minds. We can consciously encourage healthy thoughts and equally discourage the unhealthy ones. It is wise and fruitful to guard our thinking so that our thoughts are 'obedient to Christ.' This brings a positive and hopeful attitude to our lives and helps us make wise decisions."

Thinking Like Christ

Lloyd again contributed at this point. "I think the Apostle Paul said something about having the same mind as Christ. Does that mean we should try to develop the same thinking patterns and mental habits that Jesus had?"

"Yes," Gladys said. "Paul talks about our hearts and personalities being transformed by the renewing of our minds. A change in thinking can truly transform the atmosphere and attitudes of our lives. We would become different people if we began to think differently. Paul also says,

> *Do not conform any longer to the pattern of this world, but be transformed by the renewing of your mind. Then you will be able to test and approve what God's will is--his good, pleasing and perfect will.* (Romans 12:2)

"Right thinking can transform you. Right thinking can clear a lot of the gloom and tension from your life. Right thinking can guide you into right decisions, right attitudes, and right obedience. So fill your mind with good things. Pursue righteousness in your thinking. Let the atmosphere of faith, hope, and love sink into the depths of your mind until more and more you think like Christ. This is wise. This is true. This is fruitful. That's why we're told, *'Be joyful always; pray continually; give thanks in all circumstances, for this is God's will for you in Christ Jesus'* (1 Thessalonians 5:16–18)."

Thoughts Affect Emotions

"Once the thoughts are established and embedded in your mind, they'll begin to affect your emotions. This is the next step. Once thoughts are welcomed and endorsed in our minds, they influence our emotional state. We feel the joy we've been thinking about. We begin to feel the goodwill for which we have been making plans. Good thinking brings about good feelings. Peace, joy, praise, love, and hope will flourish in the heart that thinks joyful and hopeful thoughts. In order to love God with all our hearts, we have to love Him with all our minds. That means He is often in our thoughts.

Gladys nodded in my direction. "The opposite is true, as Colin described. If you allow bitter thoughts to dominate, you will soon feel bitter. If you allow negative thoughts to dominate, you will soon feel discouraged. If you think pride, you will feel pride. The writer of Proverbs says it rather vividly: *'A cheerful heart is good medicine, but a crushed spirit dries up the bones'* (Proverbs 17:22)."

No Excuses, Please

"The next step in the evolution of our minds is that we begin to justify ourselves and make it look reasonable to think and feel as we do. Most people who are burning up with resentment think they have good cause to be resentful. Those who spend much time scheming revenge on others think they have good reason for doing this. Those who are consumed with doubts have concluded that they have a good basis for doubt. We can always take our unrighteousness and dress it up in the clothes of righteousness. Jesus talked about those people who *'come to you in sheep's clothing, but inwardly they are ferocious wolves'* (Matthew 7:15)."

I nodded in agreement. "Yes, I can confirm that. We can always manufacture good reasons for doing bad things."

"Beware when you start trying to construct good reasons for having a bad attitude or an unrighteous spirit," continued Gladys. "Regardless of your reasoning, bad is bad, righteous is righteous, and it is unwise to let your mind confuse you and think otherwise. Entertain thoughts of goodwill and you'll soon be thinking of ways you can do good for someone. Thoughts of gentleness and kindness soon result in plans to help and to heal. Thoughts of love and care develop into schemes whereby we can enrich and bless others. Thoughts of worship and gratitude to God will soon show us good reasons for gratitude.

"The next step in the evolution is clear. Once your feelings have been stimulated and you have convinced yourself that your thinking is justified, the next step is action. This soon results in actions, words, and attitudes that can be seen. When you've developed the mind of Christ, you begin to speak with encouragement. You perform deeds of kindness and exhibit a spirit of forgiveness. Love flows from you in understanding, goodwill, and thoughtfulness. Once you love God, you want to do His will. You act and live righteously. On the other hand, if you've let your mind be dominated by resentfulness, then the resentfulness will begin to show. You gossip. You hurt others by your words. Your attitudes become indifferent and thoughtless. You cannot keep the edge out of your voice. Your pride can be seen. You try to undercut and dismiss others. The outward actions of your life reveal the contents of your mind."

You Are a Missionary

"In the last step, like Eve, you become a missionary for your type of thinking. You consciously try to influence others, either for good or bad. If you have the mind of Christ, your influence in this world will be helpful and righteous. If you let evil control your mind, you will become a missionary for evil. Your influence will be negative. You will discourage, hurt, and demean, and try to draw others into this same attitude. Make no mistake about it, you are a missionary, one way or the other. Your thinking will eventually have an influence on others. You will act and express yourself in ways that convince others to agree with you and support you.

"Jesus summed it up very well when He said;

> *By their fruit you will recognize them. Do people pick grapes from thornbushes, or figs from thistles? Likewise every good tree bears good fruit, but a bad tree bears bad fruit. A good tree cannot bear bad fruit, and a bad tree cannot bear good fruit. Every tree that does not bear good fruit is cut down and thrown into the fire. Thus, by their fruit you will recognize them.*" (Matthew 7:16–20)

"Gladys, you've used the word 'evolution' to describe the process of developing the mind of Christ," I said. "Does that mean this is a process and we need to have patience and persevere at it over a period of time?"

"Yes," said Gladys. "Think of your mind as a big pot that's filled with water. If you drop a touch of sugar into the water, it will make little difference. But if you continually add sugar and stir it around, gradually the water in the pot will get sweeter and sweeter. The more sugar you add, the sweeter it will become. You cannot change your thinking habits or the contents of your mind overnight. But as you patiently and continually add sugar, you will begin to change the flavor of your mind. The day will come when the dominant flavor is sweet."

Gladys looked around at us all and made some concluding remarks. "Wisdom is very much a matter of the mind. Wisdom will guide your mind to think the right things and develop the right thoughts. You don't find a wise man who's foolish in his mind. The thoughts of a wise man are wise. The thoughts of a fruitful man are fruitful. The thoughts of a godly man are godly. The thoughts of a righteous man are righteous. Be wise and let your mind *be the same as that of Christ Jesus*' (Philippians 2:5), the wisest of all men."

Silence reigned. The explanation seemed quite clear to us and we had no more questions. We were impressed; a solemn atmosphere held us. It was Hermes who finally thanked Gladys for sharing her wisdom with us. In this, we all agreed. We had a time of prayer together and made preparations to leave.

As we were leaving, a knock came to the door and a young couple stood outside. They, too, wanted to visit with Gladys and seek advice from her.

"It's no wonder that people keep coming to Gladys," I commented as we made our way back to the island. "When you become that wise, you don't need to force yourself on anyone. People come to you. They recognize your value without you promoting yourself. I wish I was as wise as Gladys."

Topics for Discussion

1. Consider how easily Eve could have dismissed the devil early in the process. and how difficult it became at the end of the process. What is the lesson to be learned from this?

2. Consider the idea that Eve became a missionary for evil. Have you ever experienced people who try to convert you to their evil thinking? Have you ever tried to convert others to wrong ways of thinking?

3. Trace the development and nourishment of your thought life.

4. What are the effects of having the mind of Christ?

THIRTY

Wisdom of the Heart

THE NEXT MORNING, WE WERE GLAD TO AGAIN SEE HERMES AND CHARLES ARRIVE in their boat. They invited us to join them and we all sailed to a far part of the Sea of Tranquility.

"Today we are going to take you to a retreat center," said Hermes. "The center is a special place where people from the main community on the Great Mountain can go for a period of rest and renewal. It's not set up like a classroom; it's designed to give you an experience-centered lesson. In the center, the leader will want you to enter into the story and become a participant rather than an observer. You don't hear the lesson so much as experience it. As far as possible, we want you to feel that you are there when it's happening."

"This seems quite different," I said, sounding impressed. "I'm looking for-ward to it!"

"Indeed it is. In fact, this will be your last lesson before deciding whether to stay by the Sea of Tranquility or not. It's absolutely crucial that you grasp what is said today."

"If we decide to stay," I asked, "where will we live?"

"Most people live at the foot of the Great Mountain, on the coast. It's a most beautiful place to live. Once you're there, you won't want to live anywhere else."

This sounded very promising.

"So, what is this important lesson we will be taught today?" Peter asked.

"Today you'll hear about the wisdom of the heart. As the title suggests, we'll really get down to the heart of the matter. More than anything else, wisdom is a matter of the heart. If you don't get this, you'll never feel quite at home living here."

This statement sounded so serious that I was filled with anticipation as we approached the retreat center.

"In the center you'll visit today, you'll learn about the experience Jesus had when He was tempted by the devil in the wilderness," Hermes explained. "I'll say it to you again: to live successfully on the Great Mountain, you'll have to be sure that your hearts are set on the right things. We need to learn to love God with our minds, but also with our hearts. See, we're almost there."

A log building sat amongst the trees near the edge of the sea. We were met there by a woman named Sheila. Hermes introduced us and we understood that Sheila was to guide us in our study. She led us into a room that was quite dark and without windows. A screen was in place against one of the walls and reclining chairs were set up in front of the screen. Sheila invited us to make ourselves comfortable.

When we were settled, Sheila said, "Today we're going to focus on a very important aspect of wise living. The wise life is to seek to love God with all our hearts. A constant struggle for humanity is our need to establish the best values in our hearts, and then give adequate energy to them. Jesus understood and experienced this very human struggle. Indeed, it was at this very level, the level of His basic values and priorities, that Satan tried to derail Jesus' ministry.

"He faced a great struggle with evil at the outset of His public ministry. Jesus had to decide which things were going to be really important if He was to fulfill His mission. He had to establish in His heart those things which had to take priority. It takes great wisdom for us to know what to give our primary attention to. Other things may be legitimate but are of secondary importance. The great issue of life is determining what our prime objectives are and learning to give ourselves to meeting those objectives. Jesus' struggle wasn't simply between what was obviously good and what was obviously bad, but rather between what was essential and what was not essential, between the important and the all-important. Settling these issues in our hearts is the center of wisdom."

The Baptism

Sheila turned on a projector and a picture came up on the screen. The screen took up most of the wall, so we had the feeling of being drawn into the image, as if we were really there. It was a picture of a river, with a man in primitive clothing standing in the water. A crowd of people dressed in ancient Middle East clothing, were gathering on the banks of the river. The men were bearded and all the women, and some of the men, had shawls over their heads. All were giving attention to the man in the river.

"I want you to watch the screen and listen to the narration," Sheila said. "We can stop at any time if you have questions or want to make comments. What you see before you is the River Jordan in Palestine. The man is John the Baptist and he's talking to the crowds of people on the riverbank. Now, watch and listen."

The figures on the screen began to move and a well-modulated male voice spoke through the sound system: "It was a day like no other. Great crowds of people flocked to the lonely, desolate spot on the River Jordan to hear the message of the newest sensation in Israel, the preaching of John the Baptist. John was a strange man."

Here the picture focused on John the Baptist. "He lived most of his life in the lonely hardships of the desert. He didn't surround himself with any comforts or luxuries. His dress was a primitive, unadorned cloak made of camel's hair. His food was the basic desert fair of locusts and wild honey. Nevertheless, this strange, unlikely man stirred up a great deal of excitement in the nation.

"When he preached, John made no appeal to the comforts and greed of his audience. He was fearless, blunt and passionate. He preached a message of repentance because, he said, the long-awaited Messiah was about to appear, and people needed to prepare for this great event by forsaking their sins and getting right with God.

"In spite of the ruggedness of the man and his message, John captivated the imagination of the nation. His message of a coming Messiah awakened a deep longing in the hearts of the people for the emergence of a leader who would lead Israel to new levels of power, prosperity, and freedom. So they came to hear him. John publicly baptized those who accepted his message and were prepared to repent. Such was the success of the movement that many, from all levels of society, were baptized.

"But this day, the day you are watching, was different. By the time this day ended, everything had changed. It started out regularly enough, with John preaching to the crowds and baptizing those who wished. The picture you see shows John standing in the river. One by one, those who wished to be baptized waded out to him. Mingling with the crowd that day was Jesus of Nazareth. Not many knew him. He wasn't a national figure. He was a relatively unknown carpenter from the village of Nazareth in the distant province of Galilee. But when it came time for the baptisms, Jesus stepped out from amongst the crowd and walked towards John." The camera zoomed in on Jesus. "When John saw Jesus come towards him, he was gripped with a sense of unshakable recognition. This was the man he had been preaching about. This was the long-anticipated Messiah.

The picture on the screen showed vivid images. John stood in the water with hands trembling with excitement. John raised his arm and pointed to Jesus. An uncanny silence descended upon the crowd. They sensed that something significant was going to happen. All eyes followed the man to whom John was pointing.

The voice of the narrator took up the story: "As Jesus strode with purpose towards John, John, with his strong voice, shouted in great conviction and awe, *'Look, the Lamb of God, who takes away the sin of the world!'* (John 1:29) No one stirred. Everyone was captivated by the drama of the moment. John continued,

> *This is the one I meant when I said: 'A man who comes after me has surpassed me because he was before me.' I myself did not know him, but the reason I came baptizing with water was that he might be revealed to Israel."* (John 1:30–31)

We watched the scene unfold before us.

"When Jesus and John came together in the waters of the River Jordan, John protested to Jesus, *'I need to be baptized by you, and do you come to me?'* (Matthew 3:14) But Jesus insisted, so John dipped him under the waters of the river. As He came up, with water still dripping from his hair, and as the large crowd watched, John saw an amazing thing. The Bible says,

> *As soon as Jesus was baptized, he went up out of the water. At that moment heaven was opened, and he saw the Spirit of God descending like a dove and lighting on him. And a voice from heaven said, 'This is my Son, whom I love; with him I am well pleased.'* (Matthew 3:16–17)

"The crowds, who saw and heard this were stunned. John the Baptist felt his heart fill with excitement—his ministry and prophecies had come to fulfillment. For Jesus, it was a moment of great assurance. For years, He had been aware of a growing consciousness within Him that he was, indeed, the Son of God, and now this personal understanding was confirmed by a public affirmation, both from John the Baptist and God Himself. The convictions that had been burning in the privacy of His heart were now dramatically and publicly confirmed."

The picture on the screen pulled back until we could see the whole scene from a distance. And then the action stopped. The voice, however, continued.

"This event sealed Jesus' conviction that He was ready to begin His work and fulfill His destiny. The task God had given Him was about to start in earnest. But some issues had to be settled right at the beginning. Issues like, what methods should be adopted in order to fulfill the purposes of God? How should He conduct His ministry? He couldn't afford any mistakes or misdirection. This work had to be clear, authentic, and devoid of error. In order to fulfill the plan of God, what should He prioritize? The convictions that had grown in His heart over years of preparation now had to be expressed publicly before the world. This would take great wisdom—wisdom of the heart.

"Jesus, in response to these momentous events and to settle these questions, withdrew into the wilderness to be alone for a time." Here, the pictures on the screen changed to a desolate desert place where Jesus sat alone. "Many questions had to be answered. What was the purpose of His ministry? How best could He reveal God to the people? How could he convince the people that He really was the Son of God? Who should He choose as His disciples? How should He handle the jealous opposition that was sure to arise?"

At this point, Sheila stopped the projector. "These are the fundamental questions of wisdom that we, too, must settle in our hearts. What values should be given priority in our lives? What is most important? What should come first? And how do we conduct life in such a way that we provide the time and attention necessary for the nourishment, encouragement, growth, and development of these values? Jesus established all this in His mind for the next forty days when he was alone in the wilderness.

"The Bible indicates that these forty days were days of great struggle and testing. It was during this time that the devil tempted Him. It is important for us to notice the nature of the temptations. The devil tried to get Jesus to adopt secondary values, to accept wrong motivations, and to believe in false priorities. In many ways, as we try to absorb the wisdom of the heart, we face similar struggles. These were the temptations of the heart, touching on our values, priorities, purposes, and motives. They were temptations to do good things the wrong way and for the wrong purpose. These temptations get to the heart of what's ultimately wise, or foolish, in our basic values and purpose in life. Just as Jesus had to settle these issues in His heart, so do we, if we wish to live wisely in the twenty-first century. Jesus' example can help us to establish the same wise principles for our lives."

The First Temptation

Sheila started the machine again. The film now showed Jesus alone in a rugged and desolate country. The voice of the narrator picked up the story. "For forty days, Jesus fasted and was without solid food. Obviously, He was very hungry by the end of it."

The picture focused on Jesus. He was haggard and thin after this extended fast. He was physically depleted, all of the energy having drained out of Him.

"And so the devil came to him in this exhausted condition with the first temptation. *'If you are the Son of God, tell these stones to become bread'* (Matthew 4:3). The temptation addressed an immediate and urgent need: Jesus needed food desperately. He could meet that need, the devil suggested, by using His powers as the Son of God. This was very subtle. Jesus had abstained for forty days and now clearly needed food. This was perfectly natural and normal; there was nothing wrong with that. But what the devil was trying to do was get Jesus to use His power for His own personal benefit and to meet His own needs."

In the film, we watched as Jesus stood, raised His head, and refused the temptation.

"Jesus' response to this was immediate: *That's not what My powers are for. This would be a misuse of the power God has entrusted to Me.* Jesus actual words to the devil were, *'It is written: "Man does not live on bread alone, but on every word that comes from the mouth of God"'* (Matthew 4:4).

"Jesus established in His mind the basic but fundamental piece of spiritual wisdom that real life isn't found in material things, but in spiritual things. The devil's temptation was, 'If you be the son of God, use your powers to take care of your physical needs.' Jesus, response was that his obvious physical needs weren't really important. His powers would flow into other channels. His authority would be given to support causes greater than His own physical satisfaction."

As we watched, Jesus weakly sat down again. "The temptation, however, went beyond His immediate physical needs, and pointed to the long-term methodology Jesus would use to win the support of the people. If He could use His powers as the Son of God to create unlimited bread, or bring great prosperity and material well-being to His followers, then certainly He would quickly gain a great following. The benefits of being a follower of Jesus would be very clear to them—they would never be hungry, they would be prosperous, they would be dominant, they would be rich and influential. As long as Jesus was providing these material gains, He could guarantee that He would have followers. But that's not why Jesus wanted people to follow Him. He was going to proclaim a kingdom in which spiritual values predominated, not material values. He wanted followers who primarily pursued their relationship with God rather than the wealth and power of this world.

"In the message He was going to preach, Jesus wanted people to understand that the real life of God was found in the affairs of the spirit and soul, not in the affairs of the world. He knew material prosperity couldn't bring the satisfaction of the soul and fulfillment of the spirit, for which men longed. At the end, all this prosperity wouldn't bring them eternal life, make them right with God, or bring peace and joy to their souls."

Once again, Sheila stopped the movie.

"Jesus was wise and established in this temptation that it was faulty to make the pursuit of material and physical well-being the primary goal, even though those values are legitimate and proper," Sheila said. "Jesus was wise enough to see through this temptation and reject it. In His kingdom, other things would take priority. Life is more than meat and drink and riches and money. Wisdom sees beyond the immediate needs of physical comforts and greed, understanding that there are more important values.

"Jesus' rejection of this temptation enabled Him to preach with authority and say,

Do not store up for yourselves treasures on earth, where moth and rust destroy, and where thieves break in and steal. But store up for yourselves treasures in heaven, where moth and rust do not destroy, and where thieves do not break in and steal. For where your treasure is, there your heart will be also. (Matthew 6:19–21)

"In His teaching, He made the basic devotion and allegiance of the human heart clear when he said,

No one can serve two masters. Either he will hate the one and love the other, or he will be devoted to the one and despise the other. You cannot serve both God and Money. (Matthew 6:24)

"The wise thing is to get these priorities sorted out in your own heart, then *'seek first his kingdom and his righteousness, and all these things will be given to you as well'* (Matthew 6:33).

"The message is clear. It is foolish to make a priority out of making money and accumulating goods to the neglect of our soul. We cannot demote God. In organizing your life, priority should be given to the welfare of your soul. In conducting your affairs, space must be given for the development of your relationship with God. In the decisions you make, you must not neglect your spiritual welfare."

"It seems to me," I said, "that this is similar to the lesson we learned when we came to the Lake of Mammon. The lake was full of people who opted for the pursuit of material possession before all else, and we were tempted to stop our journey there and participate in that. If we had done so, we never would have ended up here on the Sea of Tranquility."

"That's correct," said Sheila. "This is one of the most common temptations of the human heart—to set our hearts on material possessions and all the power, pleasure, and position they bring, thinking that this is what matters most in life. But the wisdom of God would lead the human heart to prize other values.

"But the devil wasn't yet finished with Jesus. He made other attempts to divert the priorities in Jesus' heart. In a further attempt to get Him to invest His powers and position in secondary values, the devil presented another temptation."

The Second Temptation

The film began again and we watched as the scene changed. We saw shots of the magnificent temple in Jerusalem. The camera took us up to the pinnacle of the temple, which was located on the southwest corner of the temple wall. From up here, we looked down and saw great crowds of people gathering for worship. It was here, on this pinnacle, with the crowds below, that the devil presented Jesus with his second temptation.

"The devil now took Him to the holy city and had him stand on the highest point of the temple," the narrator continued.

> "'If you are the Son of God,' he said, 'throw yourself down. For it is written: "He will command his angels concerning you, and they will lift you up in their hands, so that you will not strike your foot against a stone."'" (Matthew 4:6)

"Satan's strategy here was to tempt Jesus into drawing attention to Himself by doing a sensational and public thing. Essentially, Satan was saying, 'If you want to be a leader, you need to draw attention to yourself. Very few have even heard of Jesus, the carpenter from Nazareth. Throw yourself down in full view of everyone and the whole nation will talk about you when you land softly and unharmed in the courtyard below. If you want people to follow you, you have to do something sensational. You need to make sure people understand that there's something special about you. You need to amaze them. Become a celebrity. If you do, people will listen to you and follow you.'"

We saw the scene through the eyes of Jesus. He stood on the high pinnacle of the temple, looking down. He could see great throngs of people going about their business. If he were to throw himself down and yet be unharmed, he would indeed create a sensation.

"Jesus wisely saw through this strategy and rejected it," the narrator said. "This time, Satan wanted Him to use His powers as the Son of God to glorify Himself, to make Himself the center of attention. But Jesus wasn't on earth to create popular acclaim for Himself, but to point beyond Himself to God the Father. Jesus didn't want people to follow Him because He did amazing things. He knew that what was amazing today would soon lose its luster and people would be looking for greater and greater miracles all the time. Jesus had to use His power to help and bless others and not to make Himself great.

"In the days to come, Jesus would indeed do some amazing things and perform startling miracles, but He never made them the basis of His ministry. His power wasn't there to garner attention. He was there to glorify the Father and do His will. Jesus was able, at the end of His ministry, to say to God the Father, *'I have brought you glory on earth by completing the work you gave me to do'* (John 17:4)."

Sheila stopped the movie again to make a comment. "Again, the wisdom of Jesus comes home to us as we seek to establish wisdom in the value systems of our own hearts. It is a false value to construct life around ourselves. It isn't wise to live as if we ourselves are on the throne and everything else is of secondary importance. Wisdom of the heart tells us that there are great causes beyond ourselves. There are more important issues than our own interests. There are people, including God, who should be given priority. It's foolish to try to live for our own prestige and honor. The greatest value is to live for God, to seek Him and His will first rather than satisfying our own wishes and ambitions."

The image on the screen faded away as Sheila switched off the projector. Looking at us, she said, "Love of self is a false value. That's why Jesus said the greatest commandment is:

> *'Love the Lord your God with all your heart and with all your soul and with all your mind.' This is the first and greatest commandment. And the second is like it: 'Love your neighbor as yourself.'* (Matthew 22:37–39)

"We should make time to seek and do the will of God, to give energy to serving Him and others, to bring honor and glory to Him, to dedicate resources to the service of others. This is the wisdom of the heart that Jesus understood."

Elizabeth spoke up. "But I thought the lesson we learned from the Lake of Mammon was that the care of self and the providing of material things are legitimate, just not to be the priority. I thought we weren't to say that material things are of no value."

"And you are correct," said Sheila. "The issue here was that the enthronement of material values and of self were the false values of the heart into which Satan tried to get Jesus to invest Himself. Jesus rejected both of these. To some extent, they were legitimate. They were certainly a part of life, but they were amongst the secondary values. He did, after all, perform spectacular miracles, but He left us in no doubt that His primary purpose was greater than miracles. The material should never suffocate the spiritual; the body should never outshine the soul."

The Third Temptation

"The devil still wasn't finished. He had a third temptation." Sheila turned on the projector again and the screen came alive. Jesus now stood on the top of a very high mountain. As He looked around, He could see vast distances. Snapshots of the great nations of the world flashed before His eyes.

The narrator's voice continued. "The devil now tried to convince Jesus that His real purpose was to be in control of all the nations of the world, to rule all. But in order to do that, Jesus would have to abandon His spiritual emphasis and adopt the methods of the world, which Satan would assist Him in doing. The devil implied that real power lay in the fields of military and political dominance. The Bible says,

> *Again, the devil took him to a very high mountain and showed him all the kingdoms of the world and their splendor. 'All this I will give you,' he said, 'if you will bow down and worship me.'* (Matthew 4:8–9)

"As He struggled with this offer, Jesus admitted that He had come to win the world, to save the world and bring it back to God. Here, all the nations of the world were being offered to Him, but at a price. The price was to abandon His spiritual and godly objectives and arrive at power by worldly and devilish means. There was a clear change of motivation being suggested. The motivation would change from winning the world for God to conquering the world and gaining power for Himself. Jesus would rule the world, but not for God."

The film now showed us a variety of images, with accompanying sound. There was the marching of vast armies, the shouting and yelling of war, the burning and destruction of great cities, the adulation of massive throngs of people, the piling up of gold coins, and finally a throne, with Jesus the conqueror sitting on it but with blood on his hands.

"The methods being offered were the methods of war," the narrator intoned. "Achieving world dominance would require significant compromises of Jesus' spiritual objectives and demand an endorsement of worldly concepts of power and authority. All of this would be achieved by forsaking God and giving allegiance to the devil. Jesus would gain power by military means, by political scheming. He might end up being the ruler of the whole world, but He wouldn't have the allegiance of the hearts of men. They would not be won to God. This was the most blatant subversion of Jesus' purpose that Satan attempted.

"The basic requirement Jesus was looking for was that men in their hearts love God and obey Him. He came to establish a spiritual kingdom, not a political one. Power based on military might wouldn't lead men to love God. Power gained by political manipulation wouldn't encourage men to trust in God. In fact, economic power would entice men away from the values of the Kingdom of God."

As we watched, Jesus stood on the mountaintop and viewed the geographical extent of His potential power. We then saw Him shake His head in refusal.

"Jesus rejected this temptation. He made it clear that His aspirations and ambitions weren't based on human strategies of power and might. He didn't want to dominate men, but to win their hearts and allegiance so that they would voluntarily love God, following Him freely.

"It would have been easy and alluring to accept the devil's proposition, but the kingdom He would have ended up with wouldn't have been in line with the kind of kingdom He had been sent to establish. He couldn't be diverted from establishing the Kingdom of God in the hearts of men. On a later occasion, Jesus stated His value system when He said, *'What good will it be for a man if he gains the whole world, yet forfeits his soul? Or what can a man give in exchange for his soul?'* (Matthew 16:26)

"So Jesus, in these spiritual struggles with Satan, clearly established the issues of His heart. He wouldn't use His powers to serve Himself or the material interests of people. He wouldn't glorify Himself by sensational means. He wouldn't gain power or set up His kingdom by using the accepted and expected methods of power-seekers.

"The values that emerged victorious in Jesus' heart were that He would use His power to serve others and serve God. He would focus primarily on establishing a spiritual kingdom based on love for God and others, a kingdom that would operate by obedience to, and faith in, God. Jesus refused to compromise the values and motives of His heart. He set His purpose clearly in pursuing these goals. His whole ministry was predicated on accomplishing these objectives. All of His decisions and plans were based on the principles He established in his heart during this time in the wilderness. His route for achieving His purpose wasn't going to be easy. Many wouldn't understand why He was doing things the way He was doing them, but He was following the wisdom of His heart, and He was right."

As the narrator spoke, we watched the screen and saw an exhausted but triumphant Jesus being ministered to by angels. He turned His back on the wilderness and walked towards civilization and the start of His ministry. He was physically depleted, but spiritually triumphant. He was ready now to start His work, and He knew exactly what He would seek to do and how He would go about accomplishing it. The greatest work ever done on earth was about to start, but in a way no amount of human wisdom could ever have devised.

The Wisdom of the Heart

Sheila switched the movie off and turned to us. "Wisdom of the heart is essential. It is what guides you in making decisions and helps you to implement your decisions. Wisdom of the heart is what makes you respond to people the way you respond, and treat people the way you treat them. It is the spring from which flows the actions and attitudes of your life. If the spring is sour or corrupt, the whole flow of life will be the same.

"Wisdom of the heart determines the quality, purity, and direction of your attitude. A selfish person will make selfish decisions and in many situations put his own self-interest before other interests. A proud person will often demote other values in order to maintain his own status and public image. An angry person will make many decisions that hurt and afflict others. A person of love will allow the values of love to express themselves in his attitudes and decisions. A person of God will want God and His Kingdom to take precedence over all the other values of life.

"Everything flows from the heart. Jesus made it clear in His ministry that the real issues of life go on in the heart. He said,

> *Are you still so dull?... Don't you see that whatever enters the mouth goes into the stomach and then out of the body? But the things that come out of the mouth come from the heart, and these make a man 'unclean.' For out of the heart come evil thoughts, murder, adultery, sexual immorality, theft, false testimony, slander. These are what make a man 'unclean'; but eating with unwashed hands does not make him 'unclean.'* (Matthew 15:16–20)

"It is wise then to give special attention to the state of your heart. What are your values? What are your priorities? What are your motivations? If we follow the wisdom of Jesus, in our hearts we will dethrone ourselves and not prioritize our own self-interest. We will seek out the glory of God and the help of others rather than our own glory and stature. Our fundamental desire will be to establish the Kingdom of God in our actions and purposes. This is wisdom. It's not easy, but following it leads to life that is full, different, and satisfying. Remember Jesus' statement from the Sermon on the Mount: *'Blessed are the pure in heart, for they will see God'* (Matthew 5:8)."

Throughout this presentation, our group had hardly said a word. Now we were gripped by such a spirit of reverence that talk and questions would have been out of place.

Finally, it was Elizabeth, who seemed particularly moved by the presentation, who broke the silence. "I think we should pray," she suggested. "I certainly want this kind of heart, but I need God to help create it in me. I cannot do this by myself. I need Him. I'd like you all to pray for me that God will touch my heart and create this kind of spirit within me."

"I think," said Peter, "we all need to pray the prayer that the Psalmist prayed when he cried to God, *'Create in me a pure heart, O God, and renew a steadfast spirit within me. Do not cast me from your presence or take your Holy Spirit from me'* (Psalm 51:10–11)."

And so the session ended with us bowing our heads and asking God to create within us a value system that comes from the presence of His Holy Spirit living in our hearts.

Topics for Discussion

1. In the first temptation, Jesus was tempted to use His powers for material gain. In what ways are we tempted to give priority to material things?

2. In the second temptation, Jesus was tempted to use His powers to draw attention to Himself. In what ways are we tempted to prioritize our own glory and status?

3. In the third temptation, Jesus was tempted to gain His objectives by false methods. In what ways are we tempted to gain our objectives by questionable means? Does the end justify the means?

THIRTY-ONE

Wisdom in Christ

ON THE JOURNEY BACK FROM THE RETREAT CENTER, HERMES HAD MANY THINGS to say to us.

"I want to congratulate you all on your successful journey down the River of Wisdom," he said. "You've shown courage and perseverance in finally arriving here. I'm sure the journey has been meaningful and profitable for you, and on the way you've learned and experienced many things about wisdom. Now, you must decide if you want to stay here. Is the life of wisdom for you or not?"

"You indicated that if we decide to stay, we would stay on the Mountain," said Peter. "Where on the Mountain would we live?"

Hermes pointed to the Great Mountain. "The community on the Great Mountain is near the base, on the shore of the Sea of Tranquility. You will actually live right on the mountain, not just near it."

"In our discussions on the island," I said, "we decided that the Great Mountain represented for us Jesus Christ. It was following Far Mountain that guided us down the River of Wisdom. It is the Great Mountain that dominates the Sea of Tranquility. It is the central presence here; everything revolves around it. We decided that the way to wisdom is to follow Jesus Christ, and if we are to live in wisdom, we will live in Him."

"You have stated it well," said Hermes. "The wise life is the one that is lived in the Spirit of Jesus Christ. You have learned the lessons well."

"So what happens now?" asked Peter.

"I would suggest that Charles and I drop you off on your island today. We'll give you a portion of Scripture to read and discuss, and then tomorrow we'll come to the island and talk about it. When you understand the scripture, you can decide if you want to stay or not. If you decide to stay, we will take you to the community on the Mountain. If you decide not to stay, we will help you get back to where you came from."

"Even if we decide not to stay," I said, "we will return to our homes and be wiser and better people for having made this journey. The lessons will not be forgotten."

"Hopefully that will be the case," responded Hermes. "But you know, lessons can be forgotten. The pressures of life can crowd in again. What you have learned can easily fade into the background."

"But if we decide to stay, what will we do?" Elizabeth asked. "We can't just sit around all day being spiritual and praying."

Hermes laughed at this. "The community on the Great Mountain is just like any regular community. People live their lives. They work. They marry. They have children. They build houses. They have jobs. They live regular, normal lives, except that they live in the Spirit of Jesus Christ and in His presence. If you decide to stay, you'll need to find a place to live and you'll have work to do."

"What scripture do you want us to read?" asked Lloyd.

"John 15:1–17," Hermes said.

Lloyd looked contemplative. "Oh, I know that one. That's where Jesus talks about the vine and the branches."

"Correct," said Hermes. "These verses depict the life that's lived in the Spirit of Jesus Christ, which is ultimately the wisest life a person can live. But let's not talk about it right now. All of you, take time to read the verses and discuss them together. Charles and I will come to your island tomorrow morning. If at that time you need to talk about it more, we can. If you choose to stay, then we will take you to your destination."

After we had been dropped off on the island, I turned the group. "Why don't we take time right now to read these verses by ourselves? Then, after supper tonight, we can discuss them together around the campfire."

Time Alone

This suggestion met with agreement from all, so I collected my Bible and went away by myself to a spot where I could see the Great Mountain. In silence, I began to read.

In these verses, Jesus likened Himself to a vine, while his followers were considered to be the branches. As good branches, we needed to stay connected to Him, so that the nourishment and strength of the vine could flow constantly into us. Branches that were unconnected to the main vine became useless, withering and dying.

Later on in the verses, He expanded on this to say that we should live in Him and He should live in us. I took this to mean that our connection with Him was to be so intimate that it would be like living in each other. The Spirit of Jesus was to live in my heart. He would make His home within me so that His presence and influence would be with me all the time, affecting every part of my life—my thoughts, desires, values, and ambitions. All of me was to be under the influence of His ever-present Spirit.

That's quite a life, I thought. *Very different to the way I have been living.*

As I thought upon the verses, I came to understand that the great outcome of this close presence of Jesus in my heart would be for me to have a fruitful life that would bring glory to God—just like a good, healthy branch connected to the vine produced abundant fruit. This abundant fruit was the purpose and outcome of having a close, living relationship with Jesus Christ.

Jesus went on to describe the fruit that would mature in my life. First, he said there would be the fruit of joy: *"I have told you this so that my joy may be in you and your joy may be complete"* (John 15:11). Then there was the fruit of love. The love of God would remain in us and we would love God and love each other. Surprisingly, Jesus also included the idea of freedom. He said that this relationship meant He would no longer call us servants but friends. He even connected this branch/vine relationship with effectiveness in prayer, saying, *"If you remain in me and my words remain in you, ask whatever you wish, and it will be given you"* (John 15:7).

I sat for a long time, reading this passage and looking over the sea to the Great Mountain.

So, I thought, *when all is said and done, true wisdom is centered in Jesus Christ. The wise life is lived in Him, in obedience to His guidance and in the absorbing of His Spirit.*

In my heart, I knew that this was where reality and satisfaction lay. Was I ready to live my life like this?

I slowly returned to the camp, feeling prepared for the discussion we would have that night.

Living in Christ

After supper, we gathered around the fire and Peter opened the discussion. "The thing that impressed me is that the community we are to live in is on the Great Mountain. Hermes stressed that it wasn't near the Mountain, or within easy access of the Mountain or in a place where you could look at the Mountain now and again. It was *on* the Mountain. We live in Jesus Christ. He lives in us. There is a vital connection there, like the contact between a vine and its branches. It's not that Jesus is out there or up there or over there; He lives in our hearts and in our spirits."

"And when that relationship is present, life flows from the vine into the branches," Elizabeth said. "To me, this means that the life and wisdom of Jesus Christ will flow into us and be a part of us, and if we break that connection our spiritual life will begin to wither and die. If I were a branch on a vine, I would know it was foolish to break my connection. The wisest thing we can do is stay in close fellowship with Jesus Christ, absorbing His Spirit and truth and letting Him live within us."

"You seem to understand this very well," said Lloyd humbly. "I have difficulty imagining what that kind of life would be like. But I know it must be true, for I remember the Apostle Paul saying,

> *My purpose is that they may be encouraged in heart and united in love, so that they may have the full riches of complete understanding, in order that they may know the mystery of God, namely, Christ, in whom are hidden all the treasures of wisdom and knowledge.* (Colossians 2:2–3)

"All the wisdom of God is in Christ. He wants to live within us in order to share this wisdom and life with us. But Paul calls it a mystery and it seems to be a bit of a mystery to me, too."

"There is no doubt," I said, "that Jesus is talking about a life in which we share in His life and wisdom. The branch shares with the vine. He says that He lives in us, and we live in Him. He even goes so far as to say that just the Father are one, so we can be one with Him. It's astounding!"

285

This was all rather mystical and I could see why Lloyd was having difficulty grasping it.

Elizabeth, however, had a clear understanding and was excited. "Yes, when the Spirit of Christ is living in our hearts, there flows into us a constant supply of His strength, wisdom, and grace, just like a branch living on the vine. But the important thing is that you have to stay connected. The branches that become disconnected wither and die. It would be foolish for a branch to let this relationship be ruptured and yet expect to continue to live and be fruitful."

"Well, I certainly want to be a fruitful branch," said Peter. "But what exactly do you think it means to be fruitful?"

The Fruitful Branch

I was ready for that question, for I had given it a lot of thought as I studied the passage. "Jesus outlines some of the qualities involved in this fruitful life," I said. "He says it's joyful, loving, free, pure, effective, and brings glory to God."

Peter laughed. "That's quite a mouthful. Where do you get all of that?"

I took up my Bible. "In verse three, Jesus said, *'You are already clean because of the word I have spoken to you.'* That's where I get pure. Then, in verses nine and ten, He says,

> *As the Father has loved me, so have I loved you. Now remain in my*
> *love. If you obey my commands, you will remain in my love, just as*
> *I have obeyed my Father's commands and remain in his love.*

"That's love. In verse eleven, He says, *'I have told you this so that my joy may be in you and that your joy may be complete.'* That's joy. In verse five, Jesus says,

> *I am the vine; you are the branches. If a man remains in me and I*
> *in him, he will bear much fruit; apart from me you can do nothing.*

"That's effectiveness. Included in this effectiveness is the ability to pray effectively, for Jesus says in verse seven, *'If you remain in me and my words remain in you, ask whatever you wish, and it will be given you.'* That's an amazing promise. Further to all of this, Jesus promises a new freedom. In verse fourteen and fifteen, He says,

You are my friends if you do what I command. I no longer call you servants, because a servant does not know his master's business. Instead, I have called you friends, for everything that I learned from my Father I have made known to you.

"That's freedom from servanthood to friendship. And in all of this, we live a life that brings glory to God, which is our greatest privilege."

Elizabeth quickly added, "I agree with all that. When I thought of fruitfulness, I realized that fruit is the reproductive system of the plant. It's in the fruit that you find the seeds by which the plant reproduces itself. It's the fruit that gives the new seeds their first nourishment to begin life on their own. So, the wonderful life you have just described is fruitful, in that it influences other people and is reproduced in their lives. When a branch is fruitful, it produces effects in the lives of others for the glory of God."

"Very good," said Lloyd. "Clearly, a life spent on the Mountain is a Christ-centered life, one in which the Spirit of Christ lives within us and affects all that we do, think, and value. Our spirit begins to be like the Spirit of Christ, and we love what He loves, wish what He wishes for, and desire what He desires. We trust and obey His will just as He did the Father's will. He guides and directs our lives by residing in our hearts and influencing all that we do."

I nodded. "You mentioned a verse from the Bible that says all the wisdom of God is wrapped up in Jesus Christ. We are seeking to live wisely, so if all the wisdom of God is in Christ, we must welcome Him fully into our hearts. He, in turn, will share with us all the wisdom of God. The wise life is the Christ-centered life, and the Christ-centered life is the wise life."

We all sat there around the fire, lost in our thoughts. After a long and reverent silence, I said, "So we must decide, is this the kind of life we want to live? Do we want to live on the Mountain—not near it, or close to it, but on it?

The Conditions for Living in Christ

This was the vital question we all faced, and no one responded immediately.

"What are the conditions?" Peter asked after some time had passed. "Living like this, with us in Christ and Christ in us, must have some conditions attached to it."

I had closely studied the verses Hermes had given us and felt I could answer that.

"As far as I can see, there are only two conditions," I said. "Jesus said in verse four, *'Remain in me, and I will remain in you.'* I interpret that to mean that we must have a continuous welcoming attitude in our hearts. We welcome Him and His Spirit into our hearts. There can be no resistance or unwillingness on our part. With all of our hearts, we must welcome Him and all He represents. If we do that, He will willingly come.

"The second condition is in verse nine and ten, where He says,

> *As the Father has loved me, so have I loved you. Now remain in my*
> *love. If you obey my commands, you will remain in my love, just as*
> *I have obeyed my Father's commands and remain in his love.*

"Our welcoming attitude is constant, and the authenticity of our welcome is revealed in our willingness to obey Him. Those are the two conditions—an attitude of humble welcome and a willingness to obey and follow wherever He leads."

I waited for a response to this. No one objected, but all nodded in agreement, so I solemnly continued.

"I don't know about you, but I'm ready for this. This is the kind of life I want. This is what I've been seeking. I'm ready to live on the Mountain. I set out on this journey to seek wisdom in order to live for God in a genuine and real way, and I think I now understand that true wisdom is centered in Jesus Christ. I want to live in Him and have Him live in me. To me, that's the wisest and best way to live the rest of my life, and I'm ready for it. When Hermes and Charles come tomorrow, I'm going to tell them I want to stay. I want to live on the Mountain."

The Great Decision

Peter didn't hesitate. He stood up, reached out, and took my hand. "Friend, I'm with you. This is the life I want. I want to live on the Mountain. We'll do it together."

I felt my heart leap for joy within me. I then looked over at Lloyd and Elizabeth. They were intently looking at one another. Without a word being spoken, they seemed to agree on their conclusion.

Lloyd rose and said, "Yes, we want to stay." Elizabeth then stood. With tears in her eyes, she embraced Lloyd.

So there we stood—without words, but with full hearts, in the shadow of the Great Mountain, we joined hands in united fellowship. Our journey was complete, our destination assured, and we were bursting with joy. We would be ready for Hermes and Charles when they came in the morning.

Later, I wandered away on my own and sat down again in my private spot on the beach. It was a beautiful time. The sea once again lived up to its name and was smooth and tranquil. The night was warm and the moon bright. I looked across the still water toward the Great Mountain. Even in the moonlight, I could see it clearly. It stood in solid majesty, its strength and beauty reflected on the quiet water of the sea.

I will live there. Not near it or by it, but on it. I will be part of its life and it will be part of my life. We will be joined. We will absorb one another.

As I sat in quiet contemplation, I realized that when we had started this journey into wisdom, I'd had no idea we would end up here, but I could think of no other place I would rather be. The journey had led me to the heart of Jesus Christ and had opened my heart to Him. This was my home. This was where I wanted to be. This was wisdom, indeed. I was content.

Topics for Discussion

1. Discuss ways in which we can effectively stay connected to Jesus Christ, just as a branch is connected to the stem of a vine.

2. What kind of fruit will the branches bear?

3. Elizabeth realized that the fruit is the reproductive system of the plant. How are we reproducing for the Kingdom of God? How can we improve our fruitfulness?

Also by Bill Stewart:

- *Journey into Prayer*
- *Journey into Holiness*

CPSIA information can be obtained at www.ICGtesting.com
Printed in the USA
LVOW01s0718160114

369577LV00004B/12/P